D0829885

SCENES
FROM
CLASSIC PLAYS

468 B.C. to 1970 A.D.

808.82 SCE
Scenes from classic pla
468 B.C. to 1970 A.D.

PALM BEACH COUNTY
LIBRARY SYSTEM
3650 SUMMIT BLVD
WEST PALM BEACH, FLORIDA 33406

Smith and Kraus *Books For Actors*
THE MONOLOGUE SERIES
>The Best Men's / Women's Stage Monologues of 1994
>The Best Men's / Women's Stage Monologues of 1993
>The Best Men's / Women's Stage Monologues of 1992
>The Best Men's / Women's Stage Monologues of 1991
>The Best Men's / Women's Stage Monologues of 1990
>One Hundred Men's / Women's Stage Monologues from the 1980's
>2 Minutes and Under: Character Monologues for Actors
>Street Talk: Character Monologues for Actors
>Uptown: Character Monologues for Actors
>Monologues from Contemporary Literature: Volume I
>Monologues from Classic Plays
>100 Great Monologues from the Renaissance Theatre
>100 Great Monologues from the Neo-Classical Theatre
>100 Great Monologues from the 19th C. Romantic and Realistic Theatres

FESTIVAL MONOLOGUE SERIES
>The Great Monologues from the Humana Festival
>The Great Monologues from the EST Marathon
>The Great Monologues from the Women's Project
>The Great Monologues from the Mark Taper Forum

YOUNG ACTORS SERIES
>Great Scenes and Monologues for Children
>New Plays from A.C.T.'s Young Conservatory
>Great Scenes for Young Actors from the Stage
>Great Monologues for Young Actors
>Multicultural Monologues for Young Actors
>Multicultural Scenes for Young Actors

SCENE STUDY SERIES
>Scenes From Classic Plays 468 B.C. to 1960 A.D.
>The Best Stage Scenes of 1993
>The Best Stage Scenes of 1992
>The Best Stage Scenes for Men / Women from the 1980's

CONTEMPORARY PLAYWRIGHTS SERIES
>Romulus Linney: 17 Short Plays
>Eric Overmyer: Collected Plays
>Lanford Wilson: 21 Short Plays
>William Mastrosimone: Collected Plays
>Horton Foote: 4 New Plays
>Israel Horovitz: 16 Short Plays
>Terrence McNally: 15 Short Plays
>Humana Festival '93: The Complete Plays
>Humana Festival '94: The Complete Plays
>Women Playwrights: The Best Plays of 1992
>Women Playwrights: The Best Plays of 1993

GREAT TRANSLATION FOR ACTORS SERIES
>The Wood Demon by Anton Chekhov

CAREER DEVELOPMENT SERIES
>The Camera Smart Actor
>The Sanford Meisner Approach
>The Actor's Chekhov
>Kiss and Tell: Restoration Scenes, Monologues, & History
>Cold Readings: Some Do's and Don'ts for Actors at Auditions

If you require pre-publication information about upcoming Smith and Kraus books, you may receive our semi-annual catalogue, free of charge, by sending your name and address to *Smith and Kraus Catalogue, P.O. Box 127, One Main Street, Lyme, NH 03768. Or call us at (800) 895-4331, fax (603) 795-4427*

SCENES FROM CLASSIC PLAYS

468 B.C. to 1970 A.D.

Jocelyn A. Beard, Editor

SK
A Smith and Kraus Book

Published by Smith and Kraus, Inc.
Lyme, New Hampshire
Copyright © 1993 by Smith and Kraus, Inc.
All rights reserved

Cover and Text Design by Julia Hill
Manufactured in the United States of America

First Edition: October 1993
8 7 6 5 4 3

CAUTION: Professionals and amateurs are hereby warned that the plays represented in this book are subject to a royalty. They are fully protected under the copyright laws of the United States of America, and of all countries covered by the International Copyright Union (including the Dominion of Canada and the rest of the British Commonwealth), and of all countries covered by the Pan-American Copyright Convention and the Universal Copyright Convention, and of all countries with which the United States has reciprocal copyright relations. All rights, including professional, amateur, motion picture, recitation, lecturing, public reading, radio broadcasting, television, video or sound taping, all other forms of mechanical or electronic reproductions such as information storage and retrieval systems and photocopying, and the rights of translation into foreign languages, are strictly reserved. Pages 304-309 constitute an extension of this copyright page.

Library of Congress Cataloging-in-Publication Data

Scenes from classic plays, 468 B.C. to 1970 A.D. / edited by Jocelyn A. Beard

     p. cm.
     ISBN 1-880399-36-9 : $14.95
     1. Acting. 2. Drama—Collections. I. Beard, Jocelyn.
     PN2080.S26   1993
     808.82--dc20   93-33010
                                 CIP

SCENES
FROM
CLASSIC PLAYS
468 B.C. to 1970 A.D.

Contents

FOREWORD

When Marisa and Eric first asked me to follow-up *Monologues From Classic Plays* with a book of scenes, I thought of the huge box into which I had just packed all my copies of Sophocles and Shakespeare and groaned. Not again! I thought, as visions of Antigone having tea with the Duchess of Malfi traipsed through my weary brain. Not again.

But there I was, again, reading through the treasured classics of our civilization and again being both transported and humbled by the experience. As daunting a task as selecting the classic scenes may be, I would happily do it again and again, because every time you sit down to read Wycherly or Molière you rise a wiser person. Reading classical theatre affords a unique glimpse into our past and therefore insight into our future.

I urge you to let this book be a springboard for your love affair with classical theatre. If you find a scene that inspires while it challenges – find the play and read it. Start your own box of classics that you can go back to again, and again, and again . . . .

Jocelyn A. Beard
Patterson, NY
Autumn, 1993

—I would like to dedicate this book to my glorious baby daughter, Blythe Clementine, who generously gave me time off from being a mommy to edit this book.

SCENES
FROM
CLASSIC PLAYS

468 B.C. to 1970 A.D.

PROMETHEUS BOUND
Aeschylus
468 B.C.

Dramatic / 2 Men

Prometheus: a Titan, punished by Zeus for stealing fire for man, 30-40

Hermes: a god, 30-40

The Setting: a rocky desert in European Scythia

Here, the winged messenger of the gods chastises Prometheus for having defied Zeus.

(Enter Hermes.)

HERMES: Thee, cunning sophist, dealing bitter words
Most bitterly against the gods, the friend
Of ephemeral man, the thief of sacred fire,
Thee, Father Jove commands to curb thy boats,
And say what marriage threats his stable throne.
Answer this question in plain phrase, no dark
Tangled enigmas; do not add, Prometheus,
A second journey to my first: and, mark me!
Thy obduracy cannot soften Jove.

PROMETHEUS: This solemn mouthing, the proud pomp of phrase
Beseems the lackey of the gods. New gods
Ye are, and, being new, ye ween to hold
Unshaken citadels. Have I not seen
Two Monarchs ousted from that throne! the third
I yet shall see precipitate hurled from Heaven
With baser, speedier ruin. Do I seem
To quail before this new-forged dynasty?
Fear is my farthest thought. I pray thee go
Turn up the dust again upon the road
Thou cam'st. Reply from me thou shalt have none.

HERMES: This haughty tone hath been thy sin before:
Thy pride will strand thee on a worser woe.

PROMETHEUS: And were my woe ten-fold what now it is,
I would not barter it for thy sweet chains;
For liefer would I lackey this bare rock
Than trip the messages of Father Jove.
The insolent thus with insolence I repay.

HERMES: Thou dost delight in miseries; thou art wanton.

PROMETHEUS: Wanton! delighted! would my worst enemies
Might wanton in these bonds, thyself the first!

HERMES: Must I, too, share the blame of thy distress?

PROMETHEUS: In one round sentence, every god I hate
That injures me who never injured him.

HERMES: Thou'rt mad, clean mad; thy wit's diseased, Prometheus.

PROMETHEUS: Most mad! if madness 'tis to hate our foes.

HERMES: Prosperity's too good for thee: thy temper
Could not endure't.

PROMETHEUS: Alas! this piercing pang!

HERMES: "Alas!" – this word Jove does not understand.

PROMETHEUS: As Time grows old he teaches many things.

HERMES: Yet Time that teaches all leaves thee untaught.

PROMETHEUS: Untaught in sooth, thus parleying with a slave!

HERMES: It seems thou wilt not grant great Jove's demand.

PROMETHEUS: Such love as his to me should be repaid
With like!

HERMES: Dost beard me like a boy? Beware.

PROMETHEUS: Art not a boy, and something yet more witless,
If thou expectest answer from my mouth?
Nor insult harsh, nor cunning craft of Jove
Shall force this tale from me, till he unloose
These bonds. Yea! let him dart his levin bolts,
With white-winged snows and subterranean thunders
Mix and confound the elements of things!
No threat, no fear, shall move me to reveal
The hand that hurls him from his tyrant's throne.

HERMES: Bethink thee well: thy vaunts can help thee nothing.

PROMETHEUS: I speak not rashly: what I said I said.

HERMES: If thou art not the bought and sold of folly,
Dare to learn wisdom from thy present ills.

PROMETHEUS: Speak to the waves: thou speak'st to me as vainly!
Deem not that I, to win a smile from Jove,
Will spread a maiden smoothness o'er my soul,

And importune the foe whom most I hate
With womanish upliftings of the hands.
Thou'lt see the deathless die first!

ANTIGONE
Sophocles
442 B.C.

Dramatic / 2 Women
> Antigone: princess of Thebes, 20s
> Ismene: her younger sister, 20s

The Setting: the royal palace at Thebes

When Creon takes the city of Thebes, he declares that the body of
Prince Polynices shall be left in the street outside the palace to rot.
This enrages Antigone, who here tries to convince timid Ismene to
help her bury their brother.

(*Enter Antigone and Ismene.*)
ANTIGONE: Ismene, dear in very sisterhood,
    Do you perceive how Heaven upon us two
    Means to fulfil, before we come to die,
    Out of all ills that grow from Oedipus –
    What not, indeed? for there's no sorrow or harm,
    No circumstance of scandal or of shame
    I have not seen, among your griefs, and mine.
    And now again, what is this word they say
    Our Captain-general proclaimed but now
    To the whole city! Did you hear and heed?
    Or are you blind, while pains of enemies
    Are passing on your friends?
ISMENE: Antigone, to me no tidings about friends are come,
    Pleasant or grievous, ever since we two
    Of our brothers were bereft, who died
    Both in one day, each by the other's hand.
    And since the Argive host in this same night
    Took itself hence, I have heard nothing else,
    To make me happier, or more miserable.
ANTIGONE: I knew as much; and for that reason made you
    Go out of doors – to tell you privately.

ISMENE: What is it? I see you have some mystery.

ANTIGONE: What! has not Creon to the tomb preferred
One of our brothers, and with contumely
Withheld it from the other? Eteocles
Duly, they say, even as by law was due,
He hid beneath the earth, rendering him honour
Among the dead below; but the dead body
Of Polynices, miserably slain,
They say it has been given out publicly
None may bewail, none bury, all must leave
Unwept, unsepulchred, a dainty prize
For fowl that watch, gloating upon their prey!
This is the matter he has had proclaimed –
Excellent Creon! for your heed, they say,
And mine, I tell you – mine! and he moves hither,
Meaning to announce it plainly in the ears
Of such as do not know it, and to declare
It is no matter of small moment; he
Who does any of these things shall surely die;
The citizens shall stone him in the streets.
So stands the case. Now you will quickly show
If you are worthy of your birth or no.

ISMENE: But O rash heart, what good, if it be thus,
Could I effect, helping or hindering?

ANTIGONE: Look, will you join me? will you work with me?

ISMENE: In what attempt? What mean you?

ANTIGONE: Help me lift
The body up –

ISMENE: What, would you bury him?
Against the proclamation?

ANTIGONE: My own brother
And yours I will! If you will not, I will;
I shall not prove disloyal.

ISMENE: You are mad!
When Creon has forbidden it!

ANTIGONE: From mine own
He has no right to stay me.

ISMENE: Alas, O sister,
Think how our father perished! self-convict –
Abhorred – dishonoured – blind – his eyes put out

By his own hand! How she who was at once
His wife and mother with a knotted noose
Laid violent hands on her own life! And how
Our two unhappy brothers in one day
Each on his own head by the other's hand
Wrought common ruin! We now left alone –
Do but consider how most miserably
We too shall perish, if despite of law
We traverse the behest or power of kings.
We must remember we are women born,
Unapt to cope with men; and, being ruled
By mightier than ourselves, we have to bear
These things – and worse. For my part, I will ask
Pardon of those beneath, for what perforce
I needs must do, but yield obedience
To them that walk in power; to exceed
Is madness, and not wisdom.
ANTIGONE: Then in future
I will not bid you help me; nor henceforth,
Though you desire, shall you, with my good will,
Share what I do. Be what seems right to you;
Him will I bury. Death, so met, were honour;
And for that capital crime of piety,
Loving and loved, I will lie by his side.
Far longer is there need I satisfy
Those nether Powers, than powers on earth; for there
For ever must I lie. You, if you will,
Hold up to scorn what is approved of Heaven!
ISMENE: I am not one to cover things with scorn;
But I was born too feeble to contend
Against the state.
ANTIGONE: Yes, you can put that forward;
But I will go and heap a burial mound
Over my most dear brother.
ISMENE: My poor sister,
How beyond measure do I fear for you!
ANTIGONE: Do not spend fear on me. Shape your own course.
ISMENE: At least announce it, then, to nobody,
But keep it close, as I will.
ANTIGONE: Tell it, tell it!

You'll cross me worse, by far, if you keep silence –
Not publish it to all.

ISMENE: Your heart beats hotly
For chilling work!

ANTIGONE: I know that those approve
Whom I most need to please.

ISMENE: If you could do it!
But you desire impossibilities.

ANTIGONE: Well, when I find I have no power to stir,
I will cease trying.

ISMENE: But things impossible
'Tis wrong to attempt at all.

ANTIGONE: If you will say it,
I shall detest you soon; and you will justly
Incur the dead man's hatred. Suffer me
And my unwisdom to endure the weight
Of what is threatened. I shall meet with nothing
More grievous, at the worst, than death, with honour.

ISMENE: Then go, if you will have it: and take this with you,
You go on a fool's errand!

OEDIPUS REX
Sophocles
427 B.C.

Dramatic / 2 Men
   Oedipus: a man doomed by fate, 40-50
   Tiresias: a blind prophet, 50-70

The Setting: the royal palace at Thebes

Creon has demanded vengeance for the murder of Laius, the king. Not realizing that he is the murderer being sought, Oedipus appeals to a Delphic oracle for help.

OEDIPUS: O Tiresias,
   master of all the mysteries of life,
   all you teach and all you dare not tell,
   signs in the heavens, signs that walk the earth!
   Blind as you are, you can feel all the more
   what sickness haunts our city. You, my lord,
   are the one shield, the one savior we can find.
   We asked Apollo – perhaps the messengers
   haven't told you – he sent his answer back:
   "Relief from the plague can only come one way.
   Uncover the murderers of Laius,
   put them to death or drive them into exile."
   So I get you, grudge us nothing now, no voice,
   no message plucked from the birds, the embers
   or the other mantic ways within your grasp.
   Rescue yourself, your city, rescue me –
   rescue everything infected by the dead.
   We are in your hands. For a man to help others
   with all his gifts and native strength:
   that is the noblest work.
TIRESIAS: How terrible – to see the truth
   when the truth is only pain to him who sees!
   I knew it well, but I put it from my mind,

else I never would have come.

OEDIPUS: What's this? Why so grim, so dire?

TIRESIAS: Just send me home. You bear your burdens,
I'll bear mine. It's better that way,
please believe me.

OEDIPUS: Strange response ... unlawful,
unfriendly too to the state that bred and reared you –
you withhold the word of god.

TIRESIAS: I fail to see
that your own words are so well-timed,
I'd rather not have the same thing said of me ...

OEDIPUS: For the love of god, don't turn away,
not if you know something. We beg you,
all of us on our knees.

TIRESIAS: None of you knows –
and I will never reveal my dreadful secrets,
not to say your own.

OEDIPUS: What? You know and you won't tell?
You're bent on betraying us, destroying Thebes?

TIRESIAS: I'd rather not cause pain for you or me.
So why this ... useless interrogation?
You'll get nothing from me.

OEDIPUS: Nothing! You,
you scum of the earth, you'd enrage a heart of stone!
You won't talk? Nothing moves you?
Out with it, once and for all!

TIRESIAS: You criticize my temper ... unaware
of the one *you* live with, you revile me.

OEDIPUS: Who could restrain his anger hearing you?
What outrage – you spurn the city!

TIRESIAS: What will come will come.
Even if I shroud it all in silence.

OEDIPUS: What will come? You're bound to *tell* me that.

TIRESIAS: I will say no more. Do as you like, build your anger
to whatever pitch you please, rage your worst –

OEDIPUS: Oh I'll let you loose, I have such fury in me –
now I see it all. You helped hatch the plot,
you did the work, yes, short of killing him
with your own hands – and given eyes I'd say
you did the killing single-handed!

TIRESIAS: Is that so!

I charge you, then, submit to that decree
you just laid down: from this day onward
speak to no one, not these citizens, not myself.
You are the curse, the corruption of the land!

OEDIPUS: You, shameless –

aren't you appalled to start up such a story?
You think you can get away with this?

TIRESIAS: I have already.

The truth with all its power lives inside me.

OEDIPUS: Who primed you for this? Not your prophet's trade.

TIRESIAS: You did, you forced me, twisted it out of me.

OEDIPUS: What? Say it again – I'll understand it better.

TIRESIAS: Didn't you understand, just now?

Or are you tempting me to talk?

OEDIPUS: No, I can't say I grasped your meaning.

Out with it, again!

TIRESIAS: I say you are the murderer you hunt.

OEDIPUS: That obscenity, twice – by god, you'll pay.

TIRESIAS: Shall I say more, so you can really rage?

OEDIPUS: Much as you want. Your words are nothing – futile.

TIRESIAS: You cannot imagine . . . I tell you,

you and your loved ones live together in infamy,
you cannot see how far you've gone in guilt.

OEDIPUS: You think you can keep this up and never suffer?

TIRESIAS: Indeed, if the truth has any power.

OEDIPUS: It does

but not for you, old man. You've lost your power,
stone-blind, stone-deaf – senses, eyes blind as stone!

TIRESIAS: I pity you, flinging at me the very insults

each man here will fling at you so soon.

OEDIPUS: Blind,

lost in the night, endless night that nursed you!
You can't hurt me or anyone else who sees the light –
you can never touch me.

TIRESIAS: True, it is not your fate

to fall at my hands. Apollo is quite enough,
and he will take some pains to work this out.

OEDIPUS: Creon! Is this conspiracy his or yours?

TIRESIAS: Creon is not your downfall, no, you are your own.

THE CLOUDS
Aristophanes
423 B.C.

Serio-Comic / 2 Men
Strepsiades: a dishonest farmer, 50s
Socrates: the philosopher, 50-60

The Setting: the Thinkery, Socrates' school, Athens

Always looking for the easy way out, Strepsiades enrolls in the
Thinkery, hoping that Socrates can teach him how to outwit his many
creditors via verbal trickery. Here, the farmer greets the philosopher.

STREPSIADES: Hoa! Socrates – What hoa, my little Socrates!
SOCRATES: Mortal, how now! Thou insect of a day,
    What would'st thou?
STREPSIADES: I would know what thou art doing.
SOCRATES: I tread in air, contemplating the sun.
STREPSIADES: Ah! then I see you're basketed so high,
    That you look down upon the Gods – Good hope,
    You'll lower a peg on earth.
SOCRATES: Sublime in air,
    Sublime in thought I carry my mind with me,
    Its cogitations all assimilated
    To the pure atmosphere, in which I float;
    Lower me to earth, and my mind's subtle powers,
    Seiz'd by contagious dullness, lose their spirit;
    For the dry earth drinks up the generous sap,
    The vegetating vigour of philosophy,
    And leaves it a mere husk.
STREPSIADES: What do you say?
    Philosophy has sapt your vigour? Fie upon it.
    But come, my precious fellow, come down quickly,
    And teach me those fine things I'm here in quest of.
SOCRATES: And what fine things are they?
STREPSIADES: A new receipt
    For sending off my creditors, and foiling them

By the art logical; for you shall know
By debts, pawns, pledges, usuries, executions,
I am rackt and rent in tatters.
SOCRATES: Why permit it?
What strange infatuation seiz'd your senses?
STREPSIADES: The horse-consumption, a devouring plague;
But so you'll enter me amongst your scholars,
And tutor me like them to bilk my creditors,
Name your own price, and by the Gods I swear
I'll pay you the last drachma.
SOCRATES: By what Gods?
Answer that first; for your Gods are not mine.
STREPSIADES: How swear you then?
As the Byzantians swear
By their base iron coin?
SOCRATES: Art thou ambitious
To be instructed in celestial matters,
And taught to know them clearly?
STREPSIADES: Aye, aye, in faith,
So they be to my purpose, and celestial.
SOCRATES: What, if I bring you to a conference
With my own proper Goddesses, the Clouds?
STREPSIADES: 'Tis what I wish devoutly.
SOCRATES: Come, sit down;
Repose yourself upon this couch.
STREPSIADES: 'Tis done.
SOCRATES: Now take this chaplet – wear it.
STREPSIADES: Why this chaplet?
Would'st make of me another Athamas,
And sacrifice me to a cloud?
SOCRATES: Fear nothing;
It is a ceremony indispensable
At our initiations.
STREPSIADES: What to gain?
SOCRATES: (*Assuming all the magical solemnity and tone of
voice of an adept.*) Keep silence, then, and listen to a prayer.
Which fits the gravity of age to hear –
Oh! Air, all powerful Air, which dost enfold
This pendant globe, thou vault of flaming gold.
Ye sacred Clouds, who bid the thunder roll,

Shine forth, approach, and cheer your suppliant's soul!

STREPSIADES: Hold, keep 'em off awhile, till I am ready.
Ah! luckless me, wou'd I had brought my bonnet,
And so escap'd a soaking.

SOCRATES: Come, come away!
Fly swift, ye Clouds, and give yourselves to view!
Whether on high Olympus' sacred top
Snow-crown'd ye sit, or in the azure vales
Of your own father. Ocean sporting weave
Your misty dance, or dip your golden urns
In the seven mouths of Nile; whether ye dwell
On Thracian Mimas, or Moeotis' lake,
Hear me, yet hear, and thus invok'd approach!

LYSISTRATA
Aristophanes
412 B.C.

Serio-Comic / 4 Women
   Lysistrata: a woman dedicated to ending the war, 20-30
   Calonice, Myrrhine: women of Athens, 20-30
   Lampito: a Spartan woman, 20-30

The Setting: Athens

Here, plucky Lysistrata convinces the women of Athens to band
together and withhold sex from their warring husbands in hopes that
peace will follow.

LYSISTRATA: If they'd been summoned to worship the God of
   Wine, or Pan, or to visit the Queen of Love, why, you couldn't
   have pushed your way through the streets for all the timbrels.
   But now there's not a single woman here – except my neighbor;
   here she comes.
   (*Enter Calonice.*)
   Good day to you Calonice.
CALONICE: And to you, Lysistrata. (*Noticing Lysistrata's impatient
   air.*) But what ails you? Don't scowl, my dear; it's not becoming
   to you to knit your brows like that.
LYSISTRATA: (*Sadly.*) Ah, Calonice, my heart aches; I'm so
   annoyed at us women. For among men we have a reputation for
   sly trickery –
CALONICE: And rightly too, on my word!
LYSISTRATA: – but when they were told to meet here to consider
   a matter of no small importance, they lie abed and don't come.
CALONICE: Oh, they'll come all right, my dear. It's not easy for a
   woman to get out, you know. One is working on her husband,
   another is getting up the maid, another has to put the baby to bed,
   or wash and feed it.
LYSISTRATA: But after all, there are other matters more important
   than all that.
CALONICE: My dear Lysistrata, just what is this matter you've

summoned us women to consider? What's up? Something big?

LYSISTRATA: Very big.

CALONICE: (*Interested.*) Is it stout, too?

LYSISTRATA: (*Smiling.*) Yes indeed – both big and stout.

CALONICE: What? And the women still haven't come?

LYSISTRATA: It's not what you suppose; they'd have come soon enough for *that*. But I've worked up something, and for many a sleepless night I've turned it this way and that.

CALONICE: (*In mock disappointment.*) Oh, I guess it's pretty fine and slender, if you've turned it this way and that.

LYSISTRATA: So fine that the safety of the whole of Greece lies in us women.

CALONICE: In us women? It depends on a very slender reed then.

LYSISTRATA: Our country's fortunes are in our hands; and whether the Spartans shall perish –

CALONICE: Good! Let them perish, by all means.

LYSISTRATA: – and the Boeotians shall be completely annihilated.

CALONICE: Not completely! Please spare the eels.

LYSISTRATA: As for Athens, I won't use any such unpleasant words. But you understand what I mean. But if the women will meet here – the Spartans, the Boeotians, and we Athenians – then all together we will save Greece.

CALONICE: But what could women do that's clever or distinguished? We just sit around all dolled up in silk robes, looking pretty in our sheer gowns and evening slippers.

LYSISTRATA: These are just the things I hope will save us: these silk robes, perfumes, evening slippers, rouge, and our chiffon blouses.

CALONICE: How so?

LYSISTRATA: So never a man alive will lift a spear against the foe –

CALONICE: I'll get a silk gown at once.

LYSISTRATA: – or take up his shield –

CALONICE: I'll put on my sheerest gown!

LYSISTRATA: – or sword.

CALONICE: I'll buy a pair of evening slippers.

LYSISTRATA: Well then, shouldn't the women have come?

CALONICE: Come? Why, they should have *flown* here.

LYSISTRATA: Well, my dear, just watch: they'll act in true Athenian fashion – everything so late! And now there's not a woman here from the shore or from Salamis.

CALONICE: They're coming, I'm sure; at daybreak they were laying – to their oars to cross the straits.

LYSISTRATA: And those I expected would be the first to come – the women of Acharnae – they haven't arrived.

CALONICE: Yet the wife of Theagenes means to come: she consulted Hecate about it. (*Seeing a group of women approaching.*) But look! Here come a few. And there are some more over here. Hurrah! Where do they come from?

LYSISTRATA: From Anagyra.

CALONICE: Yes indeed! We've raised up quite a stink from Anagyra anyway.

(*Enter Myrrhine in haste, followed by several other women.*)

MYRRHINE: (*Breathlessly.*) Have we come in time, Lysistrata? What do you say? Why so quiet?

LYSISTRATA: I can't say much for you, Myrrhine, coming at this hour on such important business.

MYRRHINE: Why, I had trouble finding my girdle in the dark. But if it's so important, we're here now! Tell us.

LYSISTRATA: No. Let's wait a little for the women from Boeotia and the Peloponnesus.

MYRRHINE: That's a much better suggestion. Look! Here comes Lampito now.

(*Enter Lampito with two women.*)

LYSISTRATA: Greetings, my dear Spartan friend. How pretty you look, my dear. What a smooth complexion and well-developed figure! You could throttle an ox.

LAMPITO: Faith, yes, I think I could. I take exercises and kick my heels against my bum.

(*She demonstrates with a few steps of the Spartan "bottom-kicking" dance.*)

LYSISTRATA: And what splendid breasts you have.

LAMPITO: La! You handle me like a prize steer.

LYSISTRATA: And who is this young lady with you?

LAMPITO: Faith, she's an Ambassadress from Boeotia.

LYSISTRATA: Oh yes, a Boeotian, and blooming like a garden too.

CALONICE: (*Lifting up her skirt.*) My word! How neatly her garden's weeded!

LYSISTRATA: And who is the other girl?

LAMPITO: Oh, she's a Corinthian swell.

MYRRHINE: (*After a rapid examination.*) Yes indeed. She swells very nicely (*Pointing.*) here and here.

LAMPITO: Who has gathered together this company of women?

LYSISTRATA: I have.

LAMPITO: Speak up, then. What do you want?

MYRRHINE: Yes, my dear, tell us what this important matter is.

LYSISTRATA: Very well, I'll tell you. But before I speak, let me ask you a little question.

MYRRHINE: Anything you like.

LYSISTRATA: (*Earnestly.*) Tell me: don't you yearn for the fathers of your children, who are away at the wars? I know you all have husbands abroad.

CALONICE: Why yes; mercy me! My husband's been away for five months in Thrace keeping guard on – Eucrates.

MYRRHINE: And mine for seven whole months in Pylus.

LAMPITO: And mine, as soon as ever he returns from the fray, readjusts his shield and flies out of the house again.

LYSISTRATA: And as for lovers, there's not even a ghost of one left. Since the Milesians revolted from us, I've not even seen an eight-inch dingus to be a leather consolation for us widows. Are you willing, if I can find a way, to help me end the war?

MYRRHINE: Goodness, yes! I'd do it, even if I had to pawn my dress and – get drunk on the spot!

CALONICE: And I, even if I had to let myself be split in two like a flounder.

LAMPITO: I'd climb up Mt. Taygetus if I could catch a glimpse of peace.

LYSISTRATA: I'll tell you, then, in plain and simple words. My friends, if we are going to force our men to make peace, we must do without –

MYRRHINE: Without what? Tell us.

LYSISTRATA: Will you do it?

MYRRHINE: We'll do it, if it kills us.

LYSISTRATA: Well then, we must do without sex altogether. (*General consternation.*) Why do you turn away? Where go you? Why turn so pale? Why those tears? Will you do it or not? What means this hesitation?

MYRRHINE: I won't do it! Let the war go on.

CALONICE: Nor I! Let the war go on.

LYSISTRATA: So, my little flounder? Didn't you say just now you'd split yourself in half?

CALONICE: Anything else you like. I'm willing, even if I have to walk through fire. Anything rather than sex. There's nothing like it, my dear.

LYSISTRATA: (*To Myrrhine.*) What about you?

MYRRHINE: (*Sullenly.*) I'm willing to walk through fire, too.

LYSISTRATA: Oh vile and cursed breed! No wonder they make tragedies about us: we're naught but "love-affairs and bassinets." But you, my dear Spartan friend, if you alone are with me, our enterprise might yet succeed. Will you vote with me?

LAMPITO: 'Tis cruel hard, by my faith, for a woman to sleep alone without her nooky; but for all that, we certainly do need peace.

LYSISTRATA: O my dearest friend! You're the only real woman here.

CALONICE: (*Wavering.*) Well, if we do refrain from – (*Shuddering.*) what you say (God forbid!), would that bring peace?

LYSISTRATA: My goodness, yes! If we sit at home all rouged and powdered, dressed in our sheerest gowns, and neatly depilated, our men will get excited and want to take us; but if you don't come to them and keep away, they'll soon make a truce.

LAMPITO: Aye; Menelaus caught sight of Helen's naked breast and dropped his sword, they say.

CALONICE: What if the men give us up?

LYSISTRATA: "Flay a skinned dog," as Pherecrates says.

CALONICE: Rubbish! These make-shifts are no good. But suppose they grab us and drag us into the bedroom?

LYSISTRATA: Hold on to the door.

CALONICE: And if they beat us?

LYSISTRATA: Give in with bad grace. There's no pleasure in it for them when they have to use violence. And you must torment them in every possible way. They'll give up soon enough; a man gets no joy if he doesn't get along with his wife.

MYRRHINE: If this is your opinion, we agree.

LAMPITO: As for our own men, we can persuade them to make a just and fair peace; but what about the Athenian rabble? Who will persuade them not to start any more monkey-shines?

LYSISTRATA: Don't worry. We guarantee to convince them.

LAMPITO: Not while their ships are rigged so well and they have that mighty treasure in the temple of Athene.

LYSISTRATA: We've taken good care for that too: we shall seize the Acropolis today. The older women have orders to do this, and while we are making our arrangements, they are to pretend to make a sacrifice and occupy the Acropolis.

LAMPITO: All will be well then. That's a very fine idea.

LYSISTRATA: Let's ratify this, Lampito, with the most solemn oath.

LAMPITO: Tell us what oath we shall swear.

LYSISTRATA: Well said. Where's our Policewoman? (*To a Scythian slave.*) What are you gaping at? Set a shield upside-down here in front of me, and give me the sacred meats.

CALONICE: Lysistrata, what sort of oath are we to take?

LYSISTRATA: What oath? I'm going to slaughter a sheep over the shield, as they do in Aeschylus.

CALONICE: Don't Lysistrata! No oaths about peace over a shield.

LYSISTRATA: What shall the oath be, then?

CALONICE: How about getting a white horse somewhere and cutting out its entrails for the sacrifice?

LYSISTRATA: White horse indeed!

CALONICE: Well then, how shall we swear?

MYRRHINE: I'll tell you: let's place a large black bowl upside-down and then slaughter – a flask of Thasian wine. And then let's swear – not to pour in a single drop of water.

LAMPITO: Lord! How I like that oath!

LYSISTRATA: Someone bring out a bowl and a flask.
(*A slave brings the utensils for the sacrifice.*)

CALONICE: Look, my friend! What a big jar! Here's a cup that 'twould give me joy to handle. (*She picks up the bowl.*)

LYSISTRATA: Set it down and put your hands on our victim. (*As Calonice places her hands on the flask.*) O Lady of Persuasion and dear Loving Cup, graciously vouchsafe to receive this sacrifice from us women. (*She pours the wine into the bowl.*)

CALONICE: The blood has a good colour and spurts out nicely.

LAMPITO: Faith, it has a pleasant smell, too.

MYRRHINE: Oh, let me be the first to swear, ladies!

CALONICE: No, by our Lady! Not unless you're allotted the first turn.

LYSISTRATA: Place all your hands on the cup, and one of you repeat on behalf of what I say. Then all will swear and ratify the oath. *I will suffer no man, be he husband or lover,*

CALONICE: *I will suffer no man, be he husband or lover,*

LYSISTRATA: *To approach me all hot and horny. (As Calonice hesitates.)* Say it!

CALONICE: *(Slowly and painfully:) To approach me all hot and horny.* O Lysistrata, I feel so weak in the knees!

LYSISTRATA: *I will remain at home unmated,*

CALONICE: *I will remain at home unmated,*

LYSISTRATA: *Wearing my sheerest gown and carefully adorned,*

CALONICE: *Wearing my sheerest gown and carefully adorned,*

LYSISTRATA: *That my husband may burn with desire for me.*

CALONICE: *That my husband may burn with desire for me.*

LYSISTRATA: *And if he takes me by force against my will,*

CALONICE: *And if he takes me by force against my will,*

LYSISTRATA: *I shall do it badly and keep from moving.*

CALONICE: *I shall do it badly and keep from moving.*

LYSISTRATA: *I will not stretch my slippers toward the ceiling,*

CALONICE: *I will not stretch my slippers toward the ceiling,*

LYSISTRATA: *Nor will I take the posture of the lioness on the knife-handle.*

CALONICE: *Nor will I take the posture of the lioness on the knife-handle.*

LYSISTRATA: *If I keep this oath, may I be permitted to drink from this cup,*

CALONICE: *If I keep this oath, may I be permitted to drink from this cup,*

LYSISTRATA: *But if I break it, may the cup be filled with water.*

CALONICE: *But if I break it, may the cup be filled with water.*

LYSISTRATA: Do you all swear to this?

ALL: I do, so help me!

LYSISTRATA: Come then, I'll just consummate this offering. *(She takes a long drink from the cup.)*

CALONICE: *(Snatching the cup way.)* Shares, my dear! Let's drink to our continued friendship. *(A shout is heard from off-stage.)*

LAMPITO: What's that shouting?

LYSISTRATA: That's what I was telling you; the women have just seized the Acropolis. Now, Lampito, go home and arrange matters in Sparta; and leave these two ladies here as hostages. We'll enter the Acropolis to join our friends and help them lock the gates.

CALONICE: Don't you suppose that the men will come to attack us?

LYSISTRATA: Don't worry about them. Neither threats nor fire will suffice to open the gates, except on the terms we've stated.

CALONICE: I should say not! Else we'd belie our reputation as unmanageable pests.

MILES GLORIOSUS
Plautus
205 B.C.

Serio-Comic / 2 Men
Palaestrio: a cunning slave, 30-50
Sceledrus: a stupid slave, 30-50

The Setting: Ephesus

Sceledrus has been left to guard Philocomasium, a beautiful courtesan.
When she manages to slip away, he begs Palaestrio for help.

SCELEDRUS: Unless I've just been having a nightmare,
   Walking around on top of the roof,
   Honest to Pollux I'd swear I saw
   Philocomasium, master's girl friend,
   Here, next door, up to no good.
PALAESTRIO: He's the one who saw her kissing –
   I've heard him say that much himself.
SCELEDRUS: Who's that?
PALAESTRIO: Your fellow slave, What is it,
   Sceledrus?
SCELEDRUS: Oh, Palaestrio,
   I'm so happy to see you!
PALAESTRIO: Why?
   What's the trouble? Give me a clue.
SCELEDRUS: I'm afraid –
PALAESTRIO: Of what?
SCELEDRUS: O Here! I'm afraid
   That today all the slaves in our house
   Will get lifted up to hang from the cross.
PALAESTRIO: Go lift yourself! I don't much care
   For these uplifting thoughts of yours.
SCELEDRUS: Probably you don't know the amazing
   Thing that has just happened in here.
PALAESTRIO: What thing do you mean?
SCELEDRUS: It's wicked and awful!

PALAESTRIO: Keep it to yourself, then. Don't tell me;
  I've no desire to know.
SCELEDRUS: Well,
  I won't allow you not to know.
  Today I chased our little monkey
  Over onto this man's roof.
PALAESTRIO: Great Pollux, Sceledrus, why in the world
  Would a chimp be chased by a chump like you?
SCELEDRUS: Oh, go to hell!
PALAESTRIO: Well, my advice
  To you, my friend, is go – on speaking.
SCELEDRUS: As luck would have it, through the skylight
  I looked down to the house next door.
  There I saw Philocomasium kissing
  Some young fellow I didn't know.
PALAESTRIO: Sceledrus! A scandalous, slanderous lie!
SCELEDRUS: I definitely saw her.
PALAESTRIO: You?
SCELEDRUS: Yes, me.
  I saw her with these two eyes of mine.
PALAESTRIO: Go on, you didn't! A likely story!
SCELEDRUS: Do you think there's something wrong with my eyes?
PALAESTRIO: I don't give medical advice.
  But if the gods are on your side,
  You'll have the sense to drop that tale.
  I warn you not to lose your head:
  You might not get it back again.
  Unless you stop that stupid talk
  A double death's in store for you.
SCELEDRUS: Why do you say double?
PALAESTRIO: I'll explain.
  In the first case, if you falsely charge
  Our Philocomasium, you're a goner!
  In the second, if your facts are right
  And you were the guard, you're a goner again.
SCELEDRUS: I don't know what'll become of me:
  I only know I really saw it.
PALAESTRIO: Do you still insist, you idiot?
SCELEDRUS: What
  Do you want me to say except what I saw?

Anyhow, she's still inside right here,
At the house next door.
PALAESTRIO: What, not at home?
SCELEDRUS: Take a look, go inside yourself;
I don't ask you to take my word.
PALAESTRIO: All right, I'll go. (*Exit into soldier's house.*)
SCELEDRUS: I'll wait for you here.
(*To audience.*) While I'm at it, I'll set a trap;
I'll catch that heifer and tan her hide,
As soon as she tries to return to the barn.
What am I going to do? The soldier
Put me in charge of guarding her.
If I accuse her now, I'm through;
I'm through all the same if I shut up
And the news gets out. What in the world's
More shameless and depraved than women?
While I was upon the roof, that girl
Just left her room and went outside.
Pollux! What a brazen bitch!
If the soldier finds this out,
I swear to Herc he'll hang the house
And hoist yours truly on the cross.
Whatever happens, I'll keep mum
Rather than die in agony.
How can I possibly guard a woman
Who's always got herself for sale?
PALAESTRIO: (*Emerging from the soldier's house.*)
Sceledrus, Sceledrus, what other man
Is such a barefaced liar as you?
When you were born the gods above
Must've groaned with anger!
SCELEDRUS: What is it?
PALAESTRIO: Do you want to get your eyes gouged out,
When they're seeing things that don't exist?
SCELEDRUS: That don't exist?
PALAESTRIO: I wouldn't buy
Your claim to life for a worm-eaten walnut!
SCELEDRUS: What's the trouble?
PALAESTRIO: What's the trouble,
You're asking me?

SCELEDRUS: Why not ask you?

PALAESTRIO: Wouldn't it be a good idea
To get your tattletale tongue cut out?

SCELEDRUS: My what?

PALAESTRIO: Look! Philocomasium's
At home – the girl you saw next door,
Kissing and hugging another man.

SCELEDRUS: I'm surprised you can't afford
To drink a better grade of wine.

PALAESTRIO: Come again?

SCELEDRUS: There's something wrong with your eyes.

PALAESTRIO: Well, as for you my squinting friend,
You're blind: that's all that's wrong with *your* eyes.
The woman's definitely at home.

SCELEDRUS: At home, you say?

PALAESTRIO: At home, I say.

SCELEDRUS: You're pulling my leg, Palaestrio.

PALAESTRIO: Then I'd better go home and wash my hands.

SCELEDRUS: How's that?

PALAESTRIO: 'Cause you're a muddy mess.

SCELEDRUS: You go to hell!

PALAESTRIO: You'll go to hell,
Sceledrus, I promise you,
Unless you get a new pair of eyes
And learn to sing another tune.
But look! Our door is opening here.

SCELEDRUS: (*Indicating Periplectomenus' house.*)
Well, *this* is the door I'm looking at;
There's no way that she can cross
From here to here, except by the door.

PALAESTRIO: Look! She's home! Oh, Sceledrus,
Some bee in your bonnet is bugging you.

SCELEDRUS: I see for myself, I think for myself,
I trust myself more than anyone else:
No man is going to frighten me off
From knowing she's inside this house.
I'll plant myself here, in case that girl
Crawls to her home while I'm off guard.

PALAESTRIO: (*Aside.*) I've got him now; I'll whirl him about
And hurl him down from his towering fort.

(*To Sceledrus.*) Do you want me to try to make you admit
You're feeble-sighted?

SCELEDRUS: Go ahead and try.

PALAESTRIO: That you haven't got a brain in your head –
That your eyes are useless?

SCELEDRUS: That I'd love!

PALAESTRIO: I believe you said our master's girl
Was over here?

SCELEDRUS: Yes. Furthermore,
I say I saw her playing around,
Inside the house, with another man.

PALAESTRIO: You know there isn't a passageway
From here to our house.

SCELEDRUS: Yes, I know.

PALAESTRIO: No balcony or garden route
Unless you fly through the skylight.

SCELEDRUS: I know.

PALAESTRIO: Well then, if she's home, and if
I make you see her leaving our house,
Have you earned a thumping?

SCELEDRUS: All right.

PALAESTRIO: Watch that door. Don't let her sneak out
Secretly to cross this way.

SCELEDRUS: That's just my plan.

PALAESTRIO: I'll soon produce
Her here, in person, on the street.

PSEUDOLUS
Plautus
191 B.C.

Serio-Comic / 2 Men

Pseudolus: a cunning slave, 30-50
Calidorus: his master's teenaged son, 16-18

The Setting: Athens

Calidorus is madly in love with the beautiful Phoenicium and here appeals to the crafty Pseudolus to help him win her heart.

PSEUDOLUS: Master, if only I could read your mind
    And learn the torture that's tormenting you,
    I'd gladly spare two men a lot of bother:
    I wouldn't need to ask, or you to answer.
    Now, since that's impossible, necessity
    Compels me to question you. Answer me this:
    Why have you been acting half alive
    These last few days, toting letter-tablets
    Everywhere and drenching them with tears,
    Taking no one into your confidence?
    (*Heroically.*) Give voice, that I may know what I know not.
CALIDORUS: Oh, Pseudolus, I'm suffering!
PSEUDOLUS: Jupiter forbid!
CALIDORUS: It's out of Jupiter's control;
    Venus rules the region of my pain.
PSEUDOLUS: Am I allowed some knowledge? In the past,
    You've made me privy-partner of your plans.
CALIDORUS: My attitude's unchanged.
PSEUDOLUS: Then state your problem.
    I can offer cash, concern, or kind advice.
CALIDORUS: (*Handing him the tablets.*)
    Take this message; learn for yourself
    Why I am quite consumptified with gloom and worry.
PSEUDOLUS: As you wish. (*Examining tablets.*) But oh! What's this?

CALIDORUS: What is it?

PSEUDOLUS: I think these letters must be sexy characters:
They're climbing all over each other.

CALIDORUS: Very funny.

PSEUDOLUS: Holy Pol, unless the Sibyl reads this first,
No one else could ever decipher it.

CALIDORUS: Why are you so rude to charming letters,
Charming tablets, traced with a charming hand?

PSEUDOLUS: Excuse me, sir; do chickens now have hands?
These are hen-tracts.

CALIDORUS: Oh, you make me sick.
Read it or hand it back.

PSEUDOLUS: All right, I'll read.
Take heart.

CALIDORUS: My heart is lost.

PSEUDOLUS: Well, find it again!

CALIDORUS: No, I'll keep quiet, find it yourself in the wax.
That's where my heart resides – my breast is vacant now.

PSEUDOLUS: (*Suddenly.*) I see your girl friend, Calidorus.

CALIDORUS: (*Startled.*) Where is she? Where?

PSEUDOLUS: (*Pointing to her name.*)
Here, stretched out upon the boards, relaxed in wax.

CALIDORUS: (*Furious.*) May the gods all smother you –

PSEUDOLUS: – with happiness.

CALIDORUS: (*Tragically.*)
My life's been brief, like a blade of summer grass:
Sudden was my birth, and suddenly I'm gone.

PSEUDOLUS: Shut up, I'm trying to read.

CALIDORUS: Why not begin?

PSEUDOLUS: (*Reading.*)
"Phoenicium to her darling Calidorus:
With wax and string and these appealing characters
I wish you love and health; your healing love I beg.
My eyes are moist, my heart and soul are faltering."

CALIDORUS: I'm sunk, Pseudolus! I can't find the healing love
To send her back.

PSEUDOLUS: What healing love?

CALIDORUS: The silver kind.

PSEUDOLUS: (*Waving the tablets.*)
You're willing to repay her wooden love

With silver? Keep your wits about you, please!

CALIDORUS: Read on, and soon the letter will explain
How urgently that silver must be found.

PSEUDOLUS: "My pimp has sold me to a foreigner
(A Macedonian military man)
For twenty silver minas, dearest love.
Before that soldier left, he paid out fifteen
In advance. Now there's a balance of only five.
Therefore the soldier left a token here,
A portrait wax impression from his ring.
And so, when someone brings a token like it,
I'm to be sent with him at once. A day is set
For the transaction: next Dionysia."

CALIDORUS: And that's tomorrow!! I'm on the brink of doom,
Unless you've help to offer.

PSEUDOLUS: Let me finish.

CALIDORUS: Yes! I feel as though I'm talking with her.
Read – you give me bittersweet delight.

PSEUDOLUS: (*Reading again, with increasing fervor.*)
"Now our loves, our lives, our passionate embraces,
Laughter, fun, sweet talk, and sexy face-to-faces,
Slender little hips and thighs a-jiggle,
Tender little lips and tongues a-wiggle,
Juicy jousts of bouncy-boob and titty-tickle –
All our hopes of orgiastic consummation
Face dismemberment, disaster, desolation,
If we fail to find some mutual salvation.
Everything I know I've tried to tell you clearly:
Now I'll put you to the test. One question, merely:
Are you in love or just pretending?

                                   Yours sincerely."

CALIDORUS: An awful letter, Pseudolus.

PSEUDOLUS: Absolutely awful!

CALIDORUS: Why aren't you crying?

PSEUDOLUS: I've got stony eyes; I can't
Implore them to spit out a single tear.

CALIDORUS: How's that?

PSEUDOLUS: Hereditary dry-eye-itis.

CALIDORUS: Won't you help me just a little?

PSEUDOLUS: What should I do?

CALIDORUS: *Oh, dear!*
PSEUDOLUS: "Oh, dear"? Great Herc, no need to scrimp
    In that department; go ahead.
CALIDORUS: I'm so depressed, I can't find any cash to borrow –
PSEUDOLUS: *Oh, dear!*
CALIDORUS: There's not a penny in the house –
PSEUDOLUS: *Oh, dear!*
CALIDORUS: He's going to carry off my girl tomorrow –
PSEUDOLUS: *Oh, dear!*
CALIDORUS: Do you really think that helps?
PSEUDOLUS: I give what I've got:
    I have an inexhaustible supply of groans.
CALIDORUS: It's all over for me today. But can you lend me
    A single drachma I'd pay back tomorrow?
PSEUDOLUS: Hardly – not if my life were on the line.
    What will you do with a drachma?
CALIDORUS: Buy a rope.
PSEUDOLUS: What for?
CALIDORUS: To help me learn to swing. (*Tragically.*) I plan,
    Ere shadows fall, to fall among the shades.
PSEUDOLUS: Then who'll pay back the drachma that I gave you?
    Is that why you want to hang yourself, you sneak,
    To dun me out of the drachma I've donated?
CALIDORUS: There just no way that I can go on living
    If she is grabbed from me and granted to another.
    (*Bursts into tears.*)
PSEUDOLUS: Why cry, you cuckoo? You'll survive.
CALIDORUS: I've got to cry:
    I haven't any money of my own,
    No hope on earth of scraping up a scrap.
PSEUDOLUS: If I caught the drift of the lady's billet-doux,
    Your eyes have got to shower silver tears,
    Or this pretentious crying act will help
    As much as catching raindrops in a sieve.
    Don't fear, my lovesick dear, I won't desert you.
    Somewhere, somehow, some way (maybe) today
    I'll find you silvery succor and salvation.
    Where, oh where will it come from? I don't know,
    But I know it will: I've got a twitching brow.
CALIDORUS: I only hope your deeds can match your words!

PSEUDOLUS: Holy Herc! If once I bang my holy gong,
You know the holy rumpus I can raise!

CALIDORUS: You're now the repository of all my hopes.

PSEUDOLUS: Is it enough if I get this girl for you today
As your very own, or if I give you twenty minas?

CALIDORUS: It's enough – if it happens.

PSEUDOLUS: Demand your twenty minas,
So you'll know I'll carry out my promise to you.
Make it all quite legal: I'm itching to take the oath.

CALIDORUS: (*Formally.*)
Sir, this day will you give me twenty minas?

PSEUDOLUS: Sir, I will. And now don't be a nuisance.
Listen to this, if you still have any doubts:
If all else fails, I'll pinch it from your papa.

CALIDORUS: God save you, I love you! But look: if possible,
For goodness' sake, put the pinch on Mother, too.

PSEUDOLUS: Dispel these worries from your fevered nose.

CALIDORUS: My fevered brain, do you mean?

PSEUDOLUS: I hate clichés.
(*Hailing the audience.*)
Now hear ye, hear ye! Lend an ear, ye!
These are my solemn words of public warning
For the throng assembled here this morning,
All the citizens by tribe enrolled,
All my acquaintances and friends of old:
If you should meet me, be on guard today,
And don't believe a single word I say.

CALIDORUS: (*Startled by a noise from Ballio's house.*)
Shh!
Sweet Hercules, keep quiet!

PSEUDOLUS: Why, what's up?

CALIDORUS: The pimp's front door just gave a squeaking noise.

PSEUDOLUS: I'd rather twist his legs to make *him* squeak.

CALIDORUS: He's coming out in person: Lord of Lies!

MEDEA
Seneca
1st. Century A.D.

Dramatic / 1 Man, 1 Woman
Jason: Golden Fleece thief, 30s
Medea: his unhappy wife, 20-30

The Setting: the house of Jason, Corinth

When Jason decides to repudiate his marriage to Medea in order to marry the daughter of Creon, Medea is driven to despair and madness. Here, Medea finds the perfect revenge in the murder of their two young sons.

JASON: Lo, there she stands upon the lofty battlements!
  Bring torches! fire the house, that she may fall ensnared
  By those devices she herself hath planned.
MEDEA: (*Derisively.*) Not so,
  But rather build a lofty pyre for these thy sons;
  Their funeral rites prepare. Already for they bride
  And father have I done the service due the dead;
  For in their ruined palace have I buried them.
  One son of thine has met his doom; and this shall die
  Before his father's face.
JASON: By all the gods, and by the perils of our flight,
  And by our marriage bound which I have ne'er betrayed,
  I pray thee spare the boy, for he is innocent.
  If aught of sin there be, 'tis mine. Myself I give
  To be the victim. Take my guilty soul for his.
MEDEA: 'Tis for thy prayers and tears
  I draw, not sheathe the sword.
  Go now, and take thee maids for wives, thou faithless one;
  Abandon and betray the mother of thy sons.
JASON: And yet, I pray thee, let one sacrifice atone.
MEDEA: If in the blood of one my passion could be quenched,
  No vengeance had it sought. Though both my sons I slay,
  The number still is all too small to satisfy

My boundless grief.

JASON: Then finish what thou hast begun –
I ask no more – and grant at least that no delay
Prolong my helpless agony.

MEDEA: Now hasten not,
Relentless passion, but enjoy a slow revenge.
This day is in thy hands; its fertile hours employ.

JASON: Oh, take my life, thou heartless one.

MEDEA: Thou bid'st me pity –
Well! (*Slays the second child.*) – 'Tis done!
No more atonement, passion, can I offer thee.
Now hither lift they tearful eyes ungrateful one.
Dost recognize thy wife? 'Twas thus of old I fled.
The heavens themselves provide me with a safe retreat.
(*A chariot drawn by dragons appears in the air.*)
Twin serpents bow their necks submissive to the yoke
Now, father, take thy sons; while I, upon my car,
With wingéd speed am borne aloft through realms of air.
(*Mounts her car and is borne away.*)

JASON: (*Calling after her.*) Speed on through realms of air that
mortals never see:
But, witness heaven, where thou art gone no gods can be!

ADAM

Anonymous

12th Century

Dramatic / 2 Men
    Adam: the first man, 20s
    The Devil: a fallen angel, 30-40

The Setting: the garden of Eden

Here, the Devil tries unsuccessfully to tempt Adam.

DEVIL: How liv'st thou, Adam?
ADAM: In felicity.
DEVIL: Is it well with thee?
ADAM: There's nothing vexeth me.
DEVIL: It can be better.
ADAM: Nay – I know not how.
DEVIL: Then, wouldst thou know?
ADAM: It recks me little now.
DEVIL: I know, forsooth!
ADAM: What boots it me to learn?
DEVIL: And why not, pray?
ADAM: Naught doth it me concern.
DEVIL: Concern thee 't will!
ADAM: I know not when.
DEVIL: I'll not make haste to tell thee, then.
ADAM: Nay, tell me!
DEVIL: No! I'll keep thee waiting
    Till thou art sick of supplicating.
ADAM: To know this thing I have no need.
DEVIL: Thou dost deserve no boon, indeed!
    The boon thou hast thou canst not use.
ADAM: Prithee, how's that?
DEVIL: Thou'lt not refuse
    To hear? Well, then – 'twixt thee and me, –
ADAM: I'll listen, most assuredly!
DEVIL: Now mark me, Adam. I tell thee it

For thine own good.

ADAM: That I'll admit.

DEVIL: Thou'lt trust me, then?

ADAM: Full trust I bring!

DEVIL: In every point?

ADAM: All – save one thing.

DEVIL: What thing is that?

ADAM: This: I'll do naught
Offensive to my Maker's thought.

DEVIL: Dost fear him so?

ADAM: I fear him; yes –
Both love and fear.

DEVIL: That's foolishness!
What can he do thee?

ADAM: Good and bale.

DEVIL: Thou'st listened to an idle tale!
An evil thing befall thee? Why,
In glory born, thou canst not die!

ADAM: God saith I'll die, without redress,
Whene'er his precepts I transgress.

DEVIL: What is this great transgression, pray?
I fain would learn without delay.

ADAM: I'll tell thee all in perfect truth.
This the command he gave, forsooth:
Of all the fruits of Paradise
I've leave to eat (such his advice) –
– All, save one only, which is banned;
That I'll not touch, e'en with my hand.

DEVIL: Which fruit is that?

(*Then let Adam stretch forth his hand and shew him the
forbidden fruit, saying:*)

ADAM: See'st yonder tree?
That fruit hath he forbidden me.

DEVIL: Dost know the reason?

ADAM: Certes, no!

DEVIL: The occasion of this thing I'll show:
No whit cares he for all the rest;
But yon, that hangeth loftiest,
– The fruit of Knowledge – can bestow
The gift all mysteries to know.

If thou eat'st; that, 't will profit thee.

ADAM; In what way, pray?

DEVIL: That thou shalt see:
Thine eyes will straightway be unsealed,
All future things to thee revealed;
All that thou will'st thou canst perform;
'T will bring thee blessings in a swarm.
Eat, and thou shalt repent it not;
Then thou'lt not fear thy God in aught;
Instead, thou'lt be in all his peer;
For this, he filled they soul with fear.
Wilt trust me? Then to taste proceed.

ADAM: That will I not!

DEVIL: Fine words, indeed! Thou wilt not?

ADAM: No!

DEVIL: A fool art thou!
Thou'lt yet mind what I tell thee now.
(*Then let the Devil depart; and he shall go to the other demons,
and he shall make an excursion through the square; and after
some little interval, cheerful and rejoicing, he shall return to his
tempting of Adam, and he shall say unto him:*)
How farest thou, Adam? Wilt change they mind?
Or still to stubbornness inclined?
I meant to tell thee recently
God as his almsman keepeth thee.
He put thee here the fruit to eat;
Hast other recreation sweet?

ADAM: Here nothing lacks I could desire.

DEVIL: Dost to naught loftier aspire?
Canst boast thyself a man of price!
– God's gardener of Paradise?
He made thee keeper of his park;
Wilt thou not seek a higher mark?
Filling thy belly! – Surely, he
Had nobler aims in mind for thee!
Listen now, Adam, and attend
The honest counsel that I lend:
Thou couldest from thy Lord be free,
And thy Creator's equal be.
In brief, I'll this assurance make:

If of this apple thou partake.
(*Then shall he lift his hand toward Paradise.*)
Then thou shalt reign in majesty!
In power, God's partner thou canst be!

ADAM: Go! Get thee hence!

DEVIL: What! Adam. – How!

ADAM: Go! Get thee hence! Satan art thou!
I'll counsel giv'st thou.

DEVIL: How, pray tell?

ADAM: Thou would'st deliver me to hell!
Thou would'st me with my Lord embroil,
Move me from bliss to bale and moil.
I will not trust thee! Get thee hence!!
Nor ever have the impudence
Again to come before my face!
Traitor forsworn, withouten grace!

THE FARCE OF THE WORTHY MASTER
PIERRE PATELIN

Anonymous
1469

Serio-Comic / 2 Men, 1 Woman

    Patelin: a crafty lawyer, 30-40
    Guillemette: his wife, 30-40
    The Draper: a merchant, 20-50

The Setting: a little town in France, 1400

Business has been slow for Patelin, who cannot afford to buy his wife fabric for a new dress. Clever Patelin hatches the following scheme by which he hopes to cheat the draper out of some cloth.

    (*The back curtains are drawn aside showing Patelin's chamber.*)
PATELIN: (*Running in.*) Wife, wife . . .
    (*Guillemette enters, the old gown in her hand.*)
    Well, Madam . . . now . . . I've got it . . . right here I have it. What did I tell you?
GUILLEMETTE: What have you?
PATELIN: Something you desire greatly. But what are you doing with this old rag? I think it will do well for a bed for your cat. I did promise you a new gown and get you one I did.
GUILLEMETTE: What's gotten into your head? Did you drink anything on the way?
PATELIN: And it's paid for, Madam. It's paid for, I tell you.
GUILLEMETTE: Are you making sport of me? What are you plappering?
PATELIN: I have it right here.
GUILLEMETTE: What have you?
PATELIN: Cloth fit for the Queen of Sheba. (*Displaying the cloth.*) Here it is!
GUILLEMETTE: Holy Virgin! Where did you steal it? Who'll pay for it? What kind of a scrape have you gotten into now?
PATELIN: You need not worry, good Dame. It's paid for . . . and a

good price at that.

GUILLEMETTE: Why, how much did it cost? You did not have a copper when you left.

PATELIN: It cost nine francs, fair Lady . . . a bottle of red wine . . . and the wing of a roasted goose.

GUILLEMETTE: Are you crazy? You had no money, no goose!!!

PATELIN: Aye, aye, that I did. I paid for it as it behooves one of the learned profession of law; in promissory statements. And the merchant who took them is no fool either, oh, no; not a fool at all; but a very wise man and a shrewd . . .

GUILLEMETTE: Who was he? How . . .

PATELIN: He is the king of asses, the Pope of Idiots, the chancellor of baboons . . . our worthy neighbor, the long-nosed draper, Master Joceaulme.

GUILLEMETTE: Will you cease this jabbering and tell me how it happened? How did he come to trust you? There is no worse skinflint in town than he.

PATELIN: Ah, wife! My head! My knowledge of the law! I turned him into a noble and fine lord. I told him what a jewel his father was; I laid on him all the nine virtues thick as wax, and . . . in the end he trusted me most willingly with six yards of his fine cloth.

GUILLEMETTE: Ho, ho, ho, you are a marvel! And when does he expect to get paid?

PATELIN: By noon.

GUILLEMETTE: Holy Lord, what will we do when he comes for the money?

PATELIN: He'll be here for it and soon to boot. He must be dreaming even now of his nine francs, and his wine, and the goose. Oh, we'll give him a goose! Now you get the bed ready and I'll get in.

GUILLEMETTE: What for?

PATELIN: As soon as he comes and asks for me, swear by all the Saints that I've been in bed here for the last two months. Tell it in a sad voice and with tears in your eyes. And if he says anything, shout at him to speak lower. If he cries: "My cloth, my money," tell him he is crazy, that I haven't been from bed for weeks. And if he doesn't go with that, I'll dance him a little tune that'll make him wonder whether he is on earth or in hell.

(Patelin puts on his nightgown and cap. Guillemette goes to the door and returns quickly.)

GUILLEMETTE: He is coming, he is coming; what if he arrests you?

PATELIN: Don't worry; just do what I tell you. Quick, hide this cloth under the bedclothes. Don't forget. I've been sick for two months.

GUILLEMETTE: Quick, quick, here he is.

(Patelin gets into bed and draws the curtains. Guillemette sits down and begins to mend the old dress. The Draper enters.)

THE DRAPER: Good day, fair Dame.

GUILLEMETTE: Sh . . . for the Saints' sake. Speak lower.

THE DRAPER: Why? What's the matter?

GUILLEMETTE: You don't know!

THE DRAPER: Where is he?

GUILLEMETTE: Alas! Nearer to Paradise than to Earth. *(Begins to cry.)*

THE DRAPER: Who?

GUILLEMETTE: How can you be so heartless and ask me that, when you know he has been in bed for the last eleven weeks?

THE DRAPER: Who?

GUILLEMETTE: My husband.

THE DRAPER: Who?

GUILLEMETTE: My husband – Master Pierre, once a lawyer . . . and now a sick man . . . on his death-bed.

THE DRAPER: What!!!!!

GUILLEMETTE: *(Crying.)* You have not heard of it? Alas! And . . .

THE DRAPER: And who was it just took six yards of cloth from my shop?

GUILLEMETTE: Alas! How am I to know? It was surely not he.

THE DRAPER: You must be dreaming, good woman. Are you his wife? The wife of Pierre Patelin, the lawyer?

GUILLEMETTE: That I am, good Sir.

THE DRAPER: Then it was your husband, who was such a good friend of my father, who came to my shop a quarter of an hour ago and bought six yards of cloth for nine francs. And now I am here for my money. Where is he?

GUILLEMETTE: This is no time for jesting, sir.

THE DRAPER: Are you crazy? I want my money, that's all.

GUILLEMETTE: Don't scream. It's little sleep he gets as it is, and here you come squealing like a dying pig. He has been in bed for twelve weeks and hardly slept three nights.

THE DRAPER: Who? What are you talking about?

GUILLEMETTE: Who! My poor sick husband.

(*Weeps.*)

THE DRAPER: Come! What's this? Stop that fooling. I want my money, my nine francs.

GUILLEMETTE: (*Screaming.*) Don't scream so loud. He is dying.

THE DRAPER: But that's a black lie. He was at my shop, but a quarter of an hour ago.

PATELIN: (*Groaning from behind the curtain.*) Au, au, au . . .

GUILLEMETTE: Ah, there he is on his deathbed. He has been there for thirteen weeks yesterday without eating as much as a fly.

THE DRAPER: What are you talking about? He was at my shop just now and bought six yards of cloth . . . blue cloth.

GUILLEMETTE: How can you make sport of me? Good Master Guillaume, don't you see how he is? Do speak lower. Noise puts him in agony.

THE DRAPER: The devil speak lower? It's you who are howling. Give me my money, and I'll not speak at all.

GUILLEMETTE: (*Screaming.*) He is deadly sick. This is no time for fooling. Stop screaming. What is it you want?

THE DRAPER: I want my money, or the cloth . . . the cloth he bought from me only a little while ago.

GUILLEMETTE: What are you talking about, my good man? There is something strange in your voice.

THE DRAPER: You see, good lady, your husband, Pierre Patelin, the learned counselor, who was such a good friend of my father, came to my shop but a quarter of an hour ago and chose six yards of blue cloth . . . and then told me to come to his house to get the money and . . .

GUILLEMETTE: Ha, ha, ha, what a fine joke. You seem to be in good humor today, Master Draper! Today? . . . When he has been in bed for fourteen weeks . . . on the point of death! (*She screams louder and louder all the time.*) Today, hey! Why do you come to make sport of me? Get out, get out!

THE DRAPER: I will. Give me my money first . . . or give me my cloth. Where is he with it?

GUILLEMETTE: Ah me! He is very sick and refuses to eat a bite.

THE DRAPER: I am speaking about my cloth. If he does not want it, or hasn't the money, I'll gladly take it back. He took it this morning. I'll swear to it. Ask him yourself. I saw him and spoke to him. A piece of blue cloth.

GUILLEMETTE: Are you cracked or have you been drinking?

THE DRAPER: (*Becoming frantic.*) He took six yards of cloth, blue cloth.

GUILLEMETTE: What do I care whether it is green or blue? My husband has not left the house for the last fifteen weeks.

THE DRAPER: May the Lord bless me! But I am sure I saw him. It was he I am sure.

GUILLEMETTE: Have you no heart? I have had enough of your fooling.

THE DRAPER: Damn it all! If you think I am a fool . . .

PATELIN: (*Behind the curtain.*) Au, au, au, come and raise my pillow. Stop the braying of that ass! Everything is black and yellow! Drive these black beasts away! *Marmara carimari, carimara!*

THE DRAPER: It's he!

GUILLEMETTE: Yes, it is; alas!

THE DRAPER: Good Master Patelin, I've come for my nine francs . . . which you promised me . . .

PATELIN: (*Sitting up and sticks his head out between the curtains.*) Ha, you dog . . . come here. Shut the door. Rub the soles of my feet . . . tickle my toes . . . Drive these devils away. It's a monk; there, up he goes . . .

THE DRAPER: What's this? Are you crazy?

PATELIN: (*Getting out of bed.*) Ha . . . do you see him? A black monk flying in the air with the draper hanging on his nose. Catch him . . . quick. (*Speaking right in The Draper's face, who retreats.*) The cat! The monk! Up he flies, and there are ten little devils tweaking your long nose! Heigh, ho!

(*Goes back to bed, falling on it seemingly exhausted.*)

GUILLEMETTE: (*In loud lamentations.*) Now see what you have done.

THE DRAPER: But what does this mean? . . . I don't understand it.

GUILLEMETTE: Don't you see, don't you see!

THE DRAPER: It serves me right; why did I ever sell on credit? But I sold it, I am certain of that, and I would swear 'twas to him this morning. Did he become sick since he returned?

GUILLEMETTE: Are you beginning that joke all over again?

THE DRAPER: I am sure I sold it to him. Ah, but this may be just a cooked up story. By God! . . . tell me, have you a goose on the spit?

GUILLEMETTE: A goose on the spit! No-o-o-o, not on the spit! You are the nearest . . . But I've had enough of this. Get out and leave me in peace.

THE DRAPER: Maybe you are right. I am commencing to doubt it all. Don't cry. I must think this over for a while. But . . . the devil. I am sure I had six yards of cloth . . . and he chose the blue. I gave it to him with my own hands. Yet . . . here he is in bed sick . . . fifteen weeks. But he was at my shop a little while ago. "Come to my house and eat some goose," he said. Never, never, holy Lord, will I trust any one again.

GUILLEMETTE: Perhaps your memory is getting wobbly with age. I think you had better go and look before you talk. Maybe the cloth is still there.

(*Exit The Draper, across the front stage and into his shop.*)

PATELIN: (*Getting up cautiously and speaking low*) Is he gone?

GUILLEMETTE: Take care, he may come back.

PATELIN: I can't stand this any longer. (*Jumps out.*) We put it to him heavy, didn't we, my pretty one, eh? Ho, ho, ho.
(*Laughs uproariously.*)

THE DRAPER: (*Coming from his shop, looking under the table.*) The thief, the liar, the damned liar, he did buy . . . steal it? It isn't there. This was all sham. Ha, I'll get it, though. (*Runs toward Patelin's house.*) What's this I hear . . . laughing! . . . The robbers. (*Rushes in.*) You thieves . . . I want my cloth . . .
(*Patelin, finding no time to get back into bed, gets hold of the broom, puts the frying pan on his head and begins to jump around straddling the broom stick. Guillemette can't stop laughing.*)

THE DRAPER: Laughing in my very nose, eh! Ah, my money, pay . . .

GUILLEMETTE: I am laughing for unhappiness. Look, how the poor man is, it is you who have done this, with your bellowing.

PATELIN: Ha . . Where is the Guitar? . . . The lady Guitar I married . . . She gave birth to twenty little Guitars yesterday. Ho, ho. Come, my children . . . Light the lanterns. Ho, ho, ha . . .
(*Stops, looking intently into the air.*)

THE DRAPER: Damn your jabbering. My money! Please, my money . . . for the cloth . . .

GUILLEMETTE: Again . . . Didn't you have enough before? But. . . . Oh. . . . (*Looking intently at him.*) Now I understand!!! Why I am sure of it. You are mad . . . else you wouldn't talk this way.

THE DRAPER: Oh, Holy Lord . . . perhaps I am.

PATELIN: (*Begins to jump around as if possessed, playing a thousand and one crazy antics.*) *Mére de dieu, la coronade . . . que de l'argent il ne me sonne.* Hast understood me, gentle Sir?

THE DRAPER: What's this? I want my money . . .

GUILLEMETTE: He is speaking in delirium; he once had an uncle in Limoges and it's the language of that country.
(*Patelin gives The Draper a kick and falls down as if exhausted.*)

THE DRAPER: Oh! Oh! Where am I? This is the strangest sickness I ever saw.

GUILLEMETTE: (*Who has run to her husband.*) Do you see what you have done?

PATELIN: (*Jumps up and acts still wilder.*) Ha! The devil . . . the green cat . . . with the draper. I am happy . . .
(*Chases The Draper and his wife around the room. Guillemette seeks protection, clinging to The Draper.*)

GUILLEMETTE: Oh, I am afraid, I am afraid. Help me, kind Sir, he may do me some harm.

THE DRAPER: (*Running around the room with Guillemette clinging to him.*) Holy Ghost, what's this? He is bewitching me.

PATELIN: (*Tries to talk in signs to The Draper, who retreats. Patelin follows him, whacking the floor and furniture and occasionally getting in one on The Draper. Finally, The Draper gets on one side of the bed, and Patelin on the other. In that position he addresses him in a preachy, serious voice.*) *Et bona dies sit vobis, magister amantissime, pater reverendissime, quomodo brulis?* (*Falls on the floor near the bed as if dead.*)

GUILLEMETTE: Oh, kind Sir. Help me. He is dead. Help me put him to bed . . .
(*They both drag him into bed.*)

THE DRAPER: It were well for me to go, I think. He might die and I might be blamed for it. It must have been some imps or some devils who took my cloth . . . and I came here for the money, led by an evil spirit. It's passing strange . . . but I think I had better go.
(*Exit. The Draper goes to his shop. Guillemette watches, turning every moment to Patelin who has sat up in bed, warning him not to get out. When The Draper disappears, she turns around and bursts out laughing.*)

PATELIN: (*Jumping out.*) Now, wife, what do you think of me, eh?

(*Takes the cloth.*) Oh! Didn't we play a clever game? By Saint Peter, I did not think I could do it so well. He got a hot goose, didn't he? (*Spreading the cloth.*) This'll do for both and there'll be a goodly piece left.

GUILLEMETTE: You are an angel. Oh, ho! And now let us go and begin to cut it up.

(*Both exit, and the curtain is drawn.*)

THE SUMMONING OF EVERYMAN

Anonymous

1500

Dramatic / 2 Men

Everyman: a prosperous merchant, 30-50

Death

The Setting: a roadside

God has instructed Death to reveal the eternal journey to Everyman.
Here, the dreaded specter does his Lord's bidding.

DEATH: Everyman I will beset that liveth beastly
Out of God's laws and dreadeth not folly.
He that loveth riches I will strike with my dart,
His sight to blind and from heaven to depart –
Except that alms be his good friend –
In hell for to dwell, world without end.
(Everyman, dressed as a prosperous merchant, strolls on stage.)
Lo! Yonder I see Everyman walking.
Full little he thinketh on my coming;
His mind is on fleshly lusts and his treasure,
And great pain it shall cause him to endure
Before the Lord, heaven King.
Everyman! Stand still! Whither art thou going
Thus gaily? Hast thou thy maker forgotten?

EVERYMAN: Why asketh thou?
Wouldst thou wit?

DEATH: Yea, sir I will show you:
In great haste I am sent to thee
From God out of his majesty.

EVERYMAN: What? Sent to me?

DEATH: Yes, certainly.
Though thou have forgotten Him here,
He thinketh on thee in the heavenly sphere,
As ere we depart thou shalt know.

EVERYMAN: What desireth God of me?

DEATH: That shall I show thee:
    A reckoning He will needs have
    Without longer respite.

EVERYMAN: To give a reckoning, longer leisure I crave.
    This blind matter troubleth my wit.

DEATH: On thee thou must take a long journey;
    Therefore thy book of count with thee thou bring,
    For turn again thou cannot by no way.
    And look thou be sure of they reckoning,
    For before God thou shalt answer and show
    Thy many bad deeds and good but a few,
    How thou hast spent thy life and in what wise,
    Before the chief Lord of paradise.
    Have ado that we were in that way,
    For wit thou well: Thou shalt make none attorney.

EVERYMAN: Full unready I am such reckoning to give.
    I know thee not. What messenger art thou?

DEATH: I am Death that no man dreadeth,
    For everyman I rest and no man spareth,
    For it is God's commandment
    That all to me should be obedient.

EVERYMAN: O Death, thou comest when I had thee least in mind.
    In thy power it lieth me to save;
    Yet of my good will I give thee if thou will be kind.
    Yea, a thousand pound shalt thou have,
    And defer this matter till another day.

DEATH: Everyman, it may not be by no way.
    I set not by gold, silver, nor riches,
    Nor by pope, emperor, king, duke or princes.
    For and I would receive gifts great,
    All the world I might get,
    But my custom is clean contrary.
    I give thee no respite. Come hence, and not tarry.

EVERYMAN: Alas, shall I have no longer respite?
    I may say, Death giveth no warning.
    To think on thee it maketh my heart sick,
    For all unready is my book of reckoning.
    But twelve year and I might have abiding,
    My counting book I would make so clear

That my reckoning I should not need to fear.
Wherefore, Death, I pray thee, for God's mercy,
Spare me till I be provided of remedy.

DEATH: Thee availeth not to cry, weep, and pray.
But haste thee lightly that thou were gone that journey,
And prove thy friends, if thou can,
For wit you well: The tide abideth no man,
And in the world each living creature
For Adam's sin must die of nature.

EVERYMAN: Death, if I should this pilgrimage take
And my reckoning surely make,
Show me, for Saint Charity,
Should I not come again shortly?

DEATH: No, Everyman, and thou be once there,
Thou mayst nevermore come here.
Trust me verily.

EVERYMAN: O gracious God, in high seat celestial,
Have mercy on me in this most need!
Shall I have no company from this vale terrestrial
Of mine acquaintance, that way me to lead?

DEATH: Yea, if any be so hardy
That would go with thee and bear thee company.
Hie thee, that thou were gone to God's magnificence,
Thy reckoning to give before His presence.
What? Weenest thou thy life is given thee,
And thy worldly goods also?

EVERYMAN: I had weened so, verily.

DEATH: Nay! Nay, it was but lent thee;
For as soon as thou art gone,
Another awhile shall have it and then go there from,
Even as thou hast done.
Everyman, thou art mad: Thou hast thy wits five,
And here on earth will not amend thy life?
For suddenly I do come.

EVERYMAN: O wretched caitiff! Whither shall I flee
That I might escape this endless sorrow?
Now, gentle Death, spare me till tomorrow
That I may amend me
With good advisement.

DEATH: Nay, thereto I will not consent,

Nor no man will I respite,
But to the heart suddenly I shall smite
Without any advisement.
And now out of thy sight I will me hie.
See thou make thee ready shortly,
For thou mayst say, this is the day
That no man living may escape away.

THE TRAGICAL HISTORY OF DR. FAUSTUS
Christopher Marlowe
1588-89

Dramatic / 2 Men
Faustus: a man in search of power, 30-50
Mephistophilis: a demon, 30-50

The Setting: A room in Faustus' house

Here, Faustus makes his legendary deal with the devil.

FAUSTUS: Of wealth!
　　Why, the signiory of Embden shall be mine.
　　When Mephistophilis shall stand by me,
　　What god can hurt thee, Faustus? thou art safe:
　　Cast no more doubts. – Come, Mephistophilis,
　　And bring glad tidings from great Lucifer; –
　　Is't not midnight? – come, Mephistophilis,
　　Veni, veni Mephistophile!
　　(*Enter Mephistophilis.*)
　　Now tell me what says Lucifer, thy lord?
MEPHISTOPHILIS: That I shall wait on Faustus whilst he lives.
　　So he will buy my service with his soul.
FAUSTUS: Already Faustus hath hazarded that for thee.
MEPHISTOPHILIS: But, Faustus, thou must bequeath it solemnly,
　　And write a deed of gift with thine own blood;
　　For that security craves great Lucifer.
　　If thou deny it, I will back to hell.
FAUSTUS: Stay, Mephistophilis, and tell me, what good will my soul
　　do thy lord?
MEPHISTOPHILIS: Enlarge his kingdom.
FAUSTUS: Is that the reason why he tempts us thus?
MEPHISTOPHILIS: *Solamen miseris socios habuisse doloris.*
FAUSTUS: Why, have you any pain that torture others!
MEPHISTOPHILIS: As great as have the human souls of men.
　　But, tell me, Faustus, shall I have thy soul?
　　And I will be thy slave, and wait on thee,

And give thee more than thou hast wit to ask.

FAUSTUS: Ay, Mephistophilis, I give it thee.

MEPHISTOPHILIS: Then, Faustus, stab thy arm courageously,
And bind thy soul, that at some certain day
Great Lucifer may claim it as his own;
And then be thou as great as Lucifer.

FAUSTUS: (*Stabbing his arm.*) Lo, Mephistophilis, for love of thee
I cut mine arm, and with my proper blood
Assure my soul to be great Lucifer's,
Chief lord and regent of perpetual night!
View here the blood that trickles from mine arm,
And let it be propitious for my wish.

MEPHISTOPHILIS: But, Faustus, thou must
Write it in manner of a deed of gift.

FAUSTUS: Ay, so I will. (*Writes.*)
But, Mephistophilis,
My blood congeals, and I can write no more.

MEPHISTOPHILIS: I'll fetch thee fire to dissolve it straight.
(*Exit.*)

FAUSTUS: Why might the staying of my blood portend?
Is it unwilling I should write this bill?
Why streams it not, that I may write afresh?
Faustus gives to thee his soul: ah, there it stay'd!
Why shouldst thou not? is not thy soul thine own?
Then write again, *Faustus gives to thee his soul.*
(*Reenter Mephistophilis with a chafer of coals.*)

MEPHISTOPHILIS: Here's fire; come, Faustus, set it on.

FAUSTUS: So, now the blood begins to clear again;
Now will I make an end immediately.
(*Writes.*)

MEPHISTOPHILIS: (*Aside.*) O, what will not I do to obtain his
soul!

FAUSTUS: *Consummatum est;* this bill is ended,
And Faustus hath bequeathed his soul to Lucifer.
But what is this inscription on mine arm?
Homo, fuge: whither should I fly?
If unto God, he'll throw me down to hell.
My senses are deceiv'd; here's nothing writ: —
I see it plain; here in this place is writ,
Homo, fuge: yet shall not Faustus fly.

MEPHISTOPHILIS: (*Aside.*) I'll fetch him somewhat to delight his mind. (*Exit.*)

(*Reenter Mephistophilis with Devils, who give crowns and rich apparel to Faustus, dance, and then depart.*)

FAUSTUS: Speak, Mephistophilis, what means this show?

MEPHISTOPHILIS: Nothing, Faustus, but to delight thy mind withal.

And to show thee what magic can perform.

FAUSTUS: But may I raise up spirits when I please?

MEPHISTOPHILIS: Ay, Faustus, and do greater things than these.

FAUSTUS: Then there's enough for a thousand souls.

Here, Mephistophilis, receive this scroll,

A deed of gift of body and of soul:

But yet conditionally that thou perform

All articles prescrib'd between us both.

MEPHISTOPHILIS: Faustus, I swear by hell and Lucifer

To effect all promises between us made!

FAUSTUS: Then hear me read them. (*Reads.*)

On these conditions following.

First, that Faustus may be a spirit in form and substance.
Secondly, that Mephistophilis shall be his servant, and at his command. Thirdly, that Mephistophilis shall do for him, and bring him whatsoever he desires. Fourthly, that he shall be in his chamber or house invisible. Lastly, that he shall appear to the said John Faustus, at all times, in what form or shape soever he please. I, John Faustus, of Wertenberg, Doctor, by these presents, do give both body and soul to Lucifer prince of the east, and his minister Mephistophilis; and furthermore grant unto them, that, twenty-four years being expired, the articles above written inviolate, full power to fetch or carry the said John Faustus, body and soul, flesh, blood, or goods, into their habitation wheresoever. By me, John Faustus.

MEPHISTOPHILIS: Speak, Faustus, do you deliver this as your deed?

FAUSTUS: Ay, take it, and the devil give thee good on't!

MEPHISTOPHILIS: Now, Faustus, ask what thou wilt.

FAUSTUS: First will I question with thee about hell.

Tell me, where is the place that men call hell?

MEPHISTOPHILIS: Under the heavens.

FAUSTUS: Ay, but whereabout?

MEPHISTOPHILIS: Within the bowels of these elements,

Where we are tortur'd and remain for ever:
Hell hath no limits, nor is circumscrib'd
In one self place; for where we are is hell,
And where hell is, there must we ever be:
And, to conclude, when all the world dissolves,
And every creature shall be purified,
All places shall be hell that are not heaven.

FAUSTUS: Come, I think hell's a fable.

MEPHISTOPHILIS: Ay, think so still, till experience change thy mind.

FAUSTUS: Why, think'st thou, then, that Faustus shall be damn'd?

MEPHISTOPHILIS: Ay, of necessity, for here's the scroll!
Wherein thou hast given thy soul to Lucifer.

FAUSTUS: Ay, and body too: but what of that:?
Think'st thou that Faustus is so fond to imagine
That, after this life, there is any pain?
Tush, these are trifles and mere old wives' tales.

MEPHISTOPHILIS: But, Faustus, I am an instance to prove the contrary.
For I am damn'd, and am now in hell.

FAUSTUS: How! now in hell!
Nay, an this be hell, I'll willingly be damn'd here:
What! walking, disputing, etc.
But, leaving off this, let me have a wife,
The fairest maid in Germany.

MEPHISTOPHILIS: How! a wife!
I prithee, Faustus, talk not of a wife.

FAUSTUS: Nay, sweet Mephistophilis, fetch me one, for I will have one.

MEPHISTOPHILIS: Well, thou wilt have one? Sit there till I come:
I'll fetch thee a wife in the devil's name.
(*Exit.*)

THE TAMING OF THE SHREW
William Shakespeare
1593

Serio-Comic / 1 Man, 1 Woman
>   Kate: a shrew, 20s
>   Petruchio: a shrew-tamer, 20-30

The Setting: Padua

Here is the memorable first encounter between one of the Bard's most lovable couples.

PETRUCHIO: Good morrow, Kate, for that's your name, I hear.
KATE: Well, have you heard, but something hard of hearing,
>   They call me Katherine that do talk of me.

PETRUCHIO: You lie, in faith, for you are called plain Kate,
>   And bonny Kate, and sometimes Kate the curst.
>   But, Kate, the prettiest Kate in Christendom,
>   Kate of Kate Hall, my super-dainty Kate,
>   For dainties are all Kates, and therefore, Kate,
>   Take this of me, Kate of my consolation.
>   Hearing thy mildness praised in every town,
>   Thy virtues spoke of, and thy beauty sounded –
>   Yet not so deeply as to thee belongs –
>   Myself am moved to woo thee for my wife.

KATE: Moved! In good time, let him that moved you hither
>   Remove you hence. I knew you at the first
>   You were a movable.

PETRUCHIO: Why, what's a movable?
KATE: A joint stool.
PETRUCHIO: Thou hast hit it; come sit on me.
KATE: Asses are made to bear and so are you.
PETRUCHIO: Women are made to bear and so are you.
KATE: No such jade as you, if me you mean.
PETRUCHIO: Alas, good Kate, I will not burden thee,
>   For, knowing thee to be but young and light –

KATE: Too light for such a swain as you to catch

And yet as heavy as my weight should be.

PETRUCHIO: Should be! Should – buzz!

KATE: Well ta'en, and like a buzzard.

PETRUCHIO: O Slow-winged turtle, shall a buzzard take thee?

KATE: Ay, for a turtle, as he takes a buzzard.

PETRUCHIO: Come, come, you wasp, i' faith you are too angry.

KATE: If I be waspish, best beware of my sting.

PETRUCHIO: My remedy is then to pluck it out.

KATE: Ay, if the fool could find it where it lies.

PETRUCHIO: Who knows not where a wasp does wear his sting?
  In his tail.

KATE: In his tongue.

PETRUCHIO: Whose tongue?

KATE: Yours, if you talk of tales, and so farewell.

PETRUCHIO: What, with my tongue in your tail? Nay, come again.
  Good Kate, I am a gentleman –

KATE: That I'll try.

  (*She strikes him.*)

PETRUCHIO: I swear I'll cuff you if you strike again.

KATE: So may you lose your arms:
  If you strike me you are no gentleman,
  And if no gentleman, why then no arms.

PETRUCHIO: A herald, Kate? O, put me in thy books.

KATE: What is your crest? A coxcomb?

PETRUCHIO: A combless cock, so Kate will be my hen.

KATE: No cock of mine; you crow too like a craven.

PETRUCHIO: Nay, come, Kate, come, you must not look so sour.

KATE: It is my fashion when I see a crab.

PETRUCHIO: Why, here's no crab, and therefore look not sour.

KATE: There is, there is.

PETRUCHIO: Then show it me.

KATE: Had I a glass I would.

PETRUCHIO: What, you mean my face?

KATE: Well aimed of such a young one.

PETRUCHIO: Now, by Saint George, I am too young for you.

KATE: Yet you are withered.

PETRUCHIO: 'Tis with cares.

KATE: I care not.

PETRUCHIO: Nay, hear you, Kate, in sooth you scape not so.

KATE: I chafe you if I tarry. Let me go.

PETRUCHIO: No, not a whit. I find you passing gentle.
　　'Twas told me you were rough and coy and sullen,
　　And now I find report a very liar,
　　For thou art pleasant, gamesome, passing courteous,
　　But slow in speech, yet sweet as springtime flowers.
　　Thou canst not frown, thou canst not look askance,
　　Nor bite the lip as angry wenches will,
　　Nor hast thou pleasure to be cross in talk,
　　But thou with mildness entertain'st thy wooers,
　　With gentle conference, soft and affable.
　　Why does the world report that Kate doth limp?
　　O sland'rous world! Kate like the hazel-twig
　　Is straight and slender, and as brown in hue
　　As hazelnuts and sweeter than the kernels.
　　O, let me see thee walk. Thou dost not halt.

KATE: Go, fool, and whom thou keep'st command.

PETRUCHIO: Did ever Dian so become a grove
　　As Kate this chamber with her princely gait?
　　O, be thou Dian and let her be Kate,
　　And then let Kate be chaste and Dian sportful!

KATE: Where did you study all this goodly speech?

PETRUCHIO: It is extempore, from my mother-wit.

KATE: A witty mother! Witless else her son.

PETRUCHIO: Am I not wise?

KATE: Yes, keep you warm.

PETRUCHIO: Marry, so I mean, sweet Katherine, in thy bed.
　　And therefore, setting all this chat aside,
　　Thus in plain terms: your father hath consented
　　That you shall be my wife, your dowry 'greed on,
　　And will you, nil you, I will marry you.
　　Now, Kate, I am a husband for your turn,
　　For, by this light, whereby I see thy beauty –
　　Thy beauty that doth make me like thee well –
　　Thou must be married to no man but me.
　　For I am he am born to tame you, Kate,
　　And bring you from a wild Kate to a Kate
　　Conformable as other household Kates.
　　Here comes your father. Never make a denial;
　　I must and will have Katherine to my wife.

THE SHOEMAKER'S HOLIDAY
Thomas Dekker
1600

Serio-Comic / 1 Man, 1 Woman

    Hammon: a man in love with a married woman, 20-30
    Jane: the object of his desire, 20s

The Setting: A sempster's shop

Hammon has pursued Jane relentlessly yet without success. Here, he shows her a paper which indicates that her husband has been killed in the war with France.

    (*Enter Jane in a Sempster's shop, working; and Hammon, muffled, at another door. He stands aloof.*)

HAMMON: Yonder's the shop, and there my fair love sits.
    She's fair and lovely, but she is not mine.
    O, would she were! Thrice have I courted her,
    Thrice hath my hand been moist'ned with her hand,
    Whilst my poor famish'd eyes do feed on that
    Which made them famish. I am unfortunate:
    I still love one, yet nobody loves me.
    I muse in other men what women see
    That I so want! Fine Mistress Rose was coy,
    And this too curious! Oh, no, she is chaste,
    And for she thinks me wanton, she denies
    To cheer my cold heart with her sunny eyes.
    How prettily she works! Oh pretty hand!
    Oh happy work! It doth me good to stand
    Unseen to see her. Thus I oft have stood
    In frosty evenings, a light burning by her,
    Enduring biting cold, only to eye her.
    One only look hath seem'd as rich to me
    As king's crown; such is love's lunacy.
    Muffled I'll pass along, and by that try
    Whether she know me.

JANE: Sir, what is't you buy?

What is't you lack, sir? calico, or lawn,
Fine cambric shirts, or bands? what will you buy?

HAMMON: (*Aside.*) That which thou wilt not sell. Faith, yet I'll
try: —
How do you sell this handkerchief?

JANE: Good cheap.

HAMMON: And how these ruffs?

JANE: Cheap too.

HAMMON: And how this band?

JANE: Cheap too.

HAMMON: All cheap; how sell you this hand?

JANE: My hands are not to be sold.

HAMMON: To be given then!
Nay, faith, I come to buy.

JANE: But none knows when.

HAMMON: Good sweet, leave work a little while, let's play.

JANE: I cannot live by keeping holiday.

HAMMON: I'll pay you for the time which shall be lost.

JANE: With me you shall not be at so much cost.

HAMMON: Look, how you wound this cloth, so you wound me.

JANE: It may be so.

HAMMON: 'T is so.

JANE: What remedy?

HAMMON: Nay, faith, you are too coy.

JANE: Let go my hand.

HAMMON: I will do any task at your command.
I would let go this beauty, were I not
In mind to disobey you by a power
That controls kings: I love you!

JANE: So, now part.

HAMMON: With hands I may, but never with my heart.
In faith, I love you.

JANE: I believe you do.

HAMMON: Shall a true love in me breed hate in you:

JANE: I hate you not.

HAMMON: Then you must love?

JANE: I do.
What are you better now? I love not you.

HAMMON: All this, I hope, is but a woman's fray,
That means, "Come to me," when she cries, "Away!"

In earnest, mistress, I do not jest,
A true chaste love hath ent'red in my breast.
I love you dearly, as I love my life,
I love you as a husband loves a wife;
That, and no other love, my love requires.
Thy wealth, I know, is little; my desires
Thirst not for gold. Sweet, beauteous Jane, what's mine
Shall, if thou make myself thine, all be thine.
Say, judge, what is thy sentence, life or death?
Mercy or cruelty lies in thy breath.

JANE: Good sir, I do believe you love me well;
For 't is a silly conquest, silly pride,
For one like you – I mean a gentleman –
To boast that by his love-tricks he hath brought
Such and such women to his amorous lure;
I think you do not so, yet many do,
And make it even a very trade to woo.
I could be coy, as many women be,
Feed you with sunshine smiles and wanton looks,
But I detest witchcraft; say that I
Do constantly believe you, constant have –

HAMMON: Why dost thou not believe me?

JANE: I believe you;
But yet, good sir, because I will not grieve you
With hopes to taste fruit which will never fall,
In simple truth this is the sum of all:
My husband lives, – at least, I hope he lives.
Press'd was he to these bitter wars in France;
Bitter they are to me by wanting him,
I have but one heart, and that heart's his due.
How can I then bestow the same on you?
Whilst he lives, his I live, be it ne'er so poor,
And rather be his wife than a king's whore.

HAMMON: Chaste and dear woman, I will not abuse thee,
Although it cost my life, if thou refuse me.
Thy husband, press'd for France, what was his name?

JANE: Rafe Damport.

HAMMON: Damport? – Here's a letter sent
From France to me, from a dear friend of mine,
A gentleman of place; here he doth write

Their names that have been slain in every fight.

JANE: I hope death's scroll contains not my love's name.

HAMMON: Cannot you read?

JANE: I can.

HAMMON: Peruse the same.
To my remembrance such a name I read
Amongst the rest. See here.

JANE: Ay me, he's dead!
He's dead! If this be true, my dear heart's slain!

HAMMON: Have patience, dear love.

JANE: Hence! Hence!

HAMMON: Nay, sweet Jane,
Make not poor sorrow proud with these rich tears.
I mourn thy husband's death, because thou mourn'st.

JANE: That bill is forg'd; 't is sign'd by forgery.

HAMMON: I'll bring thee letters sent besides to many,
Carrying the like report; Jane, 't is too true.
Come, weep not: mourning, though it rise from love,
Helps not the mourned, yet hurts them that mourn.

JANE: For God's sake, leave me.

HAMMON: Whither dost thou turn?
Forget the dead, love them that are alive,
His love is faded, try how mine will thrive.

JANE: 'T is now no time for me to think on love.

HAMMON: 'T is now best time for you to think on love,
Because your love lives not.

JANE: Though he be dead,
My love to him shall not be buried;
For God's sake, leave me to myself alone.

HAMMON: 'T would kill my soul, to leave thee drown'd in moan.
Answer me to my suit, and I am gone;
Say to me yea or no.

JANE: No.

HAMMON: Then farewell!
One farewell will not serve, I come again.
Come, cry these wet cheeks; tell me, faith, sweet Jane,
Yea, or no, once more.

JANE: Once more I say no;
Once more be gone, I pray; else will I go.

HAMMON: Nay, then I will grow rude, by this white hand,

Until you change that cold "no"; here I'll stand
Till by your hard heart –
JANE: Nay, for God's love, peace!
My sorrows by your presence more increase.
Not that you thus are present, but all grief
Desires to be alone; there in brief
Thus much I say, and saying bid adieu:
If ever I wed man, it shall be you.
HAMMON: O blessed voice! Dear Jane, I'll urge no more;
Thy breath hath made me rich.
JANE: Death makes me poor.

A WOMAN KILLED WITH KINDNESS
Thomas Heywood
1603

Dramatic / 1 Man, 1 Woman
Mistress Anne Frankford: a woman seduced, 20-30
Master Wendoll: a man of low morals, 30s

The Setting: the North of England

Wendoll takes advantage of Master Frankford's absence in order to seduce his lovely young wife.

MISTRESS FRANKFORD: You are well met, sir; now, in troth, my husband,
Before he took horse, had a great desire
To speak with you: we sought about the house,
Hollaed into the fields, sent every way,
But could not meet you: therefore he enjoined me
To do unto you his most kind commends.
Nay, more; he wills you, as you prize his love,
Or hold in estimation his kind friendship,
To make bold in his absence, and command
Even as himself were present in the house:
For you must keep his table, use his servants,
And be a present Frankford in his absence.
WENDOLL: I thank him for his love. –
Give me a name, you whose infectious tongues
Are tipped with gall and poison: as you would
Think on a man that had your father slain,
Murdered your children, made your wives base strumpets,
So call me, call me so; print in my face
The most stigmatic title of a villain,
For hatching treason to so true a friend.
(*Aside.*)
MISTRESS FRANKFORD: Sir, you are much beholding to my husband;
You are a man most dear in his regard.

WENDOLL: (*Aside.*) I am bound unto your husband, and you too.
  I will not speak to wrong a gentleman
  Of that good estimation, my kind friend:
  I will not; zounds! I will not. I may choose,
  And I will choose. Shall I be so misled?
  Or shall I purchase to my father's crest
  The motto of a villain? If I say
  I will not do it, what thing can enforce me?
  What can compel me? What sad destiny
  Hath such command upon my yielding thoughts?
  I will not – Ha! some fury pricks me on,
  The swift Fates drag me at their chariot-wheel,
  And hurry me to mischief. Speak I must;
  Injure myself, wrong her, deceive his trust.

MISTRESS FRANKFORD: Are you not well, sir, that you seem
  thus troubled?
  There is sedition in your countenance.

WENDOLL: And in my heart, fair angel, chaste and wise.
  I love you: start not, speak not, answer not.
  I love you: nay, let me speak the rest:
  Bid me to swear, and I will call to record
  The host of Heaven.

MISTRESS FRANKFORD: The host of Heaven forbid
  Wendoll should hatch such a disloyal thought!

WENDOLL: Such is my fate; to this suit I was born,
  To wear rich pleasure's crown, or fortune's scorn.

MISTRESS FRANKFORD: My husband loves you.

WENDOLL: I know it.

MISTRESS FRANKFORD: He esteems you
  Even as his brain, his eye-ball, or his heart.

WENDOLL: I have tried it.

MISTRESS FRANKFORD: His purse is your exchequer, and his
  table doth freely serve you.

WENDOLL: So I have found it.

MISTRESS FRANKFORD: O! with what face of brass, what brow
  of steel,
  Can you, unblushing, speak this to the face
  Of the espoused wife of so dear a friend?
  It is my husband that maintains your state;
  Will you dishonour him that in your power

Hath left his whole affairs? I am his wife,
It is to me you speak.

WENDOLL: O speak no more!
For more than this I know, and have recorded
Within the red-leaved table of my heart.
Fair, and of all beloved, I was not fearful
Bluntly to give my life into your hand,
And at one hazard all my earthly means.
Go, tell your husband; he will turn me off,
And I am then undone. I care not, I;
Beggary, shame, death scandal, an reproach,
For you I'll hazard all: why, what care I?
For you I'll live, and in your love I'll die.

MISTRESS FRANKFORD: You move me, sir, to passion and to
pity.
The love I bear my husband is as precious
As my soul's health.

WENDOLL: I love your husband too,
And for his love I will engage my life:
Mistake me not, the augmentation
Of my sincere affection borne to you
Doth no whit lessen my regard of him.
I will be secret, lady, close as night;
And not the light of one small glorious star
Shall shine here in my forehead, to betray
That act of night.

MISTRESS FRANKFORD: What shall I say?
My soul is wandering, and hath lost her way
Oh, Master Wendoll! Oh!

WENDOLL: Sigh not, sweet saint;
For every sigh you breathe draws from my heart
A drop of blood.

MISTRESS FRANKFORD: I ne'er offended yet:
My fault, I fear, will in my brow be writ.
Women that fall, not quite bereft of grace,
Have their offences noted in their face.
I blush and am ashamed. Oh, Master Wendoll,
Pray God I be not born to curse your tongue,
That hath enchanted me! This maze I am in
I fear will prove the labyrinth of sin.

THE TRAGEDY OF OTHELLO,
THE MOOR OF VENICE
William Shakespeare
1604

Dramatic / 1 Man, 2 Women
   Othello: a Moorish general in the service of Venice, 40s
   Desdemona: his wife, 20-30
   Emilia: her faithful servant, 20-30

The Setting: a seaport in Cyprus

Othello has been tricked into believing that Desdemona has betrayed
him with another man. Enraged, he strangles her.

OTHELLO: It is the cause, it is the cause, my soul.
   Let me not name it to you, you chaste stars!
   It is the cause. Yet I'll not shed her blood,
   Nor scar that whiter skin of hers than snow,
   And smooth as monumental alabaster.
   (*He takes off his sword and lays it to one side.*)
   Yet she must die, else she'll betray more men.
   Put out the light, and then – put out the light.
   (*Speaking to the lamp.*) If I quench thee, thou flaming minister,
   I can again thy former light restore,
   Should I repent me – (*Turning to Desdemona.*) But once put out
   thine,
   Thou cunning'st pattern of excelling nature,
   I know not where is that Promethean heat
   That can thy light relume. When I have plucked thy rose,
   I cannot give it vital growth again.
   It needs must wither. I'll smell it on the tree. (*He kisses her.*)
   O balmy breath that dost almost persuade
   Justice to break her sword! One more, one more. (*He kisses her
   again.*)
   Be thus when thou art dead, and I will kill thee,
   And love thee after. One more, and this the last. (*He kisses her
   again.*)

So sweet was ne'er so fatal. I must weep,
But they are cruel tears. This sorrow's heavenly:
It strikes where it doth love. She wakes!

DESDEMONA: Who's there? Othello?

OTHELLO: Aye, Desdemona.

DESDEMONA: Will you come to bed, my lord?

OTHELLO: Have you prayed tonight, Desdemona?

DESDEMONA: Aye, my lord.

OTHELLO: If you bethink yourself of any crime,
Unreconciled as yet to heaven and grace,
Solicit for it straight.

DESDEMONA: Alas, my lord, what may you mean by that?

OTHELLO: Well, do it, and be brief. I will walk by.
I would not kill thy unprepared spirit.
No, heaven forfend! I would not kill thy soul.

DESDEMONA: Talk you of killing?

OTHELLO: Aye, I do.

DESDEMONA: Then heaven
Have mercy on me!

OTHELLO: Amen, with all my heart!

DESDEMONA: If you say so, I hope you will not kill me.

OTHELLO: Humph!

DESDEMONA: And yet I fear you, for you are fatal then
When your eyes roll so. Why I should fear, I know not,
Since guiltiness I know not. But yet I feel I fear.

OTHELLO: Think on they sins.

DESDEMONA: They are loves I bear to you.

OTHELLO: Aye, and for that thou diest.

DESDEMONA: That death's unnatural, that kills for loving.
Alas, why gnaw you so your nether lip?
Some bloody passion shakes your very frame.
These are portents. But yet I hope, I hope,
They do not point on me.

OTHELLO: Peace, and be still!

DESDEMONA: I will so. What's the matter?

OTHELLO: That handkerchief which I so loved and gave thee,
Thou gav'st to Cassio.

DESDEMONA: No, by my life and soul.
Send for the man, and ask him.

OTHELLO: Sweet soul, take heed,

Take heed of perjury. Thou'rt on thy deathbed.

DESDEMONA: Aye, but not yet to die.

OTHELLO: Yes, presently.

Therefore confess thee freely of thy sin,

For to deny each article with oath,

Cannot remove nor choke the strong conception

That I do groan withal. Thou art to die.

DESDEMONA: Then Lord have mercy on me!

OTHELLO: I say, amen.

DESDEMONA: And have you mercy too! I never did

Offend you in my life – never loved Cassio,

But with such general warranty of heaven

As I might love. I never gave him token.

OTHELLO: By Heaven, I saw my handkerchief in his hand.

O perjured woman! Thou dost stone my heart,

And mak'st me call what I intend to do

A murder, which I thought a sacrifice.

I saw the handkerchief.

DESDEMONA: He found it, then.

I never gave it him. Send for him hither,

And let him confess a truth.

OTHELLO: He hath confessed.

DESDEMONA: What, my lord?

OTHELLO: That he hath – used thee.

DESDEMONA: How? Unlawfully?

OTHELLO: Aye.

DESDEMONA: He'll not say so.

OTHELLO: No, his mouth is stopped.

Honest Iago hath ta'en order for't.

DESDEMONA: My fear interprets. What, is he dead?

OTHELLO: Had all his hairs been lives, my great revenge

Had stomach for them all.

DESDEMONA: Alas! He is betrayed, and I undone.

OTHELLO: Out, strumpet! Weep't thou for him to my face?

DESDEMONA: Oh banish me, my lord, but kill me not.

OTHELLO: Down, strumpet! (*Othello attacks her, and she resists.*)

DESDEMONA: Kill me tomorrow. Let me live tonight.

OTHELLO: Nay, if you strive . . .

DESDEMONA: But half an hour.

OTHELLO: Being done,

There is no pause.

DESDEMONA: But while I say one prayer.

OTHELLO: It is to late. (*He smothers her.*)

EMILIA: (*Off-stage.*) My lord, my lord! What, ho! My lord! My lord!

OTHELLO: What noise is this?
(*Desdemona moves.*) Not dead? Not quite dead?
I that am cruel am yet merciful.
I would not have thee linger in thy pain.
So, so.

EMILIA: (*Off-stage.*) What, ho! My lord, my lord!

OTHELLO: Who's there?

EMILIA: (*Off-stage.*) O good my lord, I would speak a word with you.

OTHELLO: (*Calling.*) Yes. (*To himself.*) 'Tis Emilia. (*Calling.*) By and by.
(*To himself.*) She's dead.
'Tis like she comes to speak of Cassio's death.
The noise was high. Ha! No more moving?
Still as the grave. Shall she come in? Were't good?
I think she stirs again. No. What's the best?
If she come in, she'll sure speak to my wife.
My wife! My wife! What wife? I have no wife.
Oh insupportable! Oh heavy hour!
Methinks it should be now a huge eclipse
Of sun and moon, and that the affrighted globe
Should yawn at alteration.

EMILIA: (*Off-stage.*) I do beseech you I may speak with you.
O good my lord!

OTHELLO: I had forgot thee. Oh come in, Emilia.
Soft! By and by. Let me the curtain draw.
Where art thou? (*He unlocks the door, and Emilia enters.*)
What's the matter with thee now?

EMILIA: O good my lord, yonder's foul murder done.

OTHELLO: What? Now?

EMILIA: But now, my lord!

OTHELLO: It is the very error of the moon.
She comes more near the earth than she was wont,
And makes men mad.

EMILIA: Cassio, my lord, has killed a young Venetian

Called Roderigo.

OTHELLO: Roderigo killed!
And Cassio killed?

EMILIA: No, Cassio is not killed.

OTHELLO: Not Cassio killed? Then murder's out of tune,
And sweet revenge grows harsh.

DESDEMONA: Oh falsely, falsely murdered!

EMILIA: Alas! What cry is that?

OTHELLO: That! What?

EMILIA: Out and alas! That was my lady's voice.
(*She pulls the curtain open.*)
Help! Help! Ho! Help! O sweet mistress, speak!

DESDEMONA: A guiltless death I die.

EMILIA: Oh who hath done
This deed?

DESDEMONA: Nobody – I myself. Farewell.
Commend me to my kind lord. Oh farewell. (*She dies.*)

OTHELLO: Why, how should she be murdered?

EMILIA: Alas, who knows?

OTHELLO: You heard her say herself, it was not I.

EMILIA: She said so. I must needs report the truth.

OTHELLO: She's like a liar gone to burning hell.
'Twas I that killed her.

THE MALCONTENT
John Marston
1604

Serio-Comic / 2 Men

    Pietro: the Duke of Genoa, 30-50
    Mendoza: a member of his court, 20-30

The Setting: the palace of the Duke of Genoa

The Duke fears himself cuckolded and here confronts the man he suspects is his wife's lover.

(*Enter Pietro, his sword drawn.*)

PIETRO: A mischief fill thy throat, thou foul-jaw'd slave!
    Say thy prayers.

MENDOZA: I ha' forgot 'em.

PIETRO: Thou shalt die.

MENDOZA: So shalt thou; I am heart-mad.

PIETRO: I am horn-mad.

MENDOZA: Extreme mad.

PIETRO: Monstrously mad.

MENDOZA: Why?

PIETRO: Why? thou, thou has dishonoured my bed.

MENDOZA: I? come, come, sit, here's my bare heart to thee,
    As steady
    As is this centre to the glorious world.
    And yet hark, thou art a cornuto; but by me?

PIETRO: Yes slave, by thee.

MENDOZA: Do not, do not with tart and spleenful breath
    Lose him can loose thee: I offend the duke?
    Bear record, O ye dumb and raw-aid'd nights,
    How vigilant my sleepless eyes have bin
    To watch the traitor; record, thou spirit of truth,
    With what disbasement I ha' thrown my self
    To under offices, only to learn
    The truth, the party, time, the means, the place,
    By whom, and when, and where thou wert disgrac'd:

And am I paid with 'slave'? hath my intrusion
To places private, and prohibited,
Only to observe the closer passages –
Heaven knows with vows of revelation –
Made me suspected, made me deem'd a villain?
What rogue hath wronged us?

PIETRO: Mendoza, I may err.

MENDOZA: Err? 'tis too mild a name, but err and err,
Run giddy with suspect, for through me thou know
That which most creatures save thy self do know.
Nay, since my service hath so loath'd reject,
'Fore I'll reveal, shalt find them clipt together.

PIETRO: Mendoza, thou know'st I am a plain-breasted man.

MENDOZA: The fitter to make a cuckold; would your brows were
most plain too!

PIETRO: Tell me, indeed I heard thee rail –

MENDOZA: At women, true; why, what cold flame could choose,
Knowing a lord so honest, virtuous,
So boundless loving, bounteous, fair shap'd, sweet,
To be contemn'd, abus'd, defam'd, made cuckold?
Heart, I hate all women for't: sweet sheets, wax lights, antique
bed posts, cambric smocks, villainous curtains, arras pictures,
oil'd hinges, and all the tongue-ti'd lascivious witnesses of great
creatures' wantonness: what salvation can you expect?

PIETRO: Wilt thou tell me?

MENDOZA: Why, you may find it your self, observe, observe.

PIETRO: I ha' not the patience: wilt thou deserve me? tell, give it.

MENDOZA: Tak't. Why, Ferneze is the man, Ferneze, I'll prove't:
this night you shall take him in your sheets, will't serve?

PIETRO: It will, my bosom's in some peace; till night –

MENDOZA: What?

PIETRO: Farewell.

MENDOZA: God, how weak a lord are you!
Why, do you think there is no more but so?

PIETRO: Why?

MENDOZA: Nay, then will I presume to council you.
It should be thus;
You with some guard upon the sudden break
Into the princess's chamber: I stay behind
Without the door, through which he needs must pass:

Ferneze flies, let him, to me he comes,
He's killed
By me, observe, by me: you follow, I rail,
And seem to save the body: duchess comes
On whom (respecting her advanced birth,
And your fair nature) I know – nay, I do know –
No violence must be us'd. She comes, I storm,
I praise, excuse Ferneze, and still maintain
The duchess' honour, she for this loves me,
I honour you, shall know her soul, you mine,
Then naught shall she contrive in vengeance
(As women are most thoughtful in revenge)
Of her Ferneze, but you shall sooner know't
Than she can think't. Thus shall his death come sure;
Your duchess brain-caught; so your life secure.

PIETRO: It is too well, my bosom and my heart.
'When nothing helps, cut off the rotten part.'
(*Exit.*)

MENDOZA: 'Who cannot feign friendship can ne'er produce the effects of hatred.' Honest fool Duke, subtile lascivious Duchess, silly novice Ferneze, I do laugh at ye; my brain is in labour till it produce mischief, & I feel sudden throes, proofs sensible the issue is at hand.
'As bears shape young, so I'll form my devise,
Which grown proves horrid; vengeance makes men wise.'

THE REVENGER'S TRAGEDY
Cyril Tourneur
1607

Dramatic / 3 Men

Antonio: a lord whose wife has been ravished and murdered by
the Duchess' son, 30s
Piero and Hippolito: his friends, 20-40

The Setting: a ducal estate

When Lord Antonio discovers his wife's body, he appeals to his
companions for help in avenging her death.

ANTONIO: Draw nearer Lords and be sad witnesses
Of a fair comely building newly fall'n,
Being falsely undermined: violent rape
Has play'd a glorious act, behold my Lords
A sight that strikes man out of me.
PIERO: That virtuous lady?
ANTONIO: Precedent for wives!
HIPPOLITO: The blush of many women, whose chaste presence
Would e'en call shame up to their cheeks, and make
Pale wanton sinners have good colours, –
ANTONIO: Dead!
Her honour first drunk poison, and her life,
Being fellows in one house did pledge her honour.
PIERO: O grief of many!
ANTONIO: I mark'd not this before –
A prayer-book the pillow to her cheek,
This was her rich confection, and another
Plac'd in her right hand, with a leaf tuckt up,
Pointing to these words:
Melius virtute mori, quam per dedecus vivere.
True and effectual it is indeed.
HIPPOLITO: My Lord since you invite us to your sorrows,
Let's truly taste 'em, that with equal comfort,
As to ourselves we may relieve your wrongs.

We have grief too, that yet walks without tongue,
Curae leves loquuntur, maiores stupent.
ANTONIO: You deal with truth my Lord.
Lend me but your attentions and I'll cut
Long grief into short words: last revelling night,
When torchlight made an artificial noon
About the court, some courtiers in the masque,
Putting on better faces than their own,
Being full of fraud and flattery: amongst whom,
The Duchess' youngest son (that moth to honour)
Fill'd up a room; and with long lust to eat
Into my wearing; amongst all the ladies,
Singled out that dear form; who ever liv'd
As cold in lust, as she is now in death;
(Which that step-duchess-monster knew too well;)
And therefore in the height of all the revels,
When music was heard loudest, courtiers busiest,
And ladies great with laughter; – O vicious minute!
Unfit but for relation to be spoke of,
Then with a face more impudent than his vizard
He harried her amidst a throng of panders,
That live upon damnation of both kinds,
And fed the ravenous vulture of his lust,
(O death to think on't!) – she, her honour forc'd,
Deem'd it a nobler dowry for her name,
To die with poison than to live with shame.
HIPPOLITO: A wondrous lady; of rare fire compact,
Sh'as made her name an empress by that act.
PIERO: My Lord what judgment follows the offender?
ANTONIO: Faith none my Lord, it cools and is deferr'd.
PIERO: Delay the doom for rape?
ANTONIO: O you must note
Who 'tis should die,
The Duchess' son; she'll look to be a saver,
'Judgment in this age is near kin to favour.'
HIPPOLITO: Nay then step forth thou bribeless officer;
I bind you all in steel to bind you surely,
Here let your oaths meet, to be kept and paid,
Which else will stick like rust and shame the blade;
Strengthen my vow, that if at the next sitting,

Judgment speak all in gold, and spare the blood
Of such a serpent, e'en before their seats
To let his soul out, which long since was found
Guilty in heaven.

ALL: We swear it and will act it.

ANTONIO: Kind gentlemen, I thank you in mine ire.

HIPPOLITO: 'Twere pity
The ruins of so fair a monument,
Should not be dipt in the defacer's blood.

PIERO: Her funeral shall be wealthy, for her name
Merits a tomb of pearl; my Lord Antonio,
For this time wipe your lady from your eyes,
No doubt our grief and yours may one day court it,
When we are more familiar with revenge.

ANTONIO: That is my comfort gentlemen, and I joy
In this one happiness above the rest,
Which will be call'd a miracle at last,
That being an old man I'd a wife so chaste.

THE MAID'S TRAGEDY
Beaumont and Fletcher
1609

Serio-Comic / 3 Women

Aspatia:	a broken-hearted young woman, 20s
Evadne:	her friend, 20s
Dula:	a young maid, 20s

The Setting: the city of Rhodes

In Rhodes, the king has decreed that young Amnitor marry Evadne, the sister of his best friend. To do so, however, Amnitor must renounce his love for Aspatia. Here, Aspatia, Evadne and a winsome friend discuss love and men.

(*Enter Evadne, Aspatia, Dula and other ladies.*)

DULA: Madam, shall we undress you for this fight?
　　The wars are nak'd that you must make to-night.

EVADNE: You are very merry, Dula.

DULA: I should be merrier far, if 'twere
　　With me as 'tis with you.

EVADNE: How's that?

DULA: That I might go to bed with him
　　With the credit that you do.

EVADNE: Why, how now, wench?

DULA: Come, ladies, will you help?

EVADNE: I am soon undone.

DULA: And as soon done:
　　Good store of clothes will trouble you at both.

EVADNE: Art thou drunk, Dula?

DULA: Why, here's none but we.

EVADNE: Thou think'st belike, there is no modesty.
　　When we're alone.

DULA: Ay, by my troth, you hit my thoughts aright.

EVADNE: You prick me, lady.

DULA: 'Tis against my will.
　　Anon you must endure more, and lie still;

You're best to practise.

EVADNE: Sure, this wench is mad.

DULA: No, 'faith, this is a trick that I have had
Since I was fourteen.

EVADNE: 'Tis high time to leave it.

DULA: Nay, now I'll keep it, till the trick leave me.
A dozen wanton words, put in your head,
Will make you livelier in your husband's bed.

EVADNE: Nay, 'faith, then take it.

DULA: Take it, madam? where?
We all, I hope, will take it, that are here.

EVADNE: Nay, then, I'll give you o'er.

DULA: So will I make
The ablest man in Rhodes, or his heart ache.

EVADNE: Wilt take my place to-night?

DULA: I'll hold your cards 'gainst any two I know.

EVADNE: What wilt thou do?

DULA: Madam, we'll do't, and make 'em leave play too.

EVADNE: Aspatia, take her part.

DULA: I will refuse it.
She will pluck down a side; she does not use it.

EVADNE: Why, do.

DULA: You will find the play
Quickly, because your head lies well that way.

EVADNE: I thank thee, Dula. 'Would thou could'st instill
Some of thy mirth into Aspatia!
Nothing but sad thoughts in her breast do dwell:
Methinks, a mean betwixt you would do well.

DULA: She is in love: Hang me, if I were so.
But I could run my country. I love, too,
To do those things that people in love do.

ASPATIA: It were a timeless smile should prove my cheek:
It were a fitter hour for me to laugh,
When at the altar the religious priest
Were pacifying the offended powers
With sacrifice, than now. This should have been
My night; and all your hands have been employed
In giving me a spotless offering
To young Amintor's bed, as we are now
For you. Pardon, Evadne; 'would my worth

Were great as yours, or that the king, or he
Or both, thought so! Perhaps he found me worthless:
But, till he did so, in these ears of mine,
These credulous ears, he pour'd the sweetest words
That art or love could frame. If he were false,
Pardon it, Heaven! and if I did want
Virtue, you safely may forgive that too;
For I have lost none that I had from you.

EVADNE: Nay, leave this sad talk, madam.

ASPATIA: Would I could!
Then should I leave the cause.

EVADNE: See, if you have not spoil'd all Dula's mirth.

ASPATIA: Thou think'st thy heart hard; but if thou be'st caught,
Remember me; thou shalt perceive a fire
Shot suddenly into thee.

DULA: That's not so good; let 'em shoot anything
But fire, I fear 'em not.

ASPATIA: Well, wench, thou may'st be taken.

EVADNE: Ladies, good-night: I'll do the rest myself.

DULA: Nay, let your lord do some.

ASPATIA: (*Sings.*) Lay a garland on my hearse,
Of the dismal yew.

EVADNE: That's one of your sad songs, madam.

ASPATIA: Believe me, 'tis a very pretty one.

EVADNE: How is it, madam?

ASPATIA: (*Sings.*) Lay a garland on my hearse,
Of the dismal yew;
Maidens, willow branches bear;
Say I died true:
My love was false, but I was firm
From my hour of birth.
Upon my buried body lie
Lightly, gentle earth!

EVADNE: Fie on't, madam! The words are so strange, they are able
to make one dream of hobgoblins. "I could never have the power":
Sing that, Dula.

DULA: (*Sings.*) I could never have the power
To love one above an hour,
But my heart would prompt mine eye
On some other man to fly;

Venus, fix mine eyes fast,
Of if not, give me all that I shall see at last.

EVADNE: So, leave me now.

DULA: Nay, we must see you laid.

ASPATIA: Madam, good-night. May all the marriage joys
That longing maids imagine in their beds,
Prove so unto you! May no discontent
Grow 'twixt your love and you! But, if there do,
Inquire of me, and I will guide your moan;
Teach you an artificial way to grieve,
To keep your sorrow waking. Love your lord
No worse than I: but if you love so well,
Alas, you may displease him; so did I.
This is the last time you shall look on me. –
Ladies, farewell. As soon as I am dead,
Come all, and watch one night about my hearse,
Bring each a mournful story, and a tear,
To offer at it when I go to earth.
With flatt'ring ivy clasp my coffin round;
Write on my brow my fortune; let my bier
Be borne by virgins that shall sing, by course,
The truth of maids, and perjuries of men.
(*Exit Evadne.*)

EVADNE: Alas, I pity thee.

THE ALCHEMIST
Ben Jonson
1610

Serio-Comic / 2 Men, 1 Woman

Subtle: an alchemist, 30-50
Face: his crafty servant, 20-40
Dol Common: a bawd, 20-30

The Setting: early 17th Century England

Here, three scurrilous 17th century mountebanks form a dread partnership.

(*Enter Face, in a captain's uniform, with his sword drawn, and Subtle with a vial, quarrelling, and followed by Dol Common.*)

FACE: Believe't, I will.

SUBTLE: Thy worst. I fart at thee.

DOL COMMON: Have you your wits? why, gentleman! for love –

FACE: Sirrah, I'll strip you –

SUBTLE: What to do? lick figs
Out at my –

FACE: Rogue, rogue! – out of all your sleights.

DOL COMMON: Nay, look ye, sovereign, general, are you
madmen?

SUBTLE: O, let the wild sheep loose. I'll gum your silks
With good strong water, an you come.

DOL COMMON: Will you have
The neighbours hear you? will you betray all?
Hark! I hear somebody.

FACE: Sirrah –

SUBTLE: I shall mar
All that the tailor has made, if you approach.

FACE: You most notorious whelp, you insolent slave,
Dare you do this?

SUBTLE: Yes, faith; yes, faith.

FACE: Why, who
Am I, my mungrel? who am I?

SUBTLE: I'll tell you,
> Since you know not yourself.

FACE: Speak lower, rogue.

SUBTLE: Yes, you were once (time's not long past) the good,
> Honest, plain, livery-three-pound-thrum, that kept
> Your master's worship's house here in the Friers,
> For the vacations –

FACE: Will you be so loud?

SUBTLE: Since, by my means, translated suburb-captain.

FACE: By your means, doctor dog!

SUBTLE: Within man's memory,
> All this I speak of.

FACE: Why, I pray you, have I
> Been countenanced by you, or you by me?
> Do but collect, sir, where I met you first.

SUBTLE: I do not hear well.

FACE: Not of this, I think it.
> But I shall put you in mind, sir; – at Pie-corner,
> Taking your meal of steam in, from cooks' stalls,
> Where, like the father of hunger, you did walk
> Piteously costive, with your pinch'd-horn-nose,
> And your complexion of the Roman wash,
> Stuck full of black and melancholic worms,
> Like powder-corns shot at the artillery-yard.

SUBTLE: I wish you could advance your voice a little.

FACE: When you went pinn'd up in the several rags
> You had raked and pick'd from dunghills, before day;
> Your feet in mouldy slippers, for your kibes;
> A felt of rug, and a thin threaden cloke,
> That scarce would cover your no buttocks –

SUBTLE: So, sir!

FACE: When all your alchemy, and your algebra,
> Your minerals, vegetals, and animals,
> Your conjuring, cozening, and your dozen of trades,
> Could not relieve your corps with so much linen
> Would make you tinder, but to see a fire;
> I gave you countenance, credit for your coals,
> Your stills, your glasses, your materials;
> Built you a furnace, drew you customers,
> Advanced all your black arts; lent you, beside,

A house to practise in –

SUBTLE: Your master's house!

FACE: Where you have studied the more thriving skill
Of bawdry since.

SUBTLE: Yes, in your master's house.
You and the rats here kept possession.
Make it not strange. I know you were one could keep
The buttery-hatch still lock'd, and save the chippings,
Sell the dole beer to aqua-vitae men,
The which, together with your Christmas vails
At post-and-pair, your letting out of counters,
Made you a pretty stock, some twenty marks,
And gave you credit to converse with cobwebs,
Here, since your mistress' death hath broke up house.

FACE: You might talk softlier, rascal.

SUBTLE: No, you scarab,
I'll thunder you in pieces: I will teach you
How to beware to tempt a Fury again,
That carries tempest in his hand and voice.

FACE: The place has made you valiant.

SUBTLE: No, your clothes. –
Thou vermin, have I ta'en thee out of dung,
So poor, so wretched, when no living thing
Would keep thee company, but a spider, or worse?
Rais'd thee from brooms, and dust, and watering-pots,
Sublimed thee, and exalted thee, and fix'd thee
In the third region, call'd our state of grace?
Wrought thee to spirit, to quintessence, with pains
Would twice have won me the philosopher's work?
Put thee in words and fashion, made thee fit
For more than ordinary fellowships?
Giv'n thee thy oaths, they quarrelling dimensions,
Thy rules to cheat at horse-race, cock-pit, cards,
Dice, or whatever gallant tincture else?
Made thee a second in mine own great art?
And have I this for thanks! Do you rebel,
Do you fly out in the projection?
Would you be gone now?

DOL COMMON: Gentlemen, what mean you?
Will you mar all?

SUBTLE: Slave, thou hadst had no name –

DOL COMMON: Will you undo yourselves with civil war?

SUBTLE: Never been known, past *equi clibanum*,
 The heat of horse-dung, under ground, in cellars,
 Or an ale-house darker than deaf John's; been lost
 To all mankind, but laundresses and tapsters,
 Had not I been.

DOL COMMON: Do you know who hears you, sovereign?

FACE: Sirrah –

DOL COMMON: Nay, general, I thought you were civil.

FACE: I shall turn desperate, if you grow thus loud.

SUBTLE: And hang thyself, I care not.

FACE: Hang thee, collier,
 And all thy pots, and pans, in picture, I will,
 Since thou hast moved me –

DOL COMMON: O, this will o'erthrow all.

FACE: Write thee up bawd in Paul's, have all thy tricks
 Of cozening with a hollow cole, dust, scrapings,
 Searching for things lost, with a sieve and sheers,
 Erecting figures in your rows of houses,
 And taking in of shadows with a glass,
 Told in red letters; and a face cut for thee,
 Worse than Gamaliel Ratsey's.

DOL COMMON: Are you sound?
 Have you your senses, masters?

FACE: I will have
 A book, but barely reckoning thy impostures,
 Shall prove a true philosopher's stone to printers.

SUBTLE: Away, you trencher-rascal!

FACE: Out, you dog-leach!
 The vomit of all prisons –

DOL COMMON: Will you be
 Your own destructions, gentlemen?

FACE: Still spew'd out
 For lying too heavy on the basket.

SUBTLE: Cheater!

FACE: Bawd!

SUBTLE: Cow-herd!

FACE: Conjurer!

SUBTLE: Cut-purse!

FACE: Witch!

DOL COMMON: O me!

    We are ruin'd, lost! have you no more regard
    To your reputations? where's your judgment? 'slight,
    Have yet some care of me, of your republic –

FACE: Away, this brach! I'll bring thee, rogue, within
    The statute of sorcery, tricesimo tertio
    Of Harry the eighth: ay, and perhaps, thy neck
    Within a noose, for laundring gold and barbing it.

DOL COMMON: (*Snatches Face's sword.*) You'll bring your head
    within a coxcomb, will you?
    And you, sir, with your menstrue – (*Dashes Subtle's vial out of his
    hand.*) – gather it up. –
    'Sdeath, you abominable pair of stinkards,
    Leave off your barking, and grow one again,
    Or, by the light that shines, I'll cut your throats.
    I'll not be made a prey unto the marshal,
    For ne'er a snarling dog-bolt of you both.
    Have you together cozen'd all this while,
    And all the world, and shall it now be said,
    You've made most courteous shift to cozen yourselves?
    You will accuse him! you will *bring him in* (*To Face.*)
    Within the statute! Who shall take your word?
    A whoreson, upstart, apocryphal captain,
    Whom not a Puritan in Blackfriers will trust
    So much as for a feather: and you, too, (*To Subtle.*)
    Will give the cause, forsooth! you will insult,
    And claim a primacy in the divisions!
    You must be chief! as if you only had
    The powder to project with, and the work
    Were not begun out of equality?
    The venture tripartite? all things in common?
    Without priority? 'Sdeath! you perpetual curs,
    Fall to your couples again, and cozen kindly,
    And heartily, and lovingly, as you should,
    And lose not the beginning of a term,
    Or, by this hand, I shall grow fractious too,
    And take my part, and quit you.

FACE: 'Tis his fault;
    He ever murmurs, and objects his pains,

And says, the weight of all lies upon him.

SUBTLE: Why, so it does.

DOL COMMON: How does it? do not we
Sustain our parts?

SUBTLE: Yes, but they are not equal.

DOL COMMON: Why, if your part exceed to-day, I hope
Ours may, to-morrow, match it.

SUBTLE: Ay, they *may.*

DOL COMMON: May, murmuring mastiff! ay , and do. Death on
me!
Help me to throttle him. (*Seizes Subtle by the throat.*)

SUBTLE: Dorothy! mistress Dorothy!
'Ods precious, I'll do any thing. What do you mean?

DOL COMMON: Because o' your fermentation and cibation?

SUBTLE: Not I, by heaven –

DOL COMMON: Your Sol and Luna – help me. (*To Face.*)

SUBTLE: Would I were hang'd then! I'll conform myself.

DOL COMMON: Will you, sir? do so then, and quickly: swear.

SUBTLE: What should I swear.

DOL COMMON: To leave your faction, sir,
And labour kindly in the common work.

SUBTLE: Let me not breathe if I meant aught beside.
I only used those speeches as a spur
To him.

DOL COMMON: I hope we need no spurs, sir. Do we?

FACE: 'Slid, prove to-day, who shall shark best.

SUBTLE: Agreed.

DOL COMMON: Yes, and work close and friendly.

SUBTLE: 'Slight, the knot
Shall grow the stronger for this breach, with me.
(*They shake hands.*)

DOL COMMON: Why, so my good baboons! Shall we go make
A sort of sober, scurvy, precise neighbours,
That scarce have smiled twice since the king came in,
A feast of laughter at our follies? Rascals,
Would run themselves from breath, to see me ride,
Or you t'have but a hole to thrust your heads in,
For which you should pay ear-rent? No, agree.
And may don Provost ride a feasting long,
In his old velvet jerkin and stain'd scarfs,

My noble sovereign, and worthy general,
Ere we contribute a new crewel garter
To his most worsted worship.

SUBTLE: Royal Dol!
Spoken like Claridiana, and thyself.

FACE: For which at supper, thou shalt sit in triumph,
And not be styled Dol Common, but Dol Proper,
Dol Singular: the longest cut at night,
Shall draw thee for his Dol Particular.

THE DUCHESS OF MALFI
John Webster
1613

Dramatic / 2 Men
> Ferdinand: the Duke of Calabria, 30-40
> Bosola: his henchman, 30-40

The Setting: a ducal estate in Amalfi

Evil Ferdinand wishes to keep an eye on his sister, the recently widowed Duchess of Malfi. To that end, he sends for the sinister Bosola and charges him to spy on her.

BOSOLA: I was lur'd to you.
FERDINAND: My brother here, the cardinal, could never
    Abide you.
BOSOLA: Never since he was in my debt.
FERDINAND: May be some oblique character in your face
    Made him suspect you.
BOSOLA: Doth he study physiognomy?
    There's no more credit to be given to th' face
    Than to a sick man's urine, which some call
    The physician's whore, because she cozens him.
    He did suspect me wrongfully.
FERDINAND: For that
    You must give great men leave to take their times.
    Distrust doth cause us seldom be deceiv'd.
    You see, the oft shaking of the cedar-tree
    Fastens it more at root.
BOSOLA: Yet take heed;
    For to suspect a friend unworthily
    Instructs him the next way to suspect you,
    And prompts him to deceive you.
FERDINAND: There's gold.
BOSOLA: So:
    What follows? – (*Aside.*) Never rain'd such showers as these
    Without thunderbolts i' th' tail of them. – Whose throat must I

cut?

FERDINAND: Your inclination to shed blood rides post
    Before my occasion to use you. I give you that
    To live i' th' court here, and observe the duchess;
    To note all the particulars of her haviour,
    What suitors do solicit her for marriage,
    And whom she best affects. She's a young widow:
    I would not have her marry again.

BOSOLA: No, sir?

FERDINAND: Do not you ask the reason; but be satisfied.
    I say I would not.

BOSOLA: It seems you would create me
    One of your familiars.

FERDINAND: Familiar! What's that?

BOSOLA: Why, a very quaint invisible devil in flesh, –
    An intelligencer.

FERDINAND: Such a kind of thriving thing
    I would wish thee; and ere long thou mayst arrive
    At a higher place by 't.

BOSOLA: Take your devils,
    Which hell calls angels! These curs'd gifts would make
    You a corrupter, me an impudent traitor;
    And should I take these, they'd take me to hell.

FERDINAND: Sir, I'll take nothing from you that I have given.
    There is a place that I procur'd for you
    This morning, the provisorship o' th' horse.
    Have you heard on 't?

BOSOLA: No.

FERDINAND: 'T is yours: is 't not worth thanks?

BOSOLA: I would have you curse yourself now, that your bounty
    (Which makes men truly noble) e'er should make me
    A villain. O, that to avoid ingratitude
    For the good deed you have done me, I must do
    All the ill man can invent! Thus the devil
    Candies all sins o'er: and what heaven terms vild,
    That names he complimental.

FERDINAND: Be yourself;
    Keep your old garb of melancholy; 't will express
    You envy those that stand above your reach,
    Yet strive not to come near 'em. This will gain

Access to private lodgings, where yourself
May, like a politic dormouse –
BOSOLA: As I have seen some
Feed in a lord's dish, half asleep, not seeming
To listen to any talk; and yet these rogues
Have cut his throat in a dream. What's my place?
The provisorship o' th' horse? Say, then, my corruption
Grew out of horse-dung: I am your creature.
FERDINAND: Away!
(*Exit.*)
BOSOLA: Let good men, for good deeds, covet good fame,
Since place and riches oft are bribes of shame.
Sometimes the devil doth preach.

THE CHANGELING
Thomas Middleton & William Rowley
1621 or 22

Serio-Comic / 1 Man, 1 Woman

Beatrice: a young woman in love, 20s

Deflores: her father's ugly servant, 30-40

The Setting: Allegant

Beatrice is being forced to marry a man she doesn't love and here enlists Deflores, a servant whom she despises, to kill her unwanted suitor so that she will be free to wed the man she truly loves.

DEFLORES: (*Aside.*) I have watcht this meeting, and do wonder
    much
    What shall become of t'other, I'm sure both
    Cannot be serv'd unless she transgress; happily
    Then I'll put in for one: for if a woman
    Fly from one point, from him she makes a husband,
    She spreads and mounts then like arithmetic,
    1, 10, 100, 1000, 10,000,
    Proves in time sutler to an army royal.
    Now do I look to be most richly rail'd at,
    Yet I must see her.

BEATRICE: (*Aside.*) Why, put case I loath'd him
    As much as youth and beauty hates a sepulchre,
    Must I needs show it? Cannot I keep that secret,
    And serve my turn upon him? – See, he's here.
    – Deflores.

DEFLORES: (*Aside.*) Ha, I shall run mad with joy,
    She call'd me fairly by my name Deflores,
    And neither rogue nor rascal.

BEATRICE: What ha' you done to your face
    A-late? y'ave met with some good physician,
    Y'ave prun'd your self me thinks, you were not wont
    To look so amorously.

DEFLORES: (*Aside.*) Not I, 'tis

The same physnomy to a hair and pimple,
Which she call'd scurvy scarce an hour ago:
How is this?

BEATRICE: Come hither, nearer man.

DEFLORES: (*Aside.*) I'm up to the chin in heaven.

BEATRICE: Turn, let me see,
Vauh! 'tis but the heat of the liver, I perceiv't.
I thought it had been worse.

DEFLORES: (*Aside.*) Her fingers toucht me,
She smells all amber.

BEATRICE: I'll make a water for you shall cleanse this
Within a fortnight.

DEFLORES: With your own hands, Lady?

BEATRICE: Yes, mine own sir; in a work of cure,
I'll trust no other.

DEFLORES: (*Aside.*) 'Tis half an act of pleasure
To hear her talk thus to me.

BEATRICE: When w'are us'd
To a hard face, 'tis not so unpleasing,
It mends still in opinion, hourly mends,
I see it by experience.

DEFLORES: (*Aside.*) I was blest
To light upon this minute, I'll make use on't.

BEATRICE: Hardness becomes the visage of a man well,
It argues service, resolution,
Manhood, if cause were of employment.

DEFLORES: 'Twould be soon seen, if e'er your Ladyship
Had cause to use it.
I would but wish the honour of a service
So happy as that mounts to.

BEATRICE: We shall try you –
Oh, my Deflores!

DEFLORES: (*Aside.*) How's that?
She calls me hers already, my Deflores.
– You were about to sigh out somewhat, Madam.

BEATRICE: No, was I? I forgot – Oh!

DEFLORES: There 'tis again –
The very fellow on't.

BEATRICE: You are too quick, sir.

DEFLORES: There's no excuse for't, now I heard it twice,

Madam, that sigh would fain have utterance,
Take pity on't, and lend it a free word;
'Las how it labours
For liberty, I hear the murmur yet
Beat at your bosom.

BEATRICE: Would Creation –

DEFLORES: Ay, well said, that's it.

BEATRICE: – Had form'd me man.

DEFLORES: Nay, that's not it.

BEATRICE: Oh 'tis the soul of freedom,
I should not then be forc'd to marry one
I hate beyond all depths, I should have power
Then to oppose my loathings, nay remove 'em
For ever from my sight.

DEFLORES: (*Aside.*) Oh blest occasion!
– Without change to your sex, you have your wishes.
Claim so much man in me.

BEATRICE: In thee, Deflores? There's small cause for that.

DEFLORES: Put it not from me, it's a service that
I kneel for to you. (*Kneels.*)

BEATRICE: You are too violent to mean faithfully,
There's horror in my service, blood and danger,
Can those be things to sue for?

DEFLORES: If you knew
How sweet it were to me to be employed
In any act of yours, you would say then
I fail'd, and us'd not reverence enough
When I receive the charge on't.

BEATRICE: (*Aside.*) This is much methinks,
Belike his wants are greedy, & to such
Gold tastes like angels' food. – Rise

DEFLORES: I'll have the work first.

BEATRICE: (*Aside.*) Possible his need
Is strong upon him; (*Gives him money.*) – there's to encourage
thee:
As thou art forward and thy service dangerous,
Thy reward shall be precious.

DEFLORES: That I have thought on,
I have assur'd my self of that beforehand,
And know it will be precious, the thought ravishes.

BEATRICE: Then take him to thy fury.

DEFLORES: I thirst for him.

BEATRICE: Alonzo de Piracquo.

DEFLORES: His end's upon him,
 He shall be seen no more.

BEATRICE: How lovely now
 Dost thou appear to me! Never was a man
 Dearlier rewarded.

DEFLORES: I do think of that.

BEATRICE: Be wondrous careful in the execution.

DEFLORES: Why, are not both our lives upon the cast?

BEATRICE: Then I throw all my fears upon thy service.

DEFLORES: They ne'er shall rise to hurt you.

BEATRICE: When the deed's done,
 I'll furnish thee with all things for thy flight,
 Thou may'st live bravely in another country.

DEFLORES: Ay, ay, we'll talk of that hereafter.

BEATRICE: (*Aside.*) I shall rid my self
 Of two inveterate loathings at one time,
 Piracquo and his Dog-face.
 (*Exit.*)

DEFLORES: Oh my blood,
 Methinks I feel her in mine arms already,
 Her wanton fingers combing out this beard,
 And being pleased, praising this bad face.
 Hunger and pleasure they'll commend sometimes
 Slovenly dishes, and feed heartily on 'em,
 Nay, which is stranger, refuse daintier for 'em.
 Some women are odd feeders – I'm too loud:
 Here comes the man goes supperless to bed,
 Yet shall not rise tomorrow to his dinner.

'TIS PITY SHE'S A WHORE
John Ford
1633

Dramatic / 1 Man, 1 Woman
    Giovanni: a man in love with his sister, 20-30
    Annabella: his sister, 20s

The Setting: Parma

Here, the tormented Giovanni reveals his forbidden passion to his sister.

ANNABELLA: Why, brother, will you not speak to me?

GIOVANNI: Yes; how d'ye, sister?

ANNABELLA: Howsoever I am, methinks you are not well.

PUTANA: Bless us! Why are you so sad, sir?

GIOVANNI: Let me entreat you, leave us a while, Putana.
    Sister, I would be private with you.

ANNABELLA: Withdraw, Putana.

PUTANA: I will. (*Aside.*) If this were any other company for her, I
    should think my absence an office of some credit; but I will leave
    them together. (*Exit Putana.*)

GIOVANNI: Come, sister, lend your hand; let's walk together. I hope
    you need not blush to walk with me;
    Here's none but you and I.

ANNABELLA: How's this?

GIOVANNI: 'Faith,
    I mean no harm.

ANNABELLA: Harm?

GIOVANNI: No, good faith.
    How is't with ye?

ANNABELLA: (*Aside.*) I trust he be not frantic. –
    I am very well, brother.

GIOVANNI: Trust me, but I am sick; I fear so sick
    'Twill cost my life.

ANNABELLA: Mercy forbid it! 'Tis not so, I hope.

GIOVANNI: I think you love me, sister.

ANNABELLA: Yes, you know I do.

GIOVANNI: I know't, indeed. You're very fair.

ANNABELLA: Nay, then I see you have a merry sickness.

GIOVANNI: That's as it proves. The poets feign, I read,
That Juno for her forehead did exceed
All other goddesses; but I durst swear
Your forehead exceed hers, as hers did theirs.

ANNABELLA: 'Troth, this is pretty!

GIOVANNI: Such a pair of stars
As are thine eyes would, like Promethean fire,
If gently glanced, give life to senseless stones.

ANNABELLA: Fie upon ye!

GIOVANNI: The lily and the rose, most sweetly strange,
Upon your dimple cheeks do strive for change.
Such lips would tempt a saint; such hands as those
Would make an anchorite lascivious.

ANNABELLA: D'ye mock me or flatter me?

GIOVANNI: If you would see a beauty more exact
Than art can counterfeit or nature frame,
Look in your glass, and there behold your own.

ANNABELLA: Oh, you are a trim youth!

GIOVANNI: Here! (*Offers his dagger to her.*)

ANNABELLA: What to do?

GIOVANNI: And here's my breast; strike home!
Rip up my bosom; there thou shalt behold
A heart in which is writ the truth I speak.
Why stand ye?

ANNABELLA: Are you earnest?

GIOVANNI: Yes, most earnest.
You cannot love?

ANNABELLA: Whom?

GIOVANNI: Me. My tortured soul
Hath felt affliction in the heat of death.
Oh, Annabella, I am quite undone!
The love of thee, my sister, and the view
Of thy immortal beauty have untuned
All harmony both of my rest and life.
Why d'ye not strike?

ANNABELLA: Forbid it, my just fears!
If this be true, 'twere fitter I were dead.

GIOVANNI: True, Annabella! 'Tis no time to jest.
I have too long suppressed the hidden flames
That almost have consumed me; I have spent
Many a silent night in sighs and groans,
Ran over all my thoughts, despised my fate,
Reasoned against the reasons of my love,
Done all that smoothed-cheek virtue could advise,
But found all bootless; 'tis my destiny
That you must either love, or I must die.

ANNABELLA: Comes this in sadness from you?

GIOVANNI: Let some mischief
Befall me soon, if I dissemble aught.

ANNABELLA: You are my brother Giovanni.

GIOVANNI: You
My sister Annabella; I know this,
And could afford you instance why to love
So much the more for this; to which intent
Wise nature first in your creation meant
To make you mine, else't had been sin and foul
To share one beauty to a double soul.
Nearness in birth or blood doth but persuade
A nearer nearness in affection.
I have asked counsel of the holy church,
Who tells me I may love you; and 'tis just
That, since I may, I should; and will, yes, will.
Must I now live or die?

ANNABELLA: Live/ thou hast won
The field, and never fought; what thou has urged
My captive heart had long ago resolved.
I blush to tell thee, – but I'll tell thee now –
For every sigh that thou hast spent for me
I have sighed ten; for every tear shed twenty;
And not so much for that I loved, as that
I durst not say I loved, nor scarcely think it.

GIOVANNI: Let not this music be a dream, ye gods,
For pity's sake, I beg ye!

ANNABELLA: On my knees, (*She kneels.*)
Brother, even by our mother's dust, I charge you,
Do not betray me to your mirth or hate;
Love me or kill me, brother.

GIOVANNI: On my knees, (*He kneels.*)
>Sister, even by my mother's dust, I charge you,
>Do not betray me to your mirth or hate;
>Love me or kill me, sister.

ANNABELLA: You mean good sooth, then?

GIOVANNI: In good troth, I do;
>And so do you, I hope; say, I'm in earnest.

ANNABELLA: I'll swear it, I.

GIOVANNI: And I; and by this kiss, –
>(*Kisses her.*)
>Once more! Yet once more – ! Now let's rise by this;
>I would not change this minute for Elysium.
>What must we now do?

ANNABELLA: What you will.

GIOVANNI: Come, then;
>After so many tears as we have wept,
>Let's learn to court in smiles, to kiss, and sleep.
>(*Exeunt.*)

THE CONSTANT PRINCE
Pedro Calderón de la Barca
1635

Dramatic / 1 Man, 1 Woman
Don Fernando: a captive prince of Portugal, 20-30
Phenix: the princess of Fez, 20s

The Setting: the royal palace in the kingdom of Fez

Don Fernando has been taken prisoner by the king of Fez and forced to labor in the royal gardens. When Phenix demands flowers, she is shocked to discover that her father has turned a prince into a slave.

PHENIX: Who is this, O heavens! I view?
FERNANDO: What disturbs thee?
PHENIX: Hearing, seeing
    Such a wretched state of being?
FERNANDO: I can well believe that true:
    Wishing, lady, upon you
    To attend in humble duty,
    I have brought thee flowers, whose beauty
    Typifies my fate, Señora;
    They are born with Aurora,
    And they perish ere the dew.
PHENIX: When this *marvel* came to light
    It was given a fitting name.
FERNANDO: Is not every flower the same
    That I bear thee in this plight?
PHENIX: It is true, but say whose spite
    Caused this novelty?
FERNANDO: My fate.
PHENIX: Is it then so strong?
FERNANDO: So great.
PHENIX: You afflict me.
FERNANDO: Do not grieve.
PHENIX: Why?
FERNANDO: Because a man doth live

Death and fortune's abject mate.

PHENIX: Are you not Fernando?

FERNANDO: Yes.

PHENIX: Changed by what?

FERNANDO: The laws that wring
Captive souls.

PHENIX: By whom?

FERNANDO: The King.

PHENIX: Why?

FERNANDO: My life he doth possess.

PHENIX: To-day I saw him thee caress.

FERNANDO: And yet he doth abhor me now.

PHENIX: How can it be that he and thou
So late conjoined, twin stars of light,
But one short day could disunite?

FERNANDO: These flowers have come to tell thee how. –
These flower awoke in beauty and delight,
At early dawn, when stars began to set –
At eve they leave us but a fond regret, –
Locked in the cold embraces of the night.
These shades that shame the rainbow's arch of light.
Where gold and snow in purple pomp are met,
All give a warning, man should not forget,
When one brief day can darken things so bright.
'Tis but to wither that the roses bloom –
'Tis to grow old they bear their beauteous flowers,
One crimson bud their cradle and their tomb.
Such are man's fortunes in this world of ours;
They live, they die, one day doth end their doom.
For ages past but seem to us like hours?

PHENIX: Horror, terror, make me fear thee;
I nor wish to see nor hear thee.
Be thou then the first of those
Whose woe hath scared another's woes.

FERNANDO: And the flowers?

PHENIX: If they can bear thee
Emblems of mortality,
Let them broken, scattered be; –
They must know my wrath alone.

FERNANDO: For what fault must they atone?

PHENIX: Like to stars they seem to me.
FERNANDO: Then you do not wish them?
PHENIX: No;
    All their rosy light I scorn.
FERNANDO: Why?
PHENIX: A woman is, when born,
    Subject to life's common foe,
    And to fortune's overthrow,
    Which methought this star did figure.
FERNANDO: Are the stars like flowers?
PHENIX: 'Tis so.
FERNANDO: This I do not see, although
    I myself have wept their rigour.
PHENIX: Listen.
FERNANDO: Speak, I wish to know.
PHENIX: These points of light, these sparkles of pure fire.
    Their twinkling splendours boldly torn away
    From the reluctant sun's departing ray,
    Live when the beams in mournful gloom retire.
    These are the flowers of night that glad Heaven's choir,
    And o'er the vault their transient odours play.
    For if the life of flowers is but one day,
    In one short night the brightest stars expire.
    But still we ask the fortunes of our lives,
    Even from this flattering spring-tide of the skies,
    'Tis good or ill, as sun or star survives.
    Oh! What duration is there? who relies
    Upon a star? or hope from it derives,
    That every night is born again and dies?
    (*Exit.*)

THE CID
Pierre Corneille
1636

Dramatic / 2 Women, 1 Man

Chimène: a young woman mourning the death of her father, 20s
Elvire: her governess, 40-60
Roderick: The "Cid," marshall of the King's army, 30s

The Setting: the court of the king of Seville

Chimène's father has forbidden her engagement to Roderick. When the Cid kills the older man in a fight, Chimène laments that she will now be forced to seek vengeance from the man she loves.

CHIMÈNE: I will avenge my father, and my woe;
    I'll follow him, destroy him, then I'll – die!
    (*Enter Roderick.*)
RODERICK: Nay, madam, you shall find an easier way;
    My life is in your hand; your honor's sure.
CHIMÈNE: Elvire, where are we? Who is this I see?
    Is Roderick in my house? – before my eyes?
RODERICK: I offer you my life; taste, when you will,
    The sweetness of my death and your revenge.
CHIMÈNE: Oh, woe!
RODERICK: Pray, hear me!
CHIMÈNE: Nay, I die!
RODERICK: A moment!
CHIMÈNE: Go; let me die!
RODERICK: I would but speak a word.
    You shall reply with sword-thrust at my heart.
CHIMÈNE: What! with a blade stained with my father's blood?
RODERICK: Chimène!
CHIMÈNE: Remove that object from mine eyes!
    Its sight recalls they crime and sues for death!
RODERICK: Nay, gaze upon it; 't will excite still more
    Thy hatred and thy wrath; 't will haste my doom.
CHIMÈNE: 'T is tinged with my own blood.

RODERICK: Plunge it in mine!
Wash in my veins what it has brought from thine.
CHIMÈNE: Oh, cruel steel, which in one awful day
A father's and a daughter's life can take.
I cannot live and see it! Take it hence!
Thou did'st me hear, and yet thou strik'st me dead!
RODERICK: I do thy will, but cherish still the wish
Of ending by thy hand my wretched life.
Not even love of thee works in my soul
Craven repentance for a righteous deed.
The fatal end of wrath too swift and hot
Brought shame upon my father's honored head.
The insult of a blow what heart can bear?
The affront was mine, I sought its author swift,
And swift avenged the honor of my sire.
Were it again to do, again 't were done!
But even 'gainst the inevitable deed,
My love long struggled for supremacy.
Judge how it ruled my heart, when I could pause,
In such an hour of rage, and hesitate
Between my house, my father, and – my love,
Compelled to wound thy heart or stand disgraced.
Myself I did accuse of haste undue,
Of passions too alive to feel affront.
Thy beauty might have turned the balance still,
But for the thought that pressed itself at last –
A man disgraced had naught to offer thee,
And vainly would thy heart's voice plead for me,
If nobleness were sunk in infamy.
To yield to love, to hearken to its cry,
Proved me unworthy of thy tenderness.
With sighs I tell thee o'er and o'er again,
And with my latest breath I still would say,
With cruel hand I've hurt thee, but naught else
Could blot my shame and leave me worthy thee.
Now, honor and my father satisfied.
To thee I come, to pay my final debt;
To offer thee my life, I seek thee here.
That duty done, this only rests to do.
Thou need'st not tell me that thy father slain

Arms thee against me – see, thy victim here!
Shrink not from offering up the blood of him
Who shed thy father's nor can mourn the deed.
CHIMÈNE: Ah! Roderick, strangely does my changeful heart
Defend thee who hast saved thy father's fame.
If my distracted mind has cruel seemed,
'T is not with blame for thee, but in despair.
The ardor of a high, unbroken spirit
That cannot brook an insult, well I know.
It was thy duty taught thee, but, alas!
In doing thine, thou teachest me mine own.
The very terror of thy deed compels;
For, as thy father's name thou hast restored,
Mine also calls upon his child for vengeance.
But, oh! my love for thee drives me to madness!
My father's loss by other hand had left
The solace of thy presence and thy love,
A consolation sweet in misery.
I still had felt in grief thy sympathy,
And loved the hand that wiped my tears away.
But now, in losing him thee too I lose;
This victory o'er my love his fame demands,
And duty, with the face of an assassin,
Drives me to work thy ruin and mine own.
For in my heart no more than in thine own
Must courage yield to luring dreams of love.
My strength must equal thine. In thine offense
Thou hast proved thy worth. By thine own death
Alone can I be worthy of thy love.
RODERICK: Defer no longer what thy cause demands.
It claims my head; I offer it to thee;
Make me the victim of thy just revenge.
I welcome the decree; I hail the stroke;
The tedious course of Justice to await
Retards thy glory, as my punishment.
'T is welcome fate to die by thy dear hand.
CHIMÈNE: No, not thine executioner am I;
'T is not for me to take thine offered life;
'T is thine to make defense 'gainst my attack.
Some other hand than mine must work my will;

Challenge I must, but punish never, never!

RODERICK: However love constrains thee for my sake,
Thy spirit must be equal to mine own,
Thyself has said; then wouldst thou borrow arms
To avenge a father's death! Nay, my Chiméne,
The soul of vengeance fails. No hand but mine
Could slay thy father; thine must punish me.

CHIMÈNE: O cruelty, to stand upon this point!
Thou didst not need my aid, I need not thine!
I follow thine example, and my spirit
Will never share with thee my glory's task.
My father's fame and I will nothing owe
To love of thine, or to thy late despair.

RODERICK: 'T is thou that standest on a point of honor.
Shall I ne'er win this mercy at thy hand?
In thy dead father's name, for our love's sake,
In vengeance or in pity, slay me here!
Thy wretched lover keener pain will know
To live and feel thy hate than meet thy blow.

CHIMÈNE: Leave me, I hate thee not.

RODERICK: 'T is my desert.

CHIMÈNE: I cannot.

RODERICK: When my deed is full known,
And men can say that still thy passion burns,
Dost thou not fear the cruel, stinging words
Of censure and of malice? Silence them;
Save thine own fame by sending me to death.

CHIMÈNE: My fame will shine the brighter for thy life,
The voice of blackest slander will lift up
My honor to the heavens, and mourn my griefs,
Knowing I love thee and yet seek thy life.
Go, vex no longer my poor, troubled soul
By sight of what I love and what I lose.
Hide thy departure in the shade of night;
For calumny may touch me, art thou seen;
The sole occasion for a slanderous word
Is, that I suffer thee within my house.
See that thou guard my virtue, and withdraw.

RODERICK: Oh, let me die!

CHIMÈNE: Depart.

RODERICK: What wilt thou do?

CHIMÈNE: The fires of wrath burn with the flames of love.
My father's death demands my utmost zeal;
'T is duty drives me with its cruel goad,
And my dear wish is – nothing to achieve.

RODERICK: O miracle of love!

CHIMÈNE: O weight of woe!

RODERICK: We pay our filial debt in suffering!

CHIMÈNE: Roderick, who would have thought –

RODERICK: Or could have dreamed –

CHIMÈNE: That joy so near so soon our grasp would miss?

RODERICK: Or storm so swift, already close to port,
Should shatter the dear bark of all our hope?

CHIMÈNE: Oh, mortal griefs!

RODERICK: Regrets that count for naught!

CHIMÈNE: Pray, leave me now; I cannot longer hear.

RODERICK: Adieu! I go to drag a dying life,
Till it is ended at thine own command.

CHIMÈNE: If my dire fate e'er bring that hour to me,
Thy breath and mine together will depart.
Adieu! and let no eye have sight of thee.

THE KING, THE GREATEST ALCADE
Lope Felix de Vega Carpio
1636

Dramatic / 3 Men

Sancho: a man fighting for his wife's honor, 30s
Pelayo: his friend, 30-40
Don Tello: a self-centered aristocrat, 30-50

The Setting: a town in Galacia, Spain

When Don Tello kidnaps Sancho's bride, the brave commoner goes to the king for help. Here, Sancho and Pelayo confront the evil Don Tello with a letter of condemnation written by the king.

(*Enter Sancho and Pelayo.*)

SANCHO: Great my Lord, I cast myself before your feet.

DON TELLO: Where have you been, Sancho? Some days have passed since last you came into my presence.

SANCHO: Rather they seemed years to me. My Lord, when I found how you persisted in the passion wherewith you were consumed – or call it love for my Elvira – I betook me to appeal to the King of Castile, who is the supreme and highest judge and who has the power to right all wrongs.

DON TELLO: So? And what, pray, did you tell him of me?

SANCHO: I told him that at the moment of my marriage you stole my wife away.

DON TELLO: Your wife? You lie, base knave! How? Did the priest come in, who was there that night?

SANCHO: No, my Lord, but he was advised that we both had given consent.

DON TELLO: If he never joined your hands, how then can it be marriage!

SANCHO: I have not come to discuss whether or not it be marriage. The King has granted me this letter which is writ in his own hand.

DON TELLO: I shake with rage. (*Reads.*) "Upon receipt of this you will deliver up to this poor peasant the woman whom you have taken from him, without word of reply; remember that the loyal vassal may be known, however distant he may be from his King, and that Kings are never distant when it is their duty to punish evil.

The King"

Man! What is this that you have done?

SANCHO: Señor, I bring this letter, given me by the King.

DON TELLO: By God, I am astonished at my own forbearance! Do you think, you hind, that by this insolence you shall teach me fear in my own despite? Do you know who I am?

SANCHO: I do, my Lord, and because I am assured of your nobility, I have brought this letter, not as you suppose to do you displeasure, but as a right friendly missive from my Lord of Castile, who is our King, that you may restore to me my wife.

DON TELLO: Then out of respect to this same letter, know that you and this miserable clown who comes with you . . .

PELAYO: Saint Blas! Saint Paul!

DON TELLO: I do not string you up here to the merlons of the battlements.

PELAYO: This not being my saint's day, by all the saints though altogether it has a devilish bad look for saints!

DON TELLO: Out of my palace on the instant, and look you linger not within my lands, or I will have you done to death with clubs! You knaves, you hinds, you low, earthly rascals of the clay! . . . What? To come to me! . . .

PELAYO: He is right too, and we were great fools to put him to this displeasure.

DON TELLO: If I have taken your wife, you knave, know I am who I am, and I reign here and here I do my will as the King does his in his Castile. My forbears never owed this land to him – they won it from the Moors.

PELAYO: Yes, they won it from the Moors and from the Christians too, and you don't owe a thing to the King.

DON TELLO: I am who I am . . .

PELAYO: (Aside.) Saint Macarius!

DON TELLO: That is the reason I do not take vengeance on you by my own hand. What? Give up Elvira! What is he to Elvira? Kill them, I say! But no – let them go! It is an unworthy thing in an hidalgo to stain his sword with peasants' blood!

PELAYO: No, don't you do it, on your life!
(Exit Don Tello.)

SANCHO: Now what do you say?

PELAYO: I say out of Galicia.

SANCHO: My brain whirls round when I consider that this fellow refuses to obey his King because he has three or four henchmen gathered here about him. For so help me God . . .

PELAYO: No, contain yourself, Sancho. It is good advice – and always was – never permit yourself a quarrel with a strong man and make no friendships among servants.

SANCHO: Let us return to León.

PELAYO: Well, I have the doubloons yet which the King gave me. So come on then.

SANCHO: I shall report to him what has happened. Ah, Elvira! Who now remains to bring you succor? Fly, fly to her, my sighs, and until I come again, tell her I die of love!

PELAYO: Better hurry, Sancho, for this fellow has not yet possessed Elvira.

SANCHO: How do you know, Pelayo?

PELAYO: Because he would have given her back once he had done his will.

THE LEARNÈD LADIES
Molière
1660

Serio-Comic / 2 Women, 1 Man

    Armande: a headstrong young woman, 20s
    Henriette: her sister, 20s
    Clitandre: suitor to both young ladies, 20-30

The Setting: Le Grand Salon of Chrysale and Philamente, a bourgeois couple.

Armande has refused Clitandre's marriage proposal and yet she becomes infuriated when he turns to her younger sister for love.

ARMANDE: What's this about?
HENRIETTE: What?
ARMANDE: This! A marriage veil?
HENRIETTE: Why not?
ARMANDE: Because you might as well choose jail!
    You'd give up all the joys of single life?
HENRIETTE: I see great joy in being someone's wife.
ARMANDE: I must sit down. My sister's gone insane!
    The very thought!
HENRIETTE: But why should I restrain
    My natural choice?
ARMANDE: It's vulgar, base and lowly.
HENRIETTE: The word that springs to mind for me is holy.
ARMANDE: And you cannot conceive the great disdain
    I feel for marriage?
HENRIETTE: If I may explain,
    The images that I would choose to see
    Are pleasant ones, of home and family.
    Myself, a husband, children in a nest
    All filled with love and laughter, Heaven blessed!
    And every night in bed between the sheets,
    I'm served a fancy feast of nuptial treats.
ARMANDE: Revolting.

HENRIETTE: It does not fill me with fright.

ARMANDE: It's sad how much your mind won't see the light.

HENRIETTE: Perhaps, but what's enlightened is my heart.
    It doesn't wish to spend its life apart
    From one who's filled it with such tenderness.
    I am in love, I'm guilty, I confess!

ARMANDE: Good Lord, your mind's in such a low estate
    That you've decided you will choose this fate?
    In household's prison asking to be locked
    With spouse and screaming babies? Well, I'm shocked.
    My dear, you must give up this foolish goal.
    Through knowledge you will elevate your soul
    And leave the burdens of domestic life
    To other women who enjoy the strife.
    When one gets married, intellectual
    Pursuits are simply ineffectual.
    How can one think when all one's time is spent
    In housework and domestic argument?
    Please, set your mind at high consideration
    And think a bit of mother's liberation!
    The eyes of learnèd men are fast upon her,
    And not with lust, but deference and honor.
    I'd sing your praise as learnèd far and wide,
    Before I'd stoop to sing "Here Comes the Bride."
    Oh, Henriette, it's truly rapturous
    To study differential calculus!
    It's hard at first, but what a satisfaction
    The first time you make sense of such abstraction!
    Read Blaise Pascal on probability,
    Boyle's elements and Milton's history,
    And Newton's orbit of the moon! It's thrilling!
    Such studies are rewarding and fulfilling.
    This wealth of knowledge is what should inspire you,
    And not some man who thinks he might desire you
    And make you slave to laws devised by men.
    Philosophy must be your husband then.
    Its very nature serves to elevate
    Our souls to heights at which we may create
    Environs where our lust can have no sway,
    Where carnal passion can be kept at bay.

Thus, thoughts of pleasure have no ill effects,
And one can turn one's back on S-E-X.

HENRIETTE: Sweet sister, from above we've been ordained
With different functions. What is to be gained
From being something I'm not meant to be?
If you wish to espouse philosophy,
The heights of worthy, learned speculation,
Then I wish to embrace domestication!
Let's not disturb what Heaven has arranged.
I do not want my instincts to be changed.
I'm happy for you in your worldly flight
To great philosophy's stupendous height,
But surely flying is one of those things
For which God would endow us all with wings
If we were meant to fly. So leave me here,
In earthly bliss and pure domestic cheer
To follow mother in her lesser role,
But one which helps to elevate her soul.

ARMANDE: If mother's whom you wish to imitate,
Then use her finer parts to best create
The model.

HENRIETTE: But my sister, think on this:
We'd not be here if not for wedded bliss.
The basest parts of marriage, as you say
Are what gave all of us the light of day.
And I for one applaud the time she chose a
Moment to forget Kant and Spinoza.
Accept with grace this marriage that I want,
And soon I may produce a new savant!

ARMANDE: Well, I'm resigned. You won't give up this plan.
So tell me . . .

HENRIETTE: Yes?

ARMANDE: You know!

HENRIETTE: What?

ARMANDE: Who's the man?

HENRIETTE: My fiancé?

ARMANDE: Exactly.

HENRIETTE: Can't you guess?

ARMANDE: It couldn't be . . . I mean . . . it's not . . . unless . . .
It isn't MY Clitandre!?

HENRIETTE: I confess!

He asked me yesterday, and I said yes!

ARMANDE: But surely you're not serious!

HENRIETTE: Why not?

You gave him up already. You forgot?

ARMANDE: Oh no! We're through, it's over, I agree!

But do you think he's gotten over me?

HENRIETTE: I haven't asked. I don't think he'd deceive me.

He tells me that he's mine alone. Believe me.

ARMANDE: My dear, you're so naive to think that men

Can love, forget and then start in again.

HENRIETTE: Perhaps you're right at that. I'll tell you what:

He's on his way. We'll ask him on the spot

Exactly what his feelings are for you.

But if it fits, can you put on the shoe?

ARMANDE: Of course! Don't be absurd. But can the truth

Be gotten from a silly, shallow youth?

HENRIETTE: His openness and honesty with me

Have made me trust him quite implicitly.

(*Clitandre enters.*)

Oh, here he is. Let's ask him right away!

ARMANDE: No rush. It could be done some other day –

CLITANDRE: (*Embracing Henriette, not seeing Armande.*)

Hello!

HENRIETTE: Hello.

ARMANDE: HELLO.

CLITANDRE: (*To Armande.*) Hello. What's new?

HENRIETTE: My sister has a question.

CLITANDRE: Oh. You do?

ARMANDE: No!

HENRIETTE: She would like to know in which direction

You presently extend your heart's affection.

CLITANDRE: I –

ARMANDE: Wait a minute! It's not in my fashion

To listen to a man declare his passion.

And forcing explanations face-to-face

Would be uncouth and very out of place.

CLITANDRE: My heart, which may appear to be uncouth

Prefers to cast its fortune with the truth.

And so, if you will pardon the intrusion,

I'll speak my piece and end all this confusion.
I can declare with total certainty . . .
(*Moving to Henriette.*)
That this sweet lady's won the heart of me.
(*To Armande.*)
Don't say a word, it's you who wished it so.
Your answer to my lover's plea was no.
Although I gave you full sufficient proof
Of my sincerity, you stayed aloof.
And so, when I decided to forget
My love for you, I found that Henriette
Was kindly sympathetic to my plight,
Possessing wit and charm without the bite
I'd heard in your remarks so frequently.
In short, surrounded with gentility,
With soft and soothing womanly support,
Instead of argument and harsh retort,
A quiet, impassive, acquiescent maid,
Instead of someone always on crusade,
I soon forgot what had me so upset.
How could I help but love my Henriette?
There's no point in attempting to regain
My interest, it would only be in vain.

ARMANDE: Excuse me, sir, but do you truly dare
Insinuate to me that I might care?
I'd find this conversation too insane
If not for your remarks which are inane.

HENRIETTE: Be gentle, sister! Practice mastery,
Which serves so well to keep our spirits free
From anger's outbursts.

ARMANDE: Just a moment please.
It's not my anger you need to appease.
I'm happy for you both, but there's one catch.
Have you informed our parents of this match?
You know, we're subject to parental laws.
In marriage contracts, it's that unseen clause,
The one that says the children must agree
To bow to *their* will and authority.

HENRIETTE: Oh, be assured, my uppermost intention
Is seeking their approval, as you mention.

Would you, Clitandre, lest they have a fit
Please speak to them, and make our love legit?
So I'll be free to love you all the time
Without the feeling that my love's a crime?

CLITANDRE: Of course, I'll speak to them without delay.
This afternoon I'll tell them, if I may.
(*He moves away.*)

ARMANDE: (*To Henriette.*)
You look as if you think that I'm upset.

HENRIETTE: Well, are you?

ARMANDE: No, I've nothing to regret.

HENRIETTE: Yes, so you've said. Besides, your education
Makes you the mistress of your situation.
And in my heart I know you'll do your best
To see this marriage well-approved and blessed.

ARMANDE: You speak in such a calm, collected voice
For someone who is only second choice.

HENRIETTE: I have the feeling you'd be quite relieved
If his rejected heart could be retrieved
By you.

ARMANDE: I will not deign to answer that.
I'll take my leave and wish you well . . .
(*To Clitandre.*)
You rat!

THE MISANTHROPE
Molière
1666

Serio-Comic / 1 Man, 1 Woman
>Alceste: a misanthrope, 30-40
>Célimène: the woman he desires, 20-30

The Setting: the home of Alceste

Cranky Alceste here complains to Célimène of her many suitors.

Scene One.

ALCESTE: You must, dear friend, give me leave to complain.
>The way you behave gives me reason for pain:
>Too often your thoughtlessness raises my gall;
>Some day we shall separate once and for all.
>I shall not deceive you with sugared pretense –
>I feel I'll be forced with your love to dispense,
>And in spite of all promises you would have heard
>I might not be able to honor my word.

CÉLIMÈNE: It's to quarrel with me, I note with dismay,
>That you've wanted to come and see me today.

ALCESTE: I don't quarrel at all. But your generous soul
>To all comers, dear Madam, presents itself whole.
>Too many suitors beleaguer your door;
>I won't share you with every officious bore.

CÉLIMÈNE: Why should I be blamed for the suitors you see?
>Can I stop all these people from taking to me?
>And if someone pleads for a share of my time
>Should I reach for a stick to punish his crime?

ALCESTE: A stick, dear Madam, is not what you need
>But a heart from too facile a tenderness freed.
>True, your charms go with you wherever you walk,
>But those lured by your looks are egged on by your talk;
>And your kind reception (of those I despise)
>Completes the conquest begun by your eyes.

The radiant smile you offer to each
Gives hope to every diligent leech.
If you were to appear more discretely wise
You would soon extinguish their amorous sighs.
But at least, dear Madam, do tell in what way
Your Clitandre so pleases and charms you, I pray.
On what solid foundation of worth and of skill
Do you build the esteem you are granting him still?
Is his letting his graceful fingernails grow
The cause of the signal of fondness you show?
Have you joined those victims of fashion's cant
Whom the dazzling charms of his wig enchant?
Does his dandyish garb assure him of grace?
Does he conquer with masses of ribbon and lace?
Has he earned by the elegant cut of his pants
That servitude sweet that a woman grants?
Have his oily smile, his falsetto voice
Been attractive enough to determine your choice?

CÉLIMÈNE: How unjustly you censure the course I pursue!
Why I humor the man is no secret to you;
For he and his friends will lend me support
To help win the case I have pending in court.

ALCESTE: It were better to lose, if it came to the test,
Than to humor a rival I must detest.

CÉLIMÈNE: The whole world now attracts your jealous abuse!

ALCESTE: The whole world shares alike in your kindness profuse.

CÉLIMÈNE: Just that point should appease your tempestuous soul
Since my tender regard goes to none as a whole.
There would be juster cause for all this ado
If I spread it less widely than now I do.

ALCESTE: But I whom excessively jealous you call,
What is mine, may I ask, that's not shared by them all?

CÉLIMÈNE: The bliss of knowing my love for you.

ALCESTE: How can I convince my heart it is true?

CÉLIMÈNE: I think if I say as much to your face
My word should be more than enough in this case.

ALCESTE: But how do I know that as part of the game
All the others might not have been told the same?

CÉLIMÈNE: Your style as a lover is sweet indeed!
And how highly you think of the life that I lead!

Well then! just to grant you relief from your care
I deny the esteem I've been rash to declare;
Now none will deceive you but you alone.
Good luck!

ALCESTE: Oh, why isn't my heart made of stone?
If only my soul could regain its ease
I would thank and bless the gods on my knees.
I admit it freely. I ever try
To set myself free from this terrible tie,
But my strongest efforts are all in vain:
For my sins, I am sure, I thus groan and complain.

CÉLIMÈNE: Your ardor, indeed, is an unequaled one.

ALCESTE: Yes, it is. On this point I will yield to none.
For no one can fathom my love for you,
And never has anyone loved as I do.

CÉLIMÈNE: Your method is startling and new, I agree,
For it seems that you court me to quarrel with me.
Your love takes the form of tantrum and whim
And never before was passion so grim.

ALCESTE: But it is in your power to stop all my grief.
Let us bury right now our disputes; and in brief
Let us open our hearts, and at once let's begin . . .

Scene Two

CÉLIMÈNE: What is it?
BASQUE: Acaste is below.
CÉLIMÈNE: Show him in.

Scene Three

ALCESTE: Indeed! Are we ever alone at all?
Forever you're ready to see those who call!
For this once, it seems you might change your routine
And inform your Acaste you're not to be seen.

CÉLIMÈNE: And affront him by having him sent away?

ALCESTE: Your concern as usual is aimed the wrong way.

CÉLIMÈNE: He's a man who would never forgive me the slight
Of my having denied myself to his sight.

ALCESTE: But why should you care about what he may feel . . .

CÉLIMÈNE: Why indeed! His good will is worth a great deal.
He is one of those who – I don't know how or why –
Count for much in the King's and the public's eye.
Their constant meddling I watch with alarm;
They do us no good, but they *can* do us harm.
And no matter what other support we may find,
We should never offend loud-mouthed men of his kind.
ALCESTE: Well and good. As I only too well recall
You find reasons to suffer the presence of all;
And your pretexts, albeit transparently thin . . .

Scene Four

BASQUE: Clitandre has come, if you please.
CÉLIMÈNE: Show him in.
(*To Alceste, who is leaving.*) You are off?
ALCESTE: Yes, indeed.
CÉLIMÈNE: Please remain.
ALCESTE: Buy why?
CÉLIMÈNE: Please stay.
ALCESTE: But I can't.
CÉLIMÈNE: I insist.
ALCESTE: I won't try.
You are set for a long conversational bout.
It's unfair to require me to sweat it out.
CÉLIMÈNE: I insist, I insist!
ALCESTE: I'll be bored to tears.
CÉLIMÈNE: All right, leave! You must have your way, it appears.

BERENICE
Jean Racine
1670

Dramatic / 1 Man, 1 Woman

Titus: Emperor of Rome, 30-40
Berenice: his wife, the Queen of Palestine, 20-30

The Setting: the Imperial palace in Rome

The people of Rome are outraged when their emperor returns home with a foreign bride. Reluctantly, he agrees to separate from Berenice in order to keep the peace. Here, the soon-to-be-parted lovers confront one another.

BERENICE: (*Coming from her apartment.*) Nay, let me go.
    Your counsel all is vain to keep me back;
    And I must see him –
    Ah, my lord, you here!
    Then it is true Titus abandons me!
    And we must part! 'Tis he will have it so!
TITUS: Spare, Madam, to o'erwhelm a hapless prince.
    We must not melt each other's hearts with woe.
    I am consumed with cruel griefs enough
    Without the added torture of those tears.
    Recall that noble spirit which so oft
    Has made me recognize the voice of duty.
    Yet there is time. Reduce your love to silence;
    And, with an eye clear'd from the mists of passion,
    Regard that duty with unflinching courage.
    Strengthen this heart of mine against yourself,
    Help me to nerve its weakness, if I can;
    To keep back tears that will not cease to rise;
    Or, if we cannot stanch those tender springs,
    Let dignity at least support our woes.
    So that the whole world without blame may mark
    When weeps an Emperor and when weeps a Queen.
    For, after all, my Princess, we must part.

BERENICE: Ah, cruel Titus, you repent too late.
What have you done? You made me think you loved me,
Accustom'd me to see you with delight.
Till but for that I lived. You knew your laws
When first you brought me to such fond confession,
Why did you let my love grow to this height?
Why said you not: "Poor Princess, fix your heart
Elsewhere, nor let deceitful hopes ensnare it;
Give it to one free to accept the gift?"
You took it gladly, will you now reject it
With cruel scorn, when to your own it clings?
How oft did all the world conspire against us!
Still there was time, you should have left me then.
A thousand reasons might have soothed my woe;
I might have blamed your father for my death,
The senate, and the people, all the empire,
The whole world, rather than a hand so dear.
Their enmity, so long declared against me,
Had long prepared me to expect misfortune.
I did not look, Sir, for this cruel blow
To fall when hope seem'd crown'd with happiness,
Now, when your love can do whate'er it wishes,
When Rome is silent, and your father dead,
When all the world bends humbly at your knees,
When there is nothing left to fear but you.

TITUS: Yes, it is I who wreak my own destruction!
Till now I lived the victim of delusion,
My heart refused to look into the future,
To think that we might one day have to part.
To eager wishes nothing seems too hard,
And blinded hope grasps the impossible.
Haply I thought to die before eyes,
And so forestall more cruel separation.
All opposition made my flame burn brighter;
Rome and the empire spoke, but glory's voice
Not yet had to my heart appeal'd in tones
Like those with which it strikes an Emperor's ears.
I know what torments wait on this resolve,
I feel my heart ready to take its flight,
I cannot any longer live without you.

Come life or death, my duty is to reign.

BERENICE: Be cruel, then, and reign, a slave to glory!
I'm ready to submit. Yes, I expected,
For trusting you, to hear those lips, that swore
A thousand vows of everlasting love,
Confess before mine eyes that they were faithless.
And banish me for ever from your presence.
I wish'd to hear that sentence from yourself!
But I will hear no more. Farewell for ever –
For ever! Ah, my lord, think how those words,
Those cruel words, dismay a heart that loves!
A year, a month will be to us an age
Of suffr'ing, when the wide sea rolls between us,
And each fresh sun that dawns shall sink in darkness
Without presenting to the eyes of Titus
His Berenice, he unseen by her
The livelong day. But how am I deceived!
No sorrow feels he at the thought of absence.
He will not count the days when I am gone,
So long to me, they'll seem too short for him!

TITUS: They'll not be many I shall have to count:
I hope ere long the tidings of my death
Will bring assurance that I loved you truly.
Then you will own that Titus could not live.

BERENICE: Ah, my dear lord, why part if that be so?
I speak not now to you of happy marriage.
Has Rome condemn'd me never more to see you?
Why grudge to me the selfsame air you breath?

TITUS: I can't resist you, Madam.
Stay, I yield;
But not without a sense of mine own weakness;
Ceaseless must be the conflict and the fears,
Ceaseless the watch to keep my steps from you,
Whose charms will ever like a magnet draw me.
Ay, at this very instant, love distracts me
From memory of all things but itself.

BERENICE: Well, well, my lord, what ill can come of it?
Where see you any sign of Rome's displeasure?

TITUS: Who knows how they will look on this offence?
If they complain, if cries succeed to murmurs,

Must I shed blood to justify my choice?
If they in silence let me break their laws,
To what do you expose me? I must purchase
Their patience at the price of base compliance
With whatsoever else they dare to ask me;
Too weak t' inforce the laws I cannot keep.

BERENICE: You count as nothing Berenice's tears!

TITUS: I count them nothing! Heavens! What injustice!

BERENICE: Why then, for unjust laws that you can change,
O'erwhelm yourself in ceaseless miseries?
Have you no rights, my lord, as well as Rome?
Why should you hold her interest more sacred
Than ours? Come, tell me.

TITUS: How you read my heart!

BERENICE: You are the Emperor, and yet you weep?

TITUS: Yes, Madam, it is true, with sighs and tears
I am unnerved. But when the throne I mounted
Rome made me swear to vindicate her laws,
And I must keep them. More than once already
Her rules have been call'd on to display
Their constancy in trial. From her birth
Those whom she honour'd readily obey'd her:
See Regulus who, faithful unto death,
Return'd to Carthage to be slain with tortures,
Torquatus dooming his victorious offspring,
Brutus with tearless eyes seeing his sons
Slain by his orders 'neath the lictor's axe.
Hard lot was theirs! But patriotic duty
Has ever won the victory with Romans.
I know in leaving you unhappy Titus
Attempts what throws their virtues in the shade,
A sacrifice surpassing any other's:
But think you, after all, I am unworthy
To leave posterity a high example
Which those who follow will be task'd to equal?

BERENICE: No! To your cruel heart I deem it easy;
Worthy are you to rob me of my life.
The veil is torn aside, I read your heart.
I will not ask you more to let me stay, –
Me, who had willingly endured the shame

Of ridicule and scorn from those who hate me.
I wish'd to drive you to this harsh refusal.
'Tis done, and soon you'll have no more to fear me.
Think not that I shall vent my wrongs in fury,
Or call on Heav'n to punish perjury:
No, if a wretch's tears still move the gods,
I pray them to forget the pangs I suffer.
If, ere I die, victim of your injustice,
I cherish any wish to leave behind me
Avengers of poor Berenice's death,
I need but seek them in your cruel heart;
Remorse will dwell there, all my love recalling,
Paint my past kindness, and my present anguish,
Show you my blood staining your royal palace,
And haunt you with abiding memories:
I have made every effort to dissuade you,
'Tis vain: to your own heart I trust for vengeance.
Farewell.

LE BOURGEOIS GENTILHOMME
Molière
1670

Serio-Comic / 3 Men
> Monsieur Jourdain: a bourgeois gentleman, 40-50
> Music Master and Dancing Master: opportunistic synchopants,
> 30-50

The Setting: the house of Monsieur Jourdain, Paris

Monsieur Jourdain is eager to adopt the airs of the upper class and therefore uses his wealth to surround himself with masters in the arts and sciences. Here, he discusses music and dance with two of his employees.

MONSIEUR JOURDAIN: Right, are we set for the knees-up?

DANCING MASTER: Excuse me?

MONSIEUR JOURDAIN: The sing-song?

MUSIC MASTER: Sing-song?

MONSIEUR JOURDAIN: What do you call it, then? Spot of singing, spot of dancing, all on the go at once? You know: the show.

DANCING MASTER: Ah, the show.

MUSIC MASTER: We are holding ourselves in readiness.

MONSIEUR JOURDAIN: Yes, I'm sorry to keep you waiting, but today I want to be done up nice and smart, you see, and my bloody tailor sent me a pair of silk stockings so tight I thought they'd never get over my knees. Neither of you are to leave the premises until they deliver my new suit. I want you to see me turned out from top to tail like a real gentleman. It's the very latest style, I do assure you.

MUSIC MASTER: We have no doubt of that.

MONSIEUR JOURDAIN: Meanwhile I had this oriental number run up just for me (*His dressing gown.*).

DANCING MASTER: How divine.

MONSIEUR JOURDAIN: My tailor informs me that all the class people adopt one of these before lunch. Valet!

VALET #1: Can I get you something, sir?

MONSIEUR JOURDAIN: No, must making sure that you've washed out your ears. – Marvellous people, servants. What do you think of their livery?

DANCING MASTER: Exquisite.

(*Monsieur Jourdain opens his robe to reveal red breeches and a green jacket.*)

MONSIEUR JOURDAIN: And how about this? It's quite rough and ready, I know. But it's only for my early morning workout.

MUSIC MASTER: Very dashing.

MONSIEUR JOURDAIN: Valet!

VALET #1: Sir?

MONSIEUR JOURDAIN: No, not you, the other one. What's the point of having two if the same sod does all the work?

VALET #2: Sir?

MONSIEUR JOURDAIN: Hold my dressing gown. – Do I still look the business?

DANCING MASTER: Incomparable.

MONSIEUR JOURDAIN: Then let's get on with your prologue or epigraph or whatever it is.

MUSIC MASTER: Prior to that I should like to hear the serenade which you commissioned. I set one of my most talented students to it.

MONSIEUR JOURDAIN: A student? You gave the job to a bone idle student? What's wrong with doing it yourself?

MUSIC MASTER: It is normally considered a great honour to have music composed for you by a student of mine.

MONSIEUR JOURDAIN: Oh? Well that's all right then. Off you go. (*The singer begins.*) – Give us my gown back so I can listen properly. – No, wait, I think I'll be better without it. – On second thoughts I will wear it after all.

SONG

"My heart burns with a fire that is ceaselessly roaring:
One look into your eyes, and my wits were derang'd,
If you treat thus a man, cruel love, so adoring –
Alas! what distress comes to he, who from you is estrang'd?"

MONSIEUR JOURDAIN: (*Yawns.*) What a bloody dreary song. No chance of jollying it up, I suppose?

MUSIC MASTER: Monsieur, the air must suit the mood of the words.

MONSIEUR JOURDAIN: I feared as much. I knew a song once.
Very witty it was too. How did it go again?

DANCING MASTER: Good God, how do I know?

MONSIEUR JOURDAIN: Had a girl in it. And a sheep.

DANCING MASTER: A girl and a sheep?

MONSIEUR JOURDAIN: Yes. It's coming back to me now . . .
(*Sings.*)
"Oh, Janet, Janet, Janet, Janet,
Every time I talk of love you try to ban it;
I thought your heart you'd open to me deep,
But I find that you're a wolf dressed as a sheep.
Oh, Janet;
Dear Janet;
When I see your woolly tail it makes me weep."
– Don't you think that's beautiful?

MUSIC MASTER: Very beautiful indeed.

DANCING MASTER: And you sing it beautifully.

MONSIEUR JOURDAIN: Though I never studied music.
Incredible.

MUSIC MASTER: You should study music, Monsieur, as you study
the dance. They go together as a matter of fact.

MONSIEUR JOURDAIN: Do proper people study music? I mean –
lords and ladies?

MUSIC MASTER: Yes they do.

MONSIEUR JOURDAIN: Right, then so will I. But I don't know
when I"m going to fit it into my schedule. As well as the Fencing
Instructor who's giving me lessons, I've a Philosophy chap due to
start this morning.

MUSIC MASTER: Philosophy's not bad, but music –

DANCING MASTER: Dance, music and dance, are the absolute
necessities of life –

MUSIC MASTER: The State needs music.

DANCING MASTER: People need to dance.

MUSIC MASTER: All the war, all the chaos in the world stems from
lack of the study of music.

DANCING MASTER: All the misery of mankind, all the downfall of
history, all the stupidity of politicians, all the blunders of generals,
in short, everything, comes from never having learned how to
dance.

MONSIEUR JOURDAIN: You're going to have to explain this in a little more detail.

MUSIC MASTER: Tell me what war is, if not a discord between two nations?

MONSIEUR JOURDAIN: You're right.

MUSIC MASTER: Well, if every citizen of every nation studied music, wouldn't they have a better appreciation of the potential for harmony in the world?

MONSIEUR JOURDAIN: You are right!

DANCING MASTER: And don't we always say, when a man has made a serious error in public or private life, don't we always say "He stepped out of line"?

MONSIEUR JOURDAIN: We do, don't we?

DANCING MASTER: And why did he step out of line? Because he did not know how to dance!

MONSIEUR JOURDAIN: Both of you are quite right.

MUSIC MASTER: Then would you like to see our performance now?

MONSIEUR JOURDAIN: Yes please.

MUSIC MASTER: The first piece is an exercise in the portrayal of the passions, musically. (*To singers.*) Would you mind, please? – You must envisage them dressed as shepherds.

MONSIEUR JOURDAIN: Not shepherds again. It's always bleeding shepherds. Can't I have water-nymphs?

MUSIC MASTER: No. It is called the pastoral convention. They are expressing their innermost passions in song. Would it seem natural to have water-nymphs expressing their innermost passions in song? It would not. It must be shepherds. Who are like that. (*He claps his hands and the music begins.*)
DUET

MAN: We lie in love's garden
For long, golden hours;
Two hearts young and ardent,
Two exquisite flowers.

WOMAN: This heat does delight now,
But summer wanes;
I feel winter's cold snow
Course through my veins.

BOTH: Serenade life!
Serenade love!
Sing for peace and tranquility –

Nothing on earth lasts for eternity.

MONSIEUR JOURDAIN: Is that all?

MUSIC MASTER: Yes.

MONSIEUR JOURDAIN: Strikingly, resoundingly brilliant. As far as I can tell.

DANCING MASTER: And now, for my offering, I humbly present the most beautiful movements available to the human body.

MONSIEUR JOURDAIN: Shepherds again?

DANCING MASTER: Whatever you like, Monsieur. – Begin! (*Music. A dance.*)

MONSIEUR JOURDAIN: That wasn't quite as pathetic as I expected. Some of those shepherds can wiggle very nicely.

MUSIC MASTER: When the dancing's put together with the music, the whole effect will be considerably improved.

MONSIEUR JOURDAIN: Good. It's intended for a very special lady who is doing me the honour of dropping in for a bite to eat.

DANCING MASTER: Everything's ready.

MUSIC MASTER: Except a detail which Monsieur has apparently overlooked.

MONSIEUR JOURDAIN: Oh? What?

MUSIC MASTER: A gentleman, Monsieur, of such taste and discernment as yourself, would normally at this point in the season have arranged for a recital in his salon ever Wednesday, say, or Thursday.

MONSIEUR JOURDAIN: That's what the posh do, is it?

MUSIC MASTER: Yes, Monsieur.

MONSIEUR JOURDAIN: See to it then. Make sure there's plenty of noise.

MUSIC MASTER: Oh, there will be! So long as you hire three singers – soprano, counter-tenor, and bass – accompanied by viol da gamba, lute, and harpsichord for the basso continuo, and two violins for the ritornello.

MONSIEUR JOURDAIN: I shall also require a bagpipe. The bagpipe is my favourite instrument and will sound extremely harmonious with those other things. But the crucial task for today is that you get the entertainment bang-on at dinner time.

DANCING MASTER: I am sure you will be delighted with it. The minuet especially is, forgive me for saying so, a triumph.

MONSIEUR JOURDAIN: Oh, a minuet? The minuet is my dance! You must see how I've improved! Maestro, please . . .

DANCING MASTER: Sir, you cannot dance without a hat.

MONSIEUR JOURDAIN: I can't?

MUSIC MASTER: Of course not.

(*Monsieur Jourdain puts on a hat and dances with the Dancing Master.*)

DANCING MASTER: La, la, la, la . . . (*Etc.*) . . . to the beat, Monsieur, to the beat . . . right leg . . . shoulders . . . arms . . . left leg . . . head . . . chin . . . point your toes! point your toes!

MONSIEUR JOURDAIN: I'm trying!

MUSIC MASTER: Bravo!

MONSIEUR JOURDAIN: Phew! That's enough. What I want to know is this. What's the protocol when a countess walks into the room? Am I meant to bow or what?

DANCING MASTER: A countess?

MONSIEUR JOURDAIN: A real countess, whose name is Dorimène.

DANCING MASTER: And you wish to show respect?

MONSIEUR JOURDAIN: The utmost respect.

DANCING MASTER: For the utmost respect, take a step back, and bow, then three steps forwards, bowing each time as you advance upon her, so that at the culmination of the final bow your nose is on a level with her knees.

(*The Dancing Master demonstrates. Monsieur Jourdain follows.*)

MONSIEUR JOURDAIN: Nose on a level with her knees . . . things are looking up already . . .

THE COUNTRY WIFE
William Wycherley
1673

Serio-Comic / 1 Man, 1 Woman

    Mr. & Mrs. Pinchwife: a domineering husband and his poorly used
        wife, 20-30

The Setting: a bedchamber in Pinchwife's house

Mrs. Pinchwife has confessed of an illicit assignation to her humorless
husband who demands that she write a letter to her lover.

PINCHWIFE: Come, tell me, I say.

MRS. PINCHWIFE: Lord! han't I told it a hundred times over?

PINCHWIFE: (*Aside.*) I would try, if in the repetition of the
    ungrateful tale, I could find her altering it in the least
    circumstance; for if her story be false, she is so too. – (*Aloud.*)
    Come, how was't, baggage?

MRS. PINCHWIFE: Lord, what pleasure you take to hear it sure!

PINCHWIFE: No, you take more in telling it I find; but speak, how
    was't?

MRS. PINCHWIFE: He carried me up into the house next to the
    Exchange.

PINCHWIFE: So, and you two were only in the room!

MRS. PINCHWIFE: Yes, for he sent away a youth that was there,
    for some dried fruit, and China oranges.

PINCHWIFE: Did he so? Damn him for it – and for –

MRS. PINCHWIFE: But presently came up the gentlewoman of the
    house.

PINCHWIFE: O, 'twas well she did; but what did he do whilst the
    fruit came?

MRS. PINCHWIFE: He kissed me a hundred times, and told me he
    fancied he kissed my fine sister, meaning me, you know, whom he
    said he loved with all his soul, and bid me to be sure to tell her so,
    and to desire her to be at her window by eleven of the clock this
    morning, and he would walk under it at that time.

PINCHWIFE: (*Aside.*) And he was as good as his word, very punctual; a pox reward him for't.

MRS. PINCHWIFE: Well, and he said if you were not within, he would come up to her, meaning me, you know, bud, still.

PINCHWIFE: (*Aside.*) So – he knew her certainly; but for this confession, I am obliged to her simplicity. – (*Aloud.*) But what, you stood very still when he kissed you?

MRS. PINCHWIFE: Yes, I warrant you; would you have had me discovered myself?

PINCHWIFE: But you told me he did some beastliness to you, as you call it; what was't?

MRS. PINCHWIFE: Why, he put –

PINCHWIFE: What?

MRS. PINCHWIFE: Why, he put the tip of his tongue between my lips, and so mousled me – and I said, I'd bite it.

PINCHWIFE: An eternal canker seize it, for a dog!

MRS. PINCHWIFE: Nay, you need not be so angry with him neither, for to say truth, he has the sweetest breath I ever knew.

PINCHWIFE: The devil! you were satisfied with it then, and would do it again?

MRS. PINCHWIFE: Not unless he should force me.

PINCHWIFE: Force you, changeling! I tell you, no woman can be forced.

MRS. PINCHWIFE: Yes, but she may sure, by such a one as he, for he's a proper, goodly, strong man; 'tis hard, let me tell you, to resist him.

PINCHWIFE: (*Aside.*) So, 'tis plain she loves him, yet she has not love enough to make her conceal it from me; but the sight of him will increase her aversion for me and love for him; and that love instruct her how to deceive me and satisfy him, all idiot that she is. Love! 'twas he gave women first their craft, their art of deluding. Out of Nature's hands they came plain, open, silly, and fit for slaves, as she and Heaven intended 'em; but damned Love – well – I must strangle that little monster whilst I can deal with him. – (*Aloud.*) Go fetch pen, ink, and paper out of the next room.

MRS. PINCHWIFE: Yes, bud. (*Exit.*)

PINCHWIFE: Why should women have more invention in love than men? It can only be, because they have more desires, more soliciting passions, more lust, and more of the devil.

(*Re-enter Mrs. Pinchwife.*)

Come, minx, sit down and write.

MRS. PINCHWIFE: Ay, dear bud, but I can't do't very well.

PINCHWIFE: I wish you could not at all.

MRS. PINCHWIFE: But what should I write for?

PINCHWIFE: I'll have you write a letter to your lover.

MRS. PINCHWIFE: Oh Lord, to the fine gentleman a letter!

PINCHWIFE: Yes, to the fine gentleman.

MRS. PINCHWIFE: Lord, you do but jeer; sure you jest.

PINCHWIFE: I am not so merry: come, write as I bid you.

MRS. PINCHWIFE: What, do you think I am a fool?

PINCHWIFE: (*Aside.*) She's afraid I would not dictate any love to him, therefore she's unwilling. – (*Aloud.*) But you had best begin.

MRS. PINCHWIFE: Indeed, and indeed, but I won't, so I won't.

PINCHWIFE: Why?

MRS. PINCHWIFE: Because he's in town; you may send for him if you will.

PINCHWIFE: Very well, you would have him brought to you; is it come to this? I say, take the pen and write, or you'll provoke me.

MRS. PINCHWIFE: Lord, what d'ye make a fool of me for? Don't I know that letters are never writ but from the country to London, and from London into the country? Now he's in town, and I am in town too; therefore I can't write to him, you know.

PINCHWIFE: (*Aside.*) So, I am glad it is no worse; she is innocent enough yet. – (*Aloud.*) Yes, you may, when your husband bids you, write letters to people that are in town.

MRS. PINCHWIFE: O, may I so? then I'm satisfied.

PINCHWIFE: Come, begin: (*Dictates.*) – "Sir" –

MRS. PINCHWIFE: Shan't I say, "Dear Sir?" – You know one says always something more than bare "Sir."

PINCHWIFE: Write as I bid you, or I will write whore with this penknife in your face.

MRS. PINCHWIFE: Nay, good bud (*Writes.*) – "Sir" –

PINCHWIFE: "Though I suffered last night your nauseous, loathed kisses and embraces" – Write!

MRS. PINCHWIFE: Nay, why should I say so? You know I told you he had a sweet breath.

PINCHWIFE: Write!

MRS. PINCHWIFE: Let me but put out "loathed."

PINCHWIFE: Write, I say!

MRS. PINCHWIFE: Well then. (*Writes.*)

PINCHWIFE: Let's see, what have you writ? – (*Takes the paper and*

reads.) "Though I suffered last night your kisses and embraces" –
Thou impudent creature! where is "nauseous" and "loathed"?

MRS. PINCHWIFE: I can't abide to write such filthy words.

PINCHWIFE: Once more write as I'd have you, and question it not,
or I will spoil thy writing with this. I will stab out those eyes that
cause my mischief. (*Holds up the penknife.*)

MRS. PINCHWIFE: Oh Lord! I will.

PINCHWIFE: So – so – let's see now. – (*Reads.*) "Though I suffered
last night your nauseous, loathed kisses and embraces" – go on –
"yet I would not have you presume that you shall ever repeat
them" – so – (*She writes.*)

MRS. PINCHWIFE: I have writ it.

PINCHWIFE: Oh, then – "I then concealed myself from your
knowledge, to avoid your insolencies." – (*She writes.*)

MRS. PINCHWIFE: So –

PINCHWIFE: 'The same reason, now I am out of your hands" – (*She
writes.*)

MRS. PINCHWIFE: So –

PINCHWIFE: "Makes me own to you my unfortunate, though
innocent frolic, of being in man's clothes" – (*She writes.*)

MRS. PINCHWIFE: So –

PINCHWIFE: "That you may evermore cease to pursue her, who
hates and detests you" – (*She writes on.*)

MRS. PINCHWIFE: So – heigh! (*Sighs.*)

PINCHWIFE: What, do you sigh? – "detests you – as much as she
loves her husband and her honor."

MRS. PINCHWIFE: I vow, husband, he'll ne'er believe I should
write such a letter.

PINCHWIFE: What, he'd expect a kinder from you? Come now,
your name only.

MRS. PINCHWIFE: What, shan't I say "Your most faithful humble
servant till death"?

PINCHWIFE: No, tormenting fiend! – (*Aside.*) Her style, I find,
would be very soft. – (*Aloud.*) Come, wrap it up now, whilst I go
fetch wax and a candle; and write on the backside, "For Mr.
Horner." (*Exit.*)

MRS. PINCHWIFE: "For Mr. Horner" – So, I am glad he has told
me his name. Dear Mr. Horner! but why should I send thee such a
letter that will vex thee, and make thee angry with me? – Well, I
will not send it. – Ay, but then my husband will kill me – for I see

plainly he won't let me love Mr. Horner – but what care I for my husband? – I won't, so I won't, send poor Mr. Horner such a letter – But then my husband – but oh, what if I writ at bottom my husband made me write it? – Ay, but then my husband would see't – Can one have no shift? ah, a London woman would have had a hundred presently. Stay – what if I should write a letter, and wrap it up like this, and write upon't too? Ay, but then my husband would see't – I don't know what to do. – But yet evades I'll try, so I will – for I will not send this letter to poor Mr. Horner, come what will on't."

"Dear, sweet Mr. Horner" – (*Writes and repeats what she writes.*) – so – "my husband would have me send you a base, rude, unmannerly letter; but I won't" – so – "and would have me forbid you loving me; but I won't" – so – "and would have me say to you, I hate you, poor Mr. Horner; but I won't tell a lie for him" – there – "for I'm sure if you and I were in the country at cards together" – so – "I could not help treading on your toe under the table" – so – "or rubbing knees with you, and staring in your face, till you saw me" – very well – "and then looking down, and blushing for an hour altogether" – so – "but I must make haste before my husband comes: and now he has taught me to write letters, you shall have longer ones from me, who am, dear, dear, poor, dear Mr. Horner, your most humble friend, and servant to command till death, – Margery Pinchwife."

Stay, I must give him a hint at bottom – so – now wrap it up just like t'other – so – now write "For Mr. Horner" – But oh now, what shall I do with it? for here comes my husband.

(*Enter Pinchwife.*)

PINCHWIFE: (*Aside.*) I have been detained by a sparkish coxcomb, who pretended a visit to me; but I fear 'twas to my wife – (*Aloud.*) What, have you done?

MRS. PINCHWIFE: Ay, ay, bud, just now.

PINCHWIFE: Let's see't: what d'ye tremble for? what, you would not have it go?

MRS. PINCHWIFE: Here – (*Aside.*) No, I must not give him that: so I had been served if I had given him this.

(*He opens and reads the first letter.*)

PINCHWIFE: Come, where's the wax and seal?

MRS. PINCHWIFE: (*Aside.*) Lord, what shall I do now? Nay, then I have it – (*Aloud.*) Pray let me see't. Lord, you will think me so

arrant a fool, I cannot seal a letter; I will do't, so I will.
(*Snatches the letter from him, changes it for the other, seals it, and delivers it to him.*)

PINCHWIFE: Nay, I believe you will learn that, and other things too, which I would not have you.

MRS. PINCHWIFE: So, han't I done it curiously? – (*Aside.*) I think I have; there's my letter going to Mr. Horner, since he'll needs have me send letters to folks.

PINCHWIFE: 'Tis very well; but I warrant, you would not have it go now?

MRS. PINCHWIFE: Yes, indeed, but I would, bud, now.

PINCHWIFE: Well, you are a good girl then. Come, let me lock you in your chamber, till I come back; and be sure you come not within three strides of the window when I am gone, for I have a spy in the street. – (*Exit Mrs. Pinchwife, Pinchwife locks the door.*) At least, 'tis fit she think so. If we do not cheat women, they'll cheat us, and fraud may be justly used with secret enemies, of which a wife is the most dangerous; and he that has a handsome one to keep, and a frontier town, must provide against treachery, rather than open force. Now I have secured all within, I'll deal with the foe without, with false intelligence.

PHAEDRA

Jean Racine

1677

Dramatic / 2 Women

Phaedra: Queen of Athens, 30s
Oenone: her nurse, 40-60

The Setting: Athens

Here, the tormented queen confesses her forbidden love for
Hippolytus, her step-son.

PHAEDRA: Dearest, we'll go no further. I must rest.
   I'll sit here. My emotions shake my breast,
   the sunlight throws black bars across my eyes.
   My knees give. If I fall, why should I rise,
   Nurse?
OENONE: Heaven help us! Let me comfort you.
PHAEDRA: Tear off these gross, official rings, undo
   these royal veils. They drag me to the ground.
   Why have you frilled me, laced me, crowned me, and wound
   my hair in turrets? All your skill torments
   and chokes me. I am crushed by ornaments.
   Everything hurts me, and drags me to my knees!
OENONE: Now this, now that, Madam. You never cease
   commanding us, then cancelling your commands.
   You feel your strength return, summon all hands
   to dress you like a bride, then say you choke!
   We open all the windows, fetch a cloak,
   rush you outdoors. It's no use, you decide
   that sunlight kills you, and only want to hide.
PHAEDRA: I feel the heavens' royal radiance cool
   and fail, as if it feared my terrible
   shame has destroyed its right to shine on men.
   I'll never look upon the sun again.
OENONE: Renunciation or renunciation!
   Now you slander the source of your creation.

Why do you run to death and tear your hair?

PHAEDRA: Oh God, take me to some sunless forest lair . . .
There hoof-beats raise a dust-cloud, and my eye
follows a horseman outlined on the sky!

OENONE: What's this, my lady?

PHAEDRA: I have lost my mind.
Where am I? Oh forget my words! I find
I've lost the habit now of talking sense.
My face is red and guilty – evidence
of treason! I've betrayed my darkest fears,
Nurse, and my eyes, despite me, fill with tears.

OENONE: Lady, if you must weep, weep for your silence
that filled your days and mine with violence.
Ah deaf to argument and numb to care,
you have no mercy. Spare me, spare
yourself. Your blood is like polluted water,
fouling a mind desiring its own slaughter.
The sun had died and shadows filled the skies
thrice now, since you have closed your eyes;
the day has broken through the night's content
thrice now, since you have tasted nourishment.
Is your salvation from your terrified
conscience this passive, servile suicide?
Lady, your madness harms the gods who gave
you life, betrays your husband. Who will save
your children? Your downfall will orphan them,
deprive them of their kingdom, and condemn
their lives and future to the discipline
of one who abhors you and all your kin,
a tyrant suckled by an amazon,
Hippolytus . . .

PHAEDRA: Oh God!

OENONE: You still hate someone;
thank heaven for that, Madam!

PHAEDRA: You spoke his name!

OENONE: Hippolytus, Hippolytus! There's hope
in hatred, Lady. Give your anger rope.
I love your anger. If the winds of love
and fury stir you, you will live. Above
your children towers this foreigner, this child

of Scythian cannibals, now wild
to ruin the kingdom, master Greece, and choke
the children of the gods beneath his yoke.
Why dawdle? Why deliberate at length?
Oh, gather up your dissipated strength.

PHAEDRA: I've lived too long.

OENONE: Always, always agonized!
Is your conscience still stunned and paralyzed?
Do you think you have washed your hands in blood?

PHAEDRA: Thank God, my hands are clean still. Would to God my
heart were innocent!

OENONE: Your heart, your heart!
What have you done that tears your soul apart?

PHAEDRA: I've said too much. Oenone, let me die;
by dying I shall escape blasphemy.

OENONE: Search for another hand to close your eyes.
Oh cruel Queen, I see that you despise
my sorrow and devotion. I'll die first,
and end the anguish of this service cursed
by your perversity. A thousand roads
always lie open to the killing gods.
I'll choose the nearest. Lady, tell me how
Oenone's love has failed you. Will you allow
your nurse to die, your nurse, who gave up all –
nation, parents, children, to serve in thrall.
I saved you from your mother, King Minos' wife!
Will your death pay me for giving up my life?

PHAEDRA: What I could tell you, I have told you. Nurse,
only my silences saves me from the curse
of heaven.

OENONE: How could you tell me anything
worse than watching you dying?

PHAEDRA: I would bring
my life and rank dishonor. What can I say
to save myself, or put off death a day.

OENONE: Ah Lady, I implore you by my tears,
and by my suffering body. Heaven hears,
and knows the truth already. Let me see.

PHAEDRA: Stand up.

OENONE: Your hesitation's killing me!

PHAEDRA: What can I tell you? How the gods reprove me!

OENONE: Speak!

PHAEDRA: Oh Venus, murdering Venus! love gored Pasiphaë with
    the bull.

OENONE: Forget
    your mother! When she died, she paid her debt.

PHAEDRA: Oh Ariadne, oh my Sister, lost
    for love of Theseus on that rocky coast.

OENONE: Lady, what nervous languor makes you rave
    against your family; they are in the grave.

PHAEDRA: Remorseless Aphrodite drives me. I,
    my race's last and worst love-victim, die.

OENONE: Are you in love?

PHAEDRA: I am insane with love!

OENONE: Who is he?

PHAEDRA: I'll tell you. Nothing love can do
    could equal . . . Nurse, I am in love. The shame
    kills me. I love the . . . Do not ask his name.

OENONE: Who?

PHAEDRA: Nurse, you know my old loathing for the son
    of Theseus and the barbarous amazon?

OENONE: Hippolytus! My God, oh my God!

PHAEDRA: You,
    not I, have named him.

OENONE: What can you do,
    but die? Your words have turned my blood to ice.
    Oh righteous heavens, must the blasphemies
    of Pasiphaë fall upon her daughter?
    Her Furies strike us down across the water.
    Why did we come here?

PHAEDRA: My evil comes from farther off. In May,
    in brilliant Athens, on my marriage day,
    I turned aside for shelter from the smile
    of Theseus. Death was frowning in an aisle –
    Hippolytus! I saw his face, turned white!
    My lost and dazzled eyes saw only night,
    capricious burnings flickered through my bleak
    abandoned flesh. I could not breathe or speak.
    I faced my flaming executioner,
    Aphrodite, my mother's murderer!

THE BEAUX-STRATEGEM
George Farquhar
1707

Serio-Comic / 2 Women
Mrs. Sullen: an unfaithful wife, 20-30
Dorinda: her sister-in-law, 20s

The Setting: Lichfield

Two charming fortune hunters have arrived in quiet Lichfield, and here the ladies they have courted discuss their newly discovered loves.

MRS. SULLEN: Well, sister!

DORINDA: And well, sister!

MRS. SULLEN: What's become of his servant?

MRS. SULLEN: Servant! he's a prettier fellow, and a finer gentleman by fifty degrees, than his master.

DORINDA: O' my conscience, I fancy you could beg that fellow at the gallows-foot!

MRS. SULLEN: O' my conscience I could, provided I could put a friend of yours in his room.

DORINDA: You desired me, sister, to leave you, when you transgressed the bounds of honour.

MRS. SULLEN: Thou dear censorious country girl! what dost mean? You can't think of the man without the bedfellow, I find.

DORINDA: I don't find anything unnatural in that thought: while the mind is conversant with flesh and blood, it must conform to the humours of the company.

MRS. SULLEN: How a little love and good company improves a woman! Why, child, you begin to live – you never spoke before.

DORINDA: Because I was never spoke to. – My lord has told me that I have more wit and beauty than any of my sex; and truly I begin to think the man is sincere.

MRS. SULLEN: You're in the right, Dorinda; pride is the life of a woman, and flattery is our daily bread; and she's a fool that won't believe a man there, as much as she that believes him in anything else. But I'll lay you a guinea that I had finer things said to me than you had.

DORINDA: Done! What did your fellow say to ye?

MRS. SULLEN: My fellow took the picture of Venus for mine.

DORINDA: But my lover took me for Venus herself.

MRS. SULLEN: Common cant! Had my spark called me a Venus directly, I should have believed him a footman in good earnest.

DORINDA: But my lover was upon his knees to me.

MRS. SULLEN: And mine was upon his tiptoes to me.

DORINDA: Mine vowed to die for me.

MRS. SULLEN: Mine swore to die with me.

DORINDA: Mine spoke the softest moving things.

MRS. SULLEN: Mine had his moving things too.

DORINDA: Mine kissed my hand ten thousand times.

MRS. SULLEN: Mine has all that pleasure to come.

DORINDA: Mine offered marriage.

MRS. SULLEN: O Lard! d'ye call that a moving thing?

DORINDA: The sharpest arrow in his quiver, my dear sister! Why, my ten thousand pounds may lie brooding here this seven years and hatch nothing at last but some ill-natured clown like yours. Whereas, if I marry my Lord Aimwell, there will be title, place, and precedence, the Park, the play, and the drawing-room, splendour, equipage, noise, and flambeaux. – *Hey, my Lady Aimwell's servants there! – Lights, lights to the stairs! – My Lady Aimwell's coach put forward! – Stand by, make room for her ladyship!* – Are not these things moving? – What! melancholy of a sudden?

MRS. SULLEN: Happy, happy sister! your angel has been watchful for your happiness, whilst mine has slept regardless of his charge. Long smiling years of circling joys for you, but not one hour for me!

(*Weeps.*)

DORINDA: Come, my dear, we'll talk of something else.

MRS. SULLEN: O Dorinda! I own myself a woman, full of my sex, a gentle, generous soul, easy and yielding to soft desires; a spacious heart, where love and all his train might lodge. And must the fair apartment of my breast be made a stable for a brute to life in?

DORINDA: Meaning your husband, I suppose?

MRS. SULLEN: Husband! no; even husband is too soft a name for him. – But, come, I expect my brother here to-night or to-morrow; he was abroad when my father married me; perhaps he'll find a way to make me easy.

DORINDA: Will you promise not to make yourself easy in the meantime with my lord's friend?

MRS. SULLEN: You mistake me, sister. It happens with us as among the men, the greatest talkers are the greatest cowards? and there's a reason for it; those spirits evaporate in prattle, which might do more mischief if they took another course. – Though, to confess the truth, I do love that fellow; – and if I met him dressed as he should be – look'ee, sister, I have no supernatural gifts – I can't swear I could resist the temptation; though I can safely promise to avoid it; and that's as much as the best of us can do. (*Exeunt.*)

SARA
Gotthold Lessing
1755

Dramatic / 2 Women
Sara Sampson: a young woman who has compromised her virtue,
      20s
Marwood: a fallen woman, 30s

The Setting: a country inn

Sara has run away with her lover, Mellefont. Here, she is confronted
by the evil Marwood, Mellefont's previous lover.

SARA: My good Mellefont sometimes gives his polite phrases quite a
    wrong accent. Do not you think so too, Madam?
MARWOOD: I am no doubt too much accustomed to his way
    already to notice anything of that sort.
SARA: Will you not take a seat, Madam?
MARWOOD: If you desire it. (*Aside, whilst they are seating
    themselves.*) I must not let this moment slip by unused.
SARA: Tell me! Shall I not be the most enviable of women with my
    Mellefont?
MARWOOD: If Mellefont knows how to appreciate his happiness,
    Miss Sampson will make him the most enviable of men. But –
SARA: A "but,' and then a pause, Madam –
MARWOOD: I am frank, Miss Sampson.
SARA: And for this reason infinitely more to be esteemed.
MARWOOD: Frank – not seldom imprudently so. My "but" is a
    proof of it. A very imprudent "but."
SARA: I do not think that my Lady Solmes can wish through this
    evasion to make me more uneasy. It must be a cruel mercy that
    only rouses suspicions of an evil which it might disclose.
MARWOOD: Not at all, Miss Sampson! You attach far too much
    importance to my "but." Mellefont is a relation of mine –
SARA: Then all the more important is the slightest charge which you
    have to make against him.
MARWOOD: But even were Mellefont my brother, I must tell you,

that I should unhesitantly side with one of my own sex against him, if I perceived that he did not act quite honestly toward her. We women ought properly to consider every insult shown to one of us as an insult to the whole sex, and to make it a common affair, in which even the sister and mother of the guilty one ought not to hesitate to share.

SARA: This remark –

MARWOOD: Has already been my guide now and then in doubtful cases.

SARA: And promises me – I tremble.

MARWOOD: No, Miss Sampson, if you mean to tremble, let us speak of something else –

SARA: Cruel woman!

MARWOOD: I am sorry to be misunderstood. I at least, if I place myself in imagination in Miss Sampson's position, would regard as a favour any more exact information which one might give me about the man with whose fate I was about to unite my own for ever.

SARA: What do you wish, Madam? Do I not know my Mellefont already? Believe me I know him, as I do my own soul. I know that he loves me –

MARWOOD: And others –

SARA: *Has* loved others. That I know also. Was he to love me, before he knew anything about me? Can I ask to be the only one who has had charm enough to attract him? Must I not confess it to myself, that I have striven to please him? Is he not so lovable, that he must have awakened this endeavor in many a breast? And isn't it but natural, if several have been successful in their endeavor?

MARWOOD: You defend him with just the same ardour and almost the same word with which I have often defended him already. It is no crime to have loved; much less still is it a crime to have been loved. But fickleness is a crime.

SARA: Not always; for often, I believe it is rendered excusable by the objects of one's love, which seldom deserve to be loved forever.

MARWOOD: Miss Sampson's doctrine of morals does not seem to be of the strictest.

SARA: It is true; the one by which I judge those who themselves confess that they have taken to bad ways is not of the strictest. Nor should it be so. For her it is not a question of fixing the limits which virtue marks out for love, but merely of excusing the human weakness that has not remained within those limits and of judging the consequences arising therefrom by the rules of wisdom. If, for example, a Mellefont loves a Marwood and eventually abandons her; this abandonment is very praiseworthy in comparison with the love itself. It would be a misfortune if he had to love a vicious person for ever because he once had loved her.

MARWOOD: But do you know this Marwood, whom you so confidently call a vicious person?

SARA: I know her from Mellefont's description.

MARWOOD: Mellefont's? Has it never occurred to you then that Mellefont must be a very invalid witness in his own affairs?

SARA: I see now, Madam, that you wish to put me to the test. Mellefont will smile, when you repeat to him how earnestly I have defended him.

MARWOOD: I beg your pardon, Miss Sampson, Mellefont must not hear anything about this conversation. You are of too noble a mind to wish out of gratitude for a well-meant warning to estrange from him a relation who speaks against him only because she looks upon his unworthy behaviour towards more than one of the most amiable of her sex as if she herself had suffered from it.

SARA: I do not wish to estrange anyone, and would that others wished it as little as I do.

MARWOOD: Shall I tell you the story of Mellefont in a few words?

SARA: I do not know. But still – yes, Madam! But under the condition that you stop as soon as Mellefont returns. He might think that I had inquired about it myself; and I should not like him to think me capable of a curiosity so prejudicial to him.

MARWOOD: I should have asked the same caution of Miss Sampson, if she had not anticipated me. He must not even be able to suspect that Marwood has been our topic; and you will be so cautious as to act in accordance with this. Hear now! Marwood is of good family. She was a young widow when Mellefont made her acquaintance at the house of one of her friends. They say, that she lacked neither beauty, nor the grace without which beauty would be nothing. Her good name was spotless. One single thing was wanting. Money. Everything that she had possessed – and she is said to have had considerable wealth – she had sacrificed for the deliverance of a husband from whom she thought it right to withhold nothing, after she had willed to give him heart and hand.

SARA: Truly a noble trait of character, which I would wish could sparkle in a better setting!

MARWOOD: In spite of her want of fortune she was sought by persons who wished nothing more than to make her happy. Mellefont appeared amongst her rich and distinguished admirers. His offer was serious, and the abundance in which he promised to place Marwood was the least on which he relied. He knew, in their earliest intimacy, that he had not to deal with an egoist but with a woman of refined feelings, who would have preferred to live in a hut with one she loved, than in a palace with one for whom she did not care.

SARA: Another trait which I grudge Miss Marwood. Do not flatter her any more, pray, Madam, or I might be led to pity her at last.

MARWOOD: Mellefont was just about to unite himself with her with due solemnity, when he received the news of the death of a cousin who left him his entire fortune on the condition that he should marry a distant relation. As Marwood had refused richer unions for his sake, he would not yield to her in generosity. He intended to tell her nothing of this inheritance, until he had forfeited it through her. That was generously planned, was it not?

SARA: Oh, Madam, who knows better than I, that Mellefont possesses the most generous of hearts?

MARWOOD: But what did Marwood do? She heard late one evening, through some friends, of Mellefont's resolution. Mellefont came in the morning to see her, and Marwood was gone.

SARA: Where to? Why?

MARWOOD: He found nothing but a letter from her, in which she told him that he must not expect ever to see her again. She did not deny, though, that she had loved him; but for this very reason she could not bring herself to be the cause of an act, of which he must necessarily repent some day. She released him from his promise, and begged him by the consummation of the union, demanded by the will to enter without further delay into the possession of a fortune, which an honorable man could employ for a better purpose than the thoughtless flattery of a woman.

SARA: But, Madam, why do you attribute such noble sentiments to Marwood? Lady Solmes may be capable of such, I daresay, but not Marwood. Certainly not Marwood.

MARWOOD: It is not surprising, that you are prejudiced against her. Mellefont was almost distracted at Marwood's resolution. He sent people in all directions to search for her, and at last found her.

SARA: No doubt, because she wished to be found!

MARWOOD: No bitter jests! They do not become a woman of such gentle disposition. I say, he found her; and found her inexorable. She would not accept his hand on any account, and the promise to return to London was all that he could get from her. They agreed to postpone their marriage until his relative, tired of the long delay, should be compelled to propose an arrangement. In the meantime Marwood could not well renounce the daily visits from Mellefont, which for a long time were nothing but the respectful visits of a suitor who has been ordered back within the bounds of friendship. But how impossible is it for a passionate temper not to transgress these bounds. Mellefont possesses everything which can make a man dangerous to us. Nobody can be more convinced of this than you yourself, Miss Sampson.

SARA: Alas.

MARWOOD: You sigh! Marwood too has sighed more than once over her weakness, and sighs yet.

SARA: Enough, Madam, enough! These words I should think, are worse than the bitter jest which you were pleased to forbid me.

MARWOOD: Its intention was not to offend you, but only to show you the unhappy Marwood in a light in which you could most correctly judge her. To be brief – love gave Mellefont the rights of a husband; and Mellefont did not any longer consider it necessary to have them made valid by the law. How happy would Marwood be, if she, Mellefont, and Heaven alone knew of her shame! How happy if a pitiable daughter did not reveal to the whole world that which she would fain be able to hide from herself.

SARA: What do you say? A daughter –

MARWOOD: Yes, through the intervention of Sara Sampson, an unhappy daughter loses all hope of ever being able to name her parents without abhorrence.

SARA: Terrible words! And Mellefont has concealed this from me? Am I to believe it, Madam?

MARWOOD: You may assuredly believe that Mellefont has perhaps concealed still more from you.

SARA: Still more? What more could he have concealed from me?

MARWOOD: This – that he still loves Marwood.

SARA: You will kill me!

MARWOOD: It is incredible that a love which has lasted more than ten years can die away so quickly. It may certainly suffer a short eclipse, but nothing but a short one, from which it breaks forth again with renewed brightness. I could name to you a Miss Oclaff, a Miss Dorcas, a Miss Moore, and several others, who one after another threatened to alienate from Marwood the man by whom they eventually saw themselves most cruelly deceived. There is a certain point beyond which he cannot go, and as soon as he gets face to face with it he draws suddenly back. But suppose, Miss Sampson, you were the one fortunate woman in whose case all circumstances declared themselves against him; suppose you succeeded in compelling him to conquer the disgust of a formal yoke which has now become innate to him; do you then expect to make sure of his heart in this way?

SARA: Miserable girl that I am! What must I hear?

MARWOOD: Nothing less than that! He would then hurry back all the more into the arms of her who had not been so jealous of his liberty. You would be called his wife and she would be it.

SARA: Do not torment me longer with such dreadful pictures! Advise me rather, Madam, I pray you, advise me what to do. You must know him! You must know by what means it may still be possible to reconcile him with a bond without which even the most sincere love remains an unholy passion.

MARWOOD: That one can catch a bird, I well know; but that one can render its cage more pleasant than the open field, I do not know. My advice, therefore, would be that one should rather not catch it, and should prepare oneself the vexation of the profitless trouble. Content yourself, young lady, with the pleasure of having seen him very near your net; and as you can foresee, that he would certainly tear it if you tempted him in altogether, spare your net and do not tempt him in.

SARA: I do not know whether I rightly understand your playful parable –

MARWOOD: If you are vexed with it, you have understood it. In one word. Your own interest as well as that of another – wisdom as well as justice, can, and must induce Miss Sampson to renounce her claims to a man to whom Marwood has the first and strongest claim. You are still in such a position with regard to him that you can withdraw, I will not say with much honour, but still without public disgrace. A short disappearance with a lover is a stain, it is true; but still a stain which time effaces. In some years all will be forgotten, and for a rich heiress there are always men to be found, who are not so scrupulous. If Marwood were in such a position, and she needed no husband for her fading charms nor father for her helpless daughter, I am sure she would act more generously toward Miss Sampson than Miss Sampson acts towards her when raising these dishonourable difficulties.

SARA: (*Rising angrily.*) This is too much! Is that the language of a relative of Mellefont's? How shamefully you are betrayed, Mellefont! Now I perceive, Madam, why he was so unwilling to leave you alone with me. He knows already, I daresay, how much one has to fear from your tongue. A poisoned tongue! I speak boldly – for your unseemly talk has continued long enough. How has Marwood been able to enlist such a mediator; a mediator who summons all her ingenuity to force upon me a dazzling romance about her; and employs every art to rouse my suspicion against the loyalty of a man, who is a man but not a monster? Was it only for this that I was told that Marwood boasted of a daughter from him; only for this that I was told of this and that forsaken girl – in order that you might be enabled to hint to me in cruel fashion that I should do well if I gave place to a hardened strumpet.

MARWOOD: Not so passionate, if you please, young lady! A hardened strumpet? You are surely using words whose full meaning you have not considered.

SARA: Does she not appear such, even from Lady Solmes' description? Well, Madam, you are her friend, perhaps her intimate friend. I do not say this as a reproach, for it may well be that it is hardly possible in this world to have virtuous friends only. Yet why should I be so humiliated for the sake of this friendship of yours? If I had had Marwood's experience, I should certainly not have committed the error which places me on such a humiliating level with her. But if I had committed it, I should certainly not have continued in it for ten years. It is one thing to fall into vice from ignorance; and another to grow intimate with it when you know it. Alas, Madam, if you knew what regret, what remorse, what anxiety my error has cost me! My error, I say, for why shall I be so cruel to myself any longer, and look upon it as a crime? Heaven itself ceases to consider it such; it withdraws my punishment, and gives me back my father. – But I am frightened, Madam; how your features are suddenly transformed! They glow – rage speaks from the fixed eye, and the quivering movement of the mouth. Ah, if I have vexed you, Madam, I beg for pardon! I am a foolish, sensitive creature; what you have said was doubtless not meant so badly. Forget my rashness! How can I pacify you? How can I also gain a friend in you as Marwood has done? Let me, let me entreat you on my knees (*Falling down upon her knees.*) for your friendship, and if I cannot have this, at least for the justice not to place me and Marwood in one and the same rank.

MARWOOD: (*Proudly stepping back and leaving Sara on her knees.*) This position of Sara Sampson is too charming for Marwood to triumph in it unrecognized. In me, Miss Sampson, behold the Marwood with whom on your knees you beg – Marwood herself – not to compare you.

SARA: (*Springing up and drawing back in terror.*) You Marwood? Ha! Now I recognize her – now I recognize the murderous deliverer, to whose dagger a warning dream exposed me. It is she! Away, unhappy Sara! Save me, Mellefont; save your beloved! And thou, sweet voice of my beloved father, call! Where does it call? Whither shall I hasten to it? – here? – there? – Help, Mellefont! Help, Betty! How she approaches me with murderous hand! Help!
(*Exit.*)

MINNA VON BARNHELM
Gotthold Lessing
1767

Serio-Comic / 2 Women, 1 Man

Minna: an heiress searching for the man she loves, 20-30
Franziska: her lively maid, 20s
Landlord: proprietor of the inn, 40-60

The Setting: a German inn, the end of the 7 Years War.

Minna's search for her fiancé brings her to a country inn, where a bizarre coincidence brings her closer to her true love.

(*The Lady's room.*)
(*Minna, Franziska*)

MINNA: (*In a negligée, looking at her watch.*) Franziska, we seem to have risen very early. The time will hang on our hands.

FRANZISKA: It's hopeless trying to sleep in these confounded big cities. What with the coaches, the watchmen, the drums, the cats, the corporals . . . there's no end to their clattering, screaming, drumming, miaowing and swearing; it seems the last thing you're meant to do at night is rest . . . a cup of tea, Madam?

MINNA: I don't like tea.

FRANZISKA: I'll get them to make some of our chocolate.

MINNA: For yourself, then, not for me.

FRANZISKA: For me? I'd just as soon talk to myself as drink by myself . . . Yes, the time's going to hang on our hands alright . . . We'll have to dress soon, and sort out which gown to wear to make the first assault.

MINNA: Why talk of assaults when I have come here merely to demand unconditional surrender?

FRANZISKA: And this officer we've driven out, and to whom we've sent our apologies; he can't have very good manners or he would have begged for permission to call on us by now.

MINNA: Not every officer is a Tellheim. To tell you the truth, it was only to gain an opportunity of making enquiries about him that I sent our apologies . . . Franziska, my heart tells me that I shall be lucky in my quest, and that I shall find him.

FRANZISKA: Your heart, Madam? People shouldn't trust their hearts too far. They are all too willing to say what you want to hear. If our mouths were as ready to flatter as our hearts, it would have become the fashion long ago to keep our mouths under lock and key.

MINNA: Ha, ha! One's mouth under lock and key? The fashion seems a good one to me.

FRANZISKA: Better to hide pretty teeth than to open your mouth and bare your heart as well!

MINNA: What? Are you so reserved?

FRANZISKA: No, Madam; but I'd like to be. People don't talk much about the virtues they have, but all the more about those they haven't got.

MINNA: You know, Franziska, you've just made a very perceptive remark.

FRANZISKA: Made? Can you make something that just occurs to you?

MINNA: And do you know why I find this remark so perceptive? It's because it applies so well to my Tellheim.

FRANZISKA: What is there for you that doesn't apply to him?

MINNA: Friend and foe alike say that he is the bravest man in the world. But who has ever heard him speak of bravery? He is the soul of integrity, but integrity and generosity are words that are never on his lips.

FRANZISKA: What virtues does he speak of, then?

MINNA: None, because he has them all.

FRANZISKA: I just wanted to hear you say that.

MINNA: Wait, Franziska; I remember now. He often speaks of economy. Between ourselves, Franziska, I believe the man's a spendthrift.

FRANZISKA: Another thing, Madam. I have often heard him talk of his faithfulness and constancy towards you. What if he was fickle?

MINNA: You wretched creature! . . . But do you mean that seriously, Franziska?

FRANZISKA: Well, how long is it since he last wrote to you?

MINNA: Ah! Since the peace he has written to me only once.

FRANZISKA: Now you're sighing against the peace! That's wonderful! Peace ought only to right the wrongs caused by war, but, instead, it's ruining the good the war brought about. Peace ought to be more considerate! . . . and how long have we been at peace now? The time will drag if it brings so little news! What's the point of the post working again, if nobody's writing, because nobody's got anything to write about?

MINNA: 'Now there's peace,' he wrote to me, 'and I am approaching the fulfilment of my wishes.' But the fact that he has written only once, one single letter . . .

FRANZISKA: That he is compelling us ourselves to hurry towards this 'fulfilment of wishes.' Just let's find him and make him pay for that! . . . What if, in the meantime, the man's 'fulfilled his wishes,' and we find out here . . .

MINNA: (*Anxious and excited.*) That he is dead?

FRANZISKA: To you, Madam, in the arms of another . . .

MINNA: Torturer! Just wait, Franziska, he'll make you pay for that! . . . But keep talking or we shall fall asleep again . . . His regiment was disbanded after the peace. Who knows what a tangle of accounts and enquiries he must be facing? Who knows to what other regiment, in what far-flung province he has been transferred? Who knows in what circumstances . . . Someone's knocking.

FRANZISKA: Come in.

(*Landlord, Minna, Franziska.*)

LANDLORD: (*Sticking his head round the door.*) Might I, your Ladyship?

FRANZISKA: Our dear Landlord? . . . Come right in.

LANDLORD: (*A pen behind his ear, a sheet of paper and an inkstand in his hand.*) I have come, your Ladyship, to wish you a humble 'Good Morning' . . . (*To Franziska.*) and you too, my pretty child . . .

FRANZISKA: What a courteous man!

MINNA: We thank you.

FRANZISKA: And wish you too a 'Good Morning.'

LANDLORD: Might I presume to enquire how your Ladyship rested the first night under my poor roof?

FRANZISKA: It's not the roof that's poor, but the beds that could do with improvement.

LANDLORD: What's that I hear? Not rested well? Perhaps the excessive exhaustion of the journey . . .

MINNA: Perhaps so.

LANDLORD: I'm sure of it, I'm sure of it! . . . Meanwhile if there is anything you lack for your Ladyship's comfort, you need only to ask.

FRANZISKA: Very well, Landlord! We're not shy, you know. Anyway, an inn is the last place where you can afford to be shy. We'll tell you what we want.

LANDLORD: And now I must also . . . (*Taking the pen from behind his ear.*)

FRANZISKA: Well?

LANDLORD: No doubt your Ladyship is already acquainted with the wise precautions taken by our police.

MINNA: Not in the least, Landlord.

LANDLORD: We landlords are directed not to accommodate any stranger, of whatever rank or station, for twenty-four hours without submitting, in writing, in the proper quarter, his name, his home, his character, his business here, the probable duration of his stay, and so on.

MINNA: Quite right.

LANDLORD: Perhaps your Ladyship will be so kind as to . . .

MINNA: With pleasure . . . My name is . . .

LANDLORD: Just one moment, please! . . . (*He writes.*) 'Date: the twenty-second of August anni currentis; arrived here at the King of Spain' . . . now your names, your Ladyship?

MINNA: Das Fräulein von Barnhelm.

LANDLORD: (*Writing:*) 'von Barnhelm' . . . Coming . . . from where, your Ladyship?

MINNA: From my estates in Saxony.

LANDLORD: (*Writing:*) 'Estates in Saxony' . . . Saxony! Ay, ay, from Saxony, your Ladyship? Saxony?

MINNA: Well? Why not? It is surely not a sin in these parts to be from Saxony?

LANDLORD: A sin? God forbid! That would be quite a new sin! . . . From Saxony then? Well, well, from Saxony! Dear old Saxony! . . . but if I remember rightly, your Ladyship, Saxony is a large place, and has several . . . what shall I say? . . . districts, provinces . . . Our police are very particular, your Ladyship.

MINNA: I understand. From my estates in Thuringia, then.

LANDLORD: From Thuringia! Yes, that's better, your Ladyship, more precise . . . (*Writes and reads.*) 'Das Fräulein von Barnhelm, coming from her estates in Thuringia, with a waiting woman and two servants . . .'

FRANZISKA: A waiting woman? That's supposed to be me, is it?

LANDLORD: Yes, my pretty child.

FRANZISKA: Now then, Landlord, instead of waiting woman, put down lady's maid. I have heard your police are very particular. There might be a misunderstanding and some trouble when my banns are called. For I *am* still a maid, and I'm called Franziska, surname Willig. I come from Thuringia too. My father was a miller on one of her Ladyship's estates. It's called Klein-Rammsdorf. My brother has the mill now. I came to court when I was very young, and was brought up with her Ladyship. We are of an age; twenty-one next Candlemas. I have learned everything her Ladyship has. I shall be delighted for the police to know everything about me.

LANDLORD: Very well, my pretty one, I'll remember that in case of further enquiries. And now, your Ladyship, your business here?

MINNA: My business?

LANDLORD: Does it concern His Majesty?

MINNA: Oh no!

LANDLORD: or the High Court of Justice?

MINNA: Nor that.

LANDLORD: Or . . .

MINNA: No, no. I am here on a purely private matter.

LANDLORD: Of course, your Ladyship, but how would you describe this private matter?

MINNA: I would describe it . . . Franziska, I believe we are being interrogated.

FRANZISKA: Surely the police won't want to learn a Lady's secrets?

LANDLORD: Certainly, my pretty one. The police want to know everything, and secrets most of all.

FRANZISKA: Well, your Ladyship, what's to be done? . . . Now listen here, Landlord, . . . as long as this stays between us and the police!

MINNA: What is the little fool going to tell him?

FRANZISKA: We have come to kidnap one of the King's officers.

LANDLORD: What? What? My child! My child!

FRANZISKA: Or to be kidnapped by the officer. It's all the same.

MINNA: Franziska, are you mad? . . . She's pulling your leg,

Landlord.

LANDLORD: I hope not! She can joke as much as she likes with your humble servant, but with the esteemed police . . .

MINNA: Do you know what, Landlord? . . . I am not sure how to handle this. I would think you could leave all this registration business until my uncle arrives. I told you yesterday the reason why he did not arrive at the same time as us. He had an accident two leagues from here, and was insistent that this unfortunate occurrence should not delay me another night. I had to proceed. He will be here no later than twenty-four hours after me.

LANDLORD: Very well, your Ladyship, we will await his arrival, then.

MINNA: He will be better able to answer your questions. He will know to whom, and how far he may declare himself; what of his affairs he may reveal, and what keep secret.

LANDLORD: All the better. You certainly can't expect a young girl (*Looking significantly at Franziska.*) to treat a serious matter in a serious way with serious people.

MINNA: And his rooms are in readiness, are they, Landlord?

LANDLORD: Completely, your Ladyship, completely; all except . . .

FRANZISKA: Which you have to throw some honest man out of first, perhaps?

LANDLORD: The lady's maids in Saxony are full of sympathy, your Ladyship.

MINNA: But it was not right of you, Landlord. You should have declined to take us in.

LANDLORD: But why, your Ladyship, why?

MINNA: I hear that the officer whom we have ousted . . .

LANDLORD: He's only a discharged officer, your Ladyship . . .

MINNA: So!

LANDLORD: Who's on his way out . . .

MINNA: So much the worse! He may be a very deserving man.

LANDLORD: I'm telling you he's been discharged.

MINNA: The King cannot know all deserving men.

LANDLORD: Oh, certainly he does, he knows them all.

MINNA: Well, he cannot reward them all.

LANDLORD: Those who have shown they deserve a reward will have got one. But during the war these gentlemen have been living as if the war would last for ever; there were no such words as 'yours' or 'mine.' Now all the inns and hotels are full of them; and a landlord has to keep a close eye on them. I did all right with this one. Even if he had no ready money left, he had stuff that was as good as cash, and I would have quite happily let him stay for two or three months more. Still, it's best to be on the safe side . . . By the way, your Ladyship, you must know something about jewelry?

MINNA: Not particularly.

LANDLORD: Your Ladyship should do, no? . . . I must show you a ring, an expensive ring. Well, I can see that your Ladyship has a very pretty ring on her finger, too, and the more I look at it, the more surprised I am at how much like mine it looks . . . Just have a look, have a look! (*Takes the ring out of its case and hands it to the ladies.*) What fire; the centre brilliant alone weights five carats.

MINNA: (*Looking at him.*) Where am I? What am I seeing? This ring . . .

LANDLORD: Is worth a good fifteen hundred Talers.

MINNA: Franziska! . . . Look here!

LANDLORD: I didn't hesitate to lend him eighty Pistoles on it.

MINNA: Don't you recognize it, Franziska?

FRANZISKA: The very one! Landlord, where did you get this ring?

LANDLORD: What, my child. Surely you've got not got a claim on it?

FRANZISKA: We have no claim on this ring?! The inside of the case must bear the Lady's monogram . . . Show him, Madam.

MINNA: It's the one, it is! . . . How did you come by this ring, Landlord?

LANDLORD: Me? In the most honest way in the world . . . Your Ladyship, your Ladyship, you're not going to ruin me, surely? How should I know where the rings comes from? During the war a lot of things changed hands, with or without the knowledge of the owners. War is war. There's more than one ring come over the border from Saxony . . . Give me it back, your Ladyship, give me it back.

FRANZISKA: Tell us first who you got it from.

LANDLORD: I wouldn't have thought he went in for that sort of thing. He's a good man otherwise . . .

MINNA: He's the best man under the sun, if you had it from its owner . . . Quickly, bring the man to me! It's him, or at least someone who knows him.

LANDLORD: Who then? Who, your Ladyship?

FRANZISKA: Aren't you listening? Our Major.

LANDLORD: Major? That's right, it was a major who had this room before you, and it was him I got it from.

MINNA: Major von Tellheim?

LANDLORD: Von Tellheim, yes! Do you know him?

MINNA: Do I know him! Is he here! Is Tellheim here? He lodged in this room? He, he pawned this ring with you? How has he got into difficulties? Where is he? Is he in debt to you? . . . Franziska, the strong box! Open it! (*Franziska puts it on the table and opens it.*) What does he owe you? Who else is he in debt to? Bring me all his creditors. Here is money. Here are bills. Everything is his!

LANDLORD: What's that you're saying?

MINNA: Where is he? Where is he?

LANDLORD: He was still here an hour ago.

MINNA: You loathsome man! How could you be so unkind, so hard, so cruel to him?

LANDLORD: Forgive me, your Ladyship . . .

MINNA: Quickly, produce him here for me.

LANDLORD: His servant might still be here. Would your Ladyship like me to go and find him?

MINNA: Would I? Hurry, run. For this service alone I will overlook the shameful way in which you have treated him . . .

FRANZISKA: Shift, Landlord, quick, off with you!
(*Pushes him out.*)

(*Minna, Franziska.*)

MINNA: I've found him again, Franziska! Do you see, I've found him! I'm beside myself with joy! Come on, rejoice with me, dear Franziska. But you're right, why should you? No, you should, you must rejoice with me. Come, my dear, I want to give you something so that you can rejoice with me. Tell me, Franziska, what shall I give you? Which of my things would suit you best? What would you like? Take whatever you want, only rejoice. I can see that you will not accept anything. Wait! (*Reaches into a satchel.*) There, my dear Franziska, (*Giving her money.*) buy something you'd like. Ask for more, if that isn't enough. Only rejoice with me. It's a sorry business being happy by oneself. Take it . . .

FRANZISKA: It would be stealing, Madam. You are drunk, drunk with happiness . . .

MINNA: I'm quarrelsome drunk, my girl. Take it or . . . (*Pressing money into her hand.*) . . . Don't you dare thank me! . . . Wait, I'm glad I thought of this. (*Reaches into her satchel for money.*) Put this aside, my dear Franziska, for the first poor wounded soldier to appeal to us for alms.

SHE STOOPS TO CONQUER
Oliver Goldsmith
1773

Serio-Comic / 2 Men, 1 Woman
  Marlow: a shy young man, 20s
  Miss Hardcastle: a clever young woman, 20s
  Hardcastle: the young woman's father, 50s

The Setting: the Hardcastle home

Marlow has been instructed by his father to court Miss Hardcastle. Unfortunately, the young man is only able to converse comfortably with bar maids and other plain folk. Miss Hardcastle therefore decides to masquerade first as a maid and then as a poor relation in order to win Marlow's heart.

MARLOW: What a bawling in every part of the house; I have scarce a moment's repose. If I go to the best room, there I find my host and his story; if I fly to the gallery, there we have my hostess with her curtsy down to the ground. I have at last got a moment to myself, and now for recollection. (*Walks and muses.*)

MISS HARDCASTLE: Did you call, sir? Did your honour call?

MARLOW: (*Musing.*) As for Miss Hardcastle, she's too grave and sentimental for me.

MISS HARDCASTLE: Did your honour call? (*She still places herself before him, he turning away.*)

MARLOW: No, child! (*Musing.*) Besides, from the glimpse I had of her, I think she squints.

MISS HARDCASTLE: I'm sure, sir, I heard the bell ring.

MARLOW: No, no! (*Musing.*) I have pleased my father, however, by coming down, and I'll to-morrow please myself by returning. (*Taking out his tablets and perusing.*)

MISS HARDCASTLE: Perhaps the other gentleman called, sir?

MARLOW: I tell you no.

MISS HARDCASTLE: I should be glad to know, sir. We have such a parcel of servants.

MARLOW: No, no, I tell you. (*Looks full in her face.*) Yes, child, I think I did call. I wanted – I wanted – I vow, child, you are vastly handsome!

MISS HARDCASTLE: O la, sir, you'll make one ashamed.

MARLOW: Never saw a more sprightly, malicious eye. Yes, yes, my dear, I did call. Have you got any of your – a – what d'ye call it in the house?

MISS HARDCASTLE: No, sir, we have been out of that these ten days.

MARLOW: One may call in this house, I find, to very little purpose. Suppose I should call for a taste, just by way of trial, of the nectar of your lips; perhaps I might be disappointed in that too.

MISS HARDCASTLE: Nectar? nectar? That's a liquor there's no call for in these parts. French, I suppose. We keep no French wines here, sir.

MARLOW: Of true English growth, I assure you.

MISS HARDCASTLE: Then it's odd I should not know it. We brew all sorts of wines in this house, and I have lived here these eighteen years.

MARLOW: Eighteen years! Why, one would think, child, you kept the bar before you were born. How old are you?

MISS HARDCASTLE: O! sir, I must not tell my age. They say women and music should never be dated.

MARLOW: To guess at this distance, you can't be much above forty. (*Approaching.*) By coming close to some women, they look younger still; but when we come very close indeed – (*Attempting to kiss her.*)

MISS HARDCASTLE: Pray, sir, keep your distance. One would think you wanted to know one's age as they do horses, by mark of mouth.

MARLOW: I protest, child, you use me extremely ill. If you keep me at this distance, how is it possible you and I can ever be acquainted?

MISS HARDCASTLE: And who wants to be acquainted with you? I want no such acquaintance, not I. I'm sure you did not treat Miss Hardcastle, that was here a while ago, in this obstropalous manner. I'll warrant me, before her you looked dashed, and kept bowing to the ground, and talked, for all the world, as if you were before a justice of the peace.

MARLOW: (*Aside.*) Egad, she has hit it, sure enough! (*To her.*) In awe of her, child. Ha! ha! ha! A mere awkward squinting thing!

No, no! I find you don't know me. I laughed and rallied her a little; but I was unwilling to be too severe. No, I could not be too severe, curse me!

MISS HARDCASTLE: Oh, then, sir, you are a favourite, I find, among the ladies?

MARLOW: Yes, my dear, a great favourite, and yet, hang me, I don't see what they find in me to follow. At the Ladies' Club in town I'm called their agreeable Rattle. Rattle, child, is not my real name, but one I'm known by. My name is Solomons; Mr. Solomons, my dear, at your service. (*Offering to salute her.*)

MISS HARDCASTLE: Hold, sir; you are introducing me to your club, not to yourself. And you're so great a favourite there, you say?

MARLOW: Yes, my dear. There's Mrs. Mantrap, Lady Betty Blackleg, the Countess of Sligo, Mrs. Longhorns, old Miss Biddy Buckskin, and your humble servant, keep up the spirit of the place.

MISS HARDCASTLE: Then it's a very merry place, I suppose?

MARLOW: Yes, as merry as cards, suppers, wine and old women can make us.

MISS HARDCASTLE: And their agreeable Rattle, ha! ha! ha!

MARLOW: (*Aside.*) Egad! I don't quite like this chit. She looks knowing, methinks. You laugh, child?

MISS HARDCASTLE: I can't but laugh to think what time they all have for minding their work or their family.

MARLOW: (*Aside.*) All's well; she don't laugh at me. (*To her.*) Do you ever work, child?

MISS HARDCASTLE: Ay, sure. There's not a screen or a quilt in the whole house but what can bear witness to that.

MARLOW: Odso! Then you must show me your embroidery. I embroider and draw patterns myself a little. If you want a judge of your work, you must apply to me. (*Seizing her hand.*)
(*Enter Hardcastle, who stands in surprise.*)

MISS HARDCASTLE: Ay, but the colours don't look well by candlelight. You shall see all in the morning. (*Struggling.*)

MARLOW: And why not now, my angel? Such beauty fires beyond the power of resistance. – Pshaw! the father here! My old luck; I never nicked seven that I did not throw ames-ace three times following.
(*Exit Marlow.*)

HARDCASTLE: So, madam! So I find *this* is your *modest* lover.

This is your humble admirer, that kept his eyes fixed on the ground, and only adored at humble distance. Kate, Kate, art thou not ashamed to deceive your father so?

MISS HARDCASTLE: Never trust me, dear papa, but he's still the modest man I first took him for; you'll be convinced of it as well as I.

HARDCASTLE: By the hand of my body, I believe his impudence is infectious! Didn't I see him seize your hand? Didn't I see him haul you about like a milk-maid? And now you talk of his respect and his modesty, forsooth!

MISS HARDCASTLE: But if I shortly convince you of his modesty, that he has only the faults that will pass off with time, and the virtues that will improve with age, I hope you'll forgive him.

HARDCASTLE: The girl would actually make one run mad! I tell you I'll not be convinced. I am convinced. He has scarcely been three hours in the house, and he has already encroached on all my prerogatives. You may like his impudence, and call it modesty; but my son-in-law, madam, must have very different qualifications.

MISS HARDCASTLE: Sir, I ask but this night to convince you.

HARDCASTLE: You shall not have half the time, for I have thoughts of turning him out this very hour.

MISS HARDCASTLE: Give me that hour, then, and I hope to satisfy you.

HARDCASTLE: Well, an hour let it be then. But I'll have no trifling with your father. All fair and open, do you mind me?

MISS HARDCASTLE: I hope, sir, you have ever found that I considered your commands as my pride; for your kindness is such that my duty as yet has been inclination. (*Exeunt.*)

THE BARBER OF SEVILLE
Pierre Augustin Caron de Beaumarchais
1775

Serio-Comic / 2 Men

    Count Almaviva: a Spanish Grandee, 02-30
    Figaro: the barber of Seville, 30-50

The Setting: Seville

The Count has become enchanted by the beautiful Rosine, a ward of Bartholo, a physician. Here, the Count conspires with crafty Figaro to gain entrance to Bartholo's house.

THE COUNT: Now that they have gone in, let's take a look at this song, in which some mystery is surely bottled up. It is a note!

FIGARO: Ha! He asked what the "Useless Precaution" was.

THE COUNT: (*Reads rapidly.*) "Your ardent attentions excite my curiosity; as soon as my guardian goes out, sing carelessly to the air of this song a few verses that will teach me the name, the rank, and the intentions of one who appears to interest himself so obstinately in the affairs of unfortunate Rosine."

FIGARO: (*Imitating Rosine's voice.*) My song! My song has fallen! Run, run now! (*He laughs.*) Ha! Ha! Ha! Ha! Ha! Oh, these women! If you want to teach cunning to the most unsophisticated, just lock her up.

THE COUNT: My darling Rosine!

FIGARO: My lord, I am no longer in doubt as to the motives of your disguise; you are making love here for future use.

THE COUNT: Well, you have caught on, but if you blab –

FIGARO: What! I blab! give away secrets! In allaying your fear, I shall not use any of the fine phrases of honor and devotion, phrases that are abused all day long; I have only a word: It is to my interest to keep silent; weigh that in the balance –

THE COUNT: Very well then, know that six months ago on the Prado I met by chance a young girl of marvellous beauty. You have just seen her. I have had her sought for all over Madrid – in vain. Just a few days ago I discovered that her name is Rosine, that she is of noble extraction, an orphan, and married to an old doctor of this city, Bartholo by name.

FIGARO: 'Pon my honor, a pretty bird, and hard to get from the nest. But who told you that she was the wife of the doctor?

THE COUNT: Everybody.

FIGARO: It is a story he patched up upon arriving from Madrid, in order to get rid of her admirers and to put her pursuers on a false trail. So far she is only his ward, but soon –

THE COUNT: (*Quickly.*) Never! Oh! What a relief! I had determined to dare all, in order to tell her how sorry I was that she was married, and I find her free! There's not a moment to lose; I must make her love me and snatch her from this unholy engagement that is in store for her. You say you know this guardian?

FIGARO: As I know my mother.

THE COUNT: What kind of a fellow is he?

FIGARO: (*Quickly.*) He's a slim, fat, short, young, doddering old fool, dappled-gray, clean shaven, cynic, who spies and peeps, and scolds and whines at the same time.

THE COUNT: Oh, come! I've seen him. His disposition?

FIGARO: Brutal, avaricious, excessively amorous and jealous of his ward who hates him like poison.

THE COUNT: His good points are – ?

FIGARO: None.

THE COUNT: So much the better. His honesty?

FIGARO: Just enough for him to escape hanging.

THE COUNT: So much the better. To punish a scoundrel, at the same time gaining my own happiness would –

FIGARO: Be both a personal and a public blessing, which is, in truth, my lord, the essence of morality.

THE COUNT: You say that fear of her lovers made him close his gates?

FIGARO: To everybody. If he could daub the chinks –

THE COUNT: Oh, the devil! So much the worse. You do not happen to have access to his house, do you?

FIGARO: Oh, yes I do! In the first place, the house in which I live belongs to the doctor, who puts me up there for nothing.

THE COUNT: Ha! Ha!

FIGARO: Yes, and I, in gratitude, promise him one hundred dollars a year for nothing also.

THE COUNT: (*Impatiently.*) You are his tenant?

FIGARO: More, his barber, his surgeon, his druggist. There isn't a razor, a lancette, or a hypodermic syringe used in his house except by the hand of your humble servant.

THE COUNT: (*Kisses him on both cheeks.*) Ah, Figaro, my friend, you shall be *my* Good Angel, my saviour, my tutelary god.

FIGARO: Plague on't! How my usefulness to you has lessened the distance between us! Talk about your impassioned people!

THE COUNT: Lucky Figaro! You are going to see my Rosine; you are going to see her. Do you realize your good fortune?

FIGARO: Now that's the speech of a lover for you. Am I the one who adores her? I wish you could take my place!

THE COUNT: If we could only get rid of all prying eyes.

FIGARO: That is what I am thinking about.

THE COUNT: To get rid of them for twelve hours only.

FIGARO: (*Meditating.*) By keeping people busy about their own affairs you keep them from meddling with others, don't you?

THE COUNT: Doubtless. Why?

FIGARO: (*Meditating.*) I am just trying to think whether the pharmacopoeia can furnish me with some little innocent means –

THE COUNT: (*In a laughing tone.*) You rascal!

FIGARO: Oh, I don't mean to harm them. They have used my services, and now to treat them all together.

THE COUNT: But this physician might smell a rat.

FIGARO: We must act so quickly that the rat will not have time to die. I have an idea. The regiment of the heir-apparent is just being quartered in this city.

THE COUNT: The Colonel is one of my friends.

FIGARO: Good. Present yourself at the doctor's house dressed like a trooper and with a quartermaster's billet. He will have to take you in, and I will take care of the rest.

THE COUNT: Excellent!

FIGARO: It would not be a bad idea for you to appear to be half drunk.

THE COUNT: What good will that do?

FIGARO: And treat him a bit cavalierly; your apparent drunkenness will be excuse enough for being unreasonable.

THE COUNT: Again I ask you why?

FIGARO: (*Patiently.*) So that he will take no offense, and so that he will believe you more in need of sleep than of love affairs in his house.

THE COUNT: Masterly conception! But why do you have no part in this plan?

FIGARO: Oh, yes, why not? We shall be lucky enough if he doesn't recognize you, you whom he has never seen. And how should I get you into the house afterwards?

THE COUNT: You are right –

FIGARO: Perhaps you will not be able to play this difficult part. A trooper – Half drunk –

THE COUNT: You are mocking me. (*Assuming the speech of a drunken person.*) Isn't the house of Doctor Bartholo around here nowhere at all, m' friend?

FIGARO: Not so bad after all; your legs ought to be a trifle more wobbly. (*With a still more drunken tone.*) Izhn't thish th' housh?

THE COUNT: Come now. You are imitating the drunkenness of a low fellow.

FIGARO: That is the best way to be drunk; it is the drunkenness of pleasure.

THE COUNT: Some one is opening the door.

FIGARO: It is our man. Let's move away till he leaves.

THE SCHOOL FOR SCANDAL
Richard Brinsley Sheridan
1777

Serio-Comic / 1 Man, 1 Woman
  Lady Teazle: a young society wife, 20s
  Sir Peter Teazle: her older husband, 40-50

The Setting: the home of Sir Peter Teazle, London

Sir Peter here takes his extravagant young wife to task for her many
foolish expenditures.

SIR PETER: Lady Teazle, Lady Teazle, I'll not bear it!

LADY TEAZLE: Sir Peter, Sir Peter, you may bear it or not, as you
please; but I ought to have my own way in every thing, and,
what's more, I will too. What! Though I was educated in the
country, I know very well that women of fashion in London are
accountable to nobody after they are married.

SIR PETER: Very well, ma'am, very well; so a husband is to have
no influence, no authority?

LADY TEAZLE: Authority! No, to be sure; if you wanted authority
over me, you should have adopted me, and not married me: I am
sure you were old enough.

SIR PETER: Old enough! – ay, there it is. Well, well, Lady Teazle,
though my life may be made unhappy by your temper, I'll not be
ruined by your extravagance!

LADY TEAZLE: My extravagance! I'm sure I'm not more
extravagant than a woman of fashion ought to be.

SIR PETER: No, no, madam, you shall throw away no more sums on
such unmeaning luxury. 'Slife! to spend as much to furnish your
dressing-room with flowers in winter as would suffice to turn the
Pantheon into a greenhouse, and give a *fête champétre* at
Christmas.

LADY TEAZLE: And am I to blame, Sir Peter, because flowers are
dear in cold weather? You should find fault with the climate, and
not with me. For my part, I'm sure I wish it was spring all the year

round, and that roses grew under our feet!

SIR PETER: 'Oons! madam – if you had been born to this, I shouldn't wonder at you talking thus; but you forget what your situation was when I married you.

LADY TEAZLE: No, no, I don't; 'twas a very disagreeable one, or I should never have married you.

SIR PETER: Yes, yes, madam, you were then in somewhat humbler style – the daughter of a plain country squire. Recollect, Lady Teazle, when I saw you first sitting at your tambour, in a pretty figured linen gown, with a bunch of keys at your side, your hair combed smooth over a roll, and your apartment hung round with fruits in worsted, of your own working.

LADY TEAZLE: Oh, yes! I remember it very well, and a curious life I led. My daily occupation to inspect the dairy, superintend the poultry, make extracts from the family receipt-book, and comb my aunt Deborah's lap-dog.

SIR PETER: Yes, yes, ma'am, 'twas so indeed.

LADY TEAZLE: And then you know, my evening amusements! To draw patterns for ruffles, which I had not materials to make up; to play Pope Joan with the curate; to read a sermon to my aunt; or to be stuck down to an old spinet to strum my father to sleep after a fox-chase.

SIR PETER: I am glad you have so good a memory. Yes, madam, these were the recreations I took you from; but now you must have your coach – *vis-á-vis* – and three powdered footmen before your chair; and, in the summer, a pair of white cats to draw you to Kensington Gardens. No recollection, I suppose, when you were content to ride double, behind the butler, on a docked coach-horse.

LADY TEAZLE: No – I swear I never did that: I deny the butler and the coach-horse.

SIR PETER: This, madam, was your situation; and what have I done for you? I have made you a woman of fashion, of fortune, of rank – in short, I have made you my wife.

LADY TEAZLE: Well, then, and there is but one thing more you can make me to add to the obligations, that is –

SIR PETER: My widow, I suppose?

LADY TEAZLE: Hem! hem!

SIR PETER: I thank you, madam – but don't flatter yourself, for, though your ill conduct may disturb my peace of mind, it shall never break my heart, I promise you: however, I am equally obliged to you for the hint.

LADY TEAZLE: Then why will you endeavour to make yourself so disagreeable to me, and thwart me in every little elegant expense?

SIR PETER: 'Slife, madam, I say, had you any of these little elegant expenses when you married me?

LADY TEAZLE: Lud, Sir Peter! would you have me be out of the fashion?

SIR PETER: The fashion, indeed! what had you to do with the fashion before you married me?

LADY TEAZLE: For my part, I should think you would like to have your wife thought a woman of taste.

SIR PETER: Ay – there again – taste! Zounds! madam, you had no taste when you married me!

LADY TEAZLE: That's very true, indeed, Sir Peter! and after having married you, I should never pretend to taste again, I allow. But now, Sir Peter, since we have finished our daily jangle, I presume I may go to my engagement at Lady Sneerwell's.

SIR PETER: Ay, there's another precious circumstance – a charming set of acquaintances you have made there!

LADY TEAZLE: Nay, Sir Peter, they are all people of rank and fortune, and remarkably tenacious of reputation.

SIR PETER: Yes, egad, they are tenacious of reputation with a vengeance; for they don't choose any body should have a character for themselves! Such a crew! Ah! many a wretch has rid on a hurdle who has done less mischief than these utterers of forged tales, coiners of scandal, and clippers of reputation.

LADY TEAZLE: What, would you restrain the freedom of speech?

SIR PETER: Ah! they have made you just as bad as any one of the society.

LADY TEAZLE: Why, I believe I do bear a part with a tolerable grace.

SIR PETER: Grace indeed!

LADY TEAZLE: But I vow I bear no malice against the people I abuse: when I say an ill-natured thing, 'tis out of pure good humour; and I take it for granted they deal exactly in the same manner with me. But, Sir Peter, you know you promised to come to Lady Sneerwell's too.

SIR PETER: Well, well, I'll call in, just to look after my own character.

LADY TEAZLE: Then, indeed, you must make haste after me, or

you'll be too late. So good-bye to ye.
(*Exit.*)

SIR PETER: So – I have gained much by my intended expostulation!
Yet with what a charming air she contradicts every thing I say, and
how pleasantly she shows her contempt for my authority! Well,
though I can't make her love me, there is great satisfaction in
quarrelling with her; and I think she never appears to such
advantage as when she is doing every thing in her power to plague
me.
(*Exit.*)

SAUL
Vittorio Alfieri
1784

Dramatic / 2 Men
Saul: the first king of Israel, 50s
Jonathan: his son, 30s

The Setting: Ancient Israel

On the eve of Saul's tragic death on Mt. Gilboa, father and son
confront one another on the subject of David – Jonathan's best friend
and the bane of Saul's existence.

SAUL: . . . Jonathan,
    Lov'st thou thy father? . . .
JONATHAN: Father! . . . yes, I love thee:
    But, loving thee, I also love thy glory:
    Hence, sometimes I oppose, far as a son
    Ought to oppose, thine impulses unjust.
SAUL: Often thy father's arm dost thou restrain:
    But, thou dost turn against thyself that sword
    Which thou avertest from another's breast.
    Yes, yes, defend that David to the utmost;
    Shortly will he . . . Dost thou not hear a voice
    That in thy heart cries: "David will be king"?
    – David? He shall be immolated first.
JONATHAN: And doth not God, with a more dreadful voice,
    Cry in thy heart: "My favorite is David;
    He is the chosen of the Lord of hosts"?
    Doth not each act of his confirm this truth?
    Was not the frantic and invidious rage
    Of Abner silenced by his mere approach?
    And thou, when thou re-enter'st in thyself,
    Dost thou not find that, only at his presence,
    All thy suspicions vanish like a cloud
    Before the sun? And dost thou fondly dream,

When the malignant spirit visits thee,
That I restrain thy arm? 'Tis God restrains it.
Scarcely wilt thou have levell'd at his breast
Thy evil-brandish'd sword, when thou wilt be
Forced to withdraw it suddenly: in tears
Thou thyself prostrate at his feet wilt fall;
Yes, father, thou, repentant: for thou art
Indeed not impious . . .

SAUL: But too true thy words.
    A strange inexplicable mystery
    This David is to me. No sooner I
    In Elah had beheld him, than he pleased
    My eyes; but never, never won my heart.
    When I might almost be disposed to love him,
    A fierce repulsion shoots athwart my breast,
    And woons me from him; scarcely do I wish
    For his destruction, than, if I behold him,
    He straight disarms me, with such wonder fills me,
    That in his presence I become a nothing . . .
    Ah! this is surely, this the vengeance is
    Of the inscrutable Almighty hand!
    Tremendous hand, I now begin to know thee . . .
    But what? why should I seek for reasons now? . . .
    God have I ne'er offended: this is then
    The vengeance of the priests. Yes, David is
    An instrument of sacerdotal malice.
    Expiring Samuel he beheld in Ramah:
    Th' implacable old man to him address'd
    His dying words. Who knows, who knows if he
    Upon the head of this my enemy
    Pour'd not the sacred oil with which before
    My brows he had anointed? P'rhaps thou knowest . . .
    Speak . . . yes, thou knowest: I conjure thee, speak.

JONATHAN: Father, I know not: but if it were so,
    Should not I, equally with thee, esteem
    Myself in this offended? Am not I
    Thy eldest son? Dost thou not mean this throne
    For me, when thou art gather'd to thy fathers?
    If I then hold my peace, who else should dare
    To make complaints at this? In fortitude

David surpasses me; in virtue, sense,
In ev'ry quality: and as the more
His worth surpasses mine, the more I love him.
Now, should that pow'r which gives and takes away
Kingdoms at will, bestow this throne on David,
What other greater proof can I require?
He is more worthy of that throne than I:
And God hath summon'd him to lofty deeds,
The shepherd of his children. – But meanwhile
I swear, that he has always been to thee
A faithful subject and a loyal son.
Now to that God to whom it doth belong,
The future yield: against that God, meanwhile,
Against the truth, ah, harden not thy heart.
If a divinity in Samuel spake not,
How could an undesigning, weak old man,
Half in the grave already, such effects
Produce by David's means? That mystery
Of love and hatred which thou feel'st for David;
That apprehension at a battle's name,
(A terror hitherto to thee unknown,)
Whence, Saul, can it proceed? Is there a power
On earth producing such effects as these? . . .

SAUL: What language dost thou hold? A son of Saul
Art thou? – Feel'st thou no int'rest for the throne? –
Know'st not the cruel rights of him who'll hold it?
My house will be abolish'd, from the roots
Torn up, by him who seizes on my sceptre.
Thy sons, thy brothers, and thyself destroy'd . . .
Not one of Saul's descendants will remain . . .
O guilty and insatiable thirst
Of pow'r, what horrors canst thou not produce?
To reign, the brother immolates the brother;
Mothers their children; wives their consorts slay;
The son his father . . . Sacrilegious throne!
Thou art the seat of blood and cruelty.

JONATHAN: Has man a shield against the sword of Heaven?
Not menaces or prayers can turn aside
The wrath of God omnipotent, who oft
The proud abases, and exalts the humble.

EGMONT

Johann Wolfgang Goethe
1786

Dramatic / 2 Women

    Clara: a young woman in love with the hero, Egmont, 20s
    Mother: her unhappy mother, 50s

The Setting: Brussels, during the 16th century revolt against Spain

Clara's mother wishes that her daughter would marry the humble
Brackenburg rather than waste time pining over the heroic Count
Egmont.

MOTHER: Do you send him away so soon!

CLARA: I long to know what is going on; and, besides, – do not be
    angry, mother, – his presence pains me. I never know how I ought
    to behave towards him. I have done him no wrong, and it goes to
    my very heart, to see how deeply he feels it. Well, – it can't be
    helped now!

MOTHER: He is such a true-hearted fellow!

CLARA: I cannot help it, I must treat him kindly. Often, without a
    thought, I return the gentle loving pressure of his hand. I reproach
    myself that I am deceiving him, that I am nourishing in his heart a
    vain hope. I am in a sad plight. God knows, I do not willingly
    deceive him. I do not wish him to hope, yet I cannot let him
    despair!

MOTHER: That is not as it should be.

CLARA: I liked him once, and in my soul I like him still. I could
    have married him; yet I believe I was never really in love with
    him.

MOTHER: You would have been always happy with him.

CLARA: I should have been provided for, and have led a quiet life.

MOTHER: And it has all been trifled away through your own folly.

CLARA: I am in a strange position. When I think how it has come to
    pass, I know it, indeed, and I know it not. But I have only to look
    upon Egmont, and I understand it all; ay, and stranger things

would seem natural then. Oh, what a man he is. All the provinces worship him. And in his arms, shall I not be the happiest creature in the world?

MOTHER: And how will it be in the future?

CLARA: I only ask, does he love me? – does he love me? – as if there were any doubt about it.

MOTHER: One has nothing but anxiety of heart with one's children. Always care and sorrow, whatever may be the end of it! It cannot come to good! Alas, you have made yourself wretched! You have made your mother wretched too.

CLARA: (*Quietly.*) Yet, you allowed it in the beginning.

MOTHER: Alas, I was too indulgent, I am always too indulgent.

CLARA: When Egmont rode by, and I ran to the window, did you chide me then? Did you not come to the window yourself? When he looked up, smiled, nodded, and greeted me; was it displeasing to you? Did you not feel honoured in your daughter?

MOTHER: Go on with your reproaches.

CLARA: (*With emotion.*) Then, when he passed more frequently, and we felt sure that it was on my account that he came this way, did you not remark it, yourself, with secret joy? Did you call me away, when I stood at the closed window waiting for him?

MOTHER: Could I imagine that it would go so far?

CLARA: (*With faltering voice, and repressed tears.*) And then, one evening, when, enveloped in his mantle, he surprised us as we sat at our lamp, who busied herself in receiving him, while I remained, lost in astonishment, as if fastened to my chair?

MOTHER: Could I imagine that the prudent Clara would so soon be carried away by this unhappy love? I must now endure that my daughter –

CLARA: (*Bursting into tears.*) Mother! How can you? You take pleasure in tormenting me.

MOTHER: (*Weeping.*) Ay, weep away! Make me yet more wretched by your grief. Is it not misery enough that my only daughter is a cast-away?

CLARA: (*Rising, and speaking coldly.*) A cast-away! The beloved of Egmont, a cast-away! – What princess but would envy the poor Clara her place in his heart? Oh, mother, – my own mother, you were not wont to speak thus! Dear mother, be kind! – Let the people think, let the neighbours whisper what they like, – this chamber, this lowly house is a paradise, since Egmont's love dwelt here.

MOTHER: One cannot help liking him! that is true. He is always so kind, frank, and open-hearted.

CLARA: There is not a drop of false blood in his veins. And then, mother, he is indeed the great Egmont; yet, when he comes to me, how tender he is, how kind! How he tries to conceal from me his rank, his bravery! How anxious he is about me! so entirely the man, the friend, the lover.

MOTHER: Do you expect him to-day?

CLARA: Have you not noticed how often I go to the window? How I listen to every noise at the door? Though I know that he will not come before night, yet, from the time when I rise in the morning, I keep expecting him every moment. Were I but a boy, to follow him always, to the court and everywhere! Could I but carry his colours in the field!

MOTHER: You were always such a lively, restless creature; even as a little child, now wild, now thoughtful. Will you not dress yourself a little better?

CLARA: Perhaps I may, if I want something to do. – Yesterday, some of his people went by, singing songs in his honour. At least his name was in the songs! I could not understand the rest. My heart leaped up in my throat, – I would fain have called them back if I had not felt ashamed.

MOTHER: Take care! Your impetuous nature will ruin all. You will betray yourself before the people; as, not long ago, at your cousin's, when you found the wood-cut with the description, and exclaimed, with a cry: "Count Egmont!" – I grew as red as fire.

CLARA: Could I help crying out? It was the battle of Gravelines, and I found in the picture, the letter C, and then looked for it in the description below. There it stood, "Count Egmont, with his horse shot under him." I shuddered, and afterwards I could not help laughing at the wood-cut figure of Egmont, as tall as the neighbouring tower of Gravelines, and the English ships at the side. – When I remember how I used to conceive of a battle, and what an idea I had, as a girl, of Count Egmont, when I listened to descriptions of him, and of all the other earls and princes; – and think how it is with me now!

HERNANI
Victor Hugo
1830

Dramatic / 2 Men, 1 Woman
    Don Ruy Gomez: a man seeking revenge, 60s
    Hernani: a bandit in love with a lady, 30s
    Doña Sol: the young woman loved by both men, 20s

The Setting: the palace of Aragon, Saragossa

When Doña Sol rejects Don Ruy in favor of Hernani, the evil Don tricks the bandit into vowing to take his own life. When Doña Sol discovers that the man she loves is about to drink poison, she impulsively joins him.

(*The Mask in black domino appears at balustrade of steps. Hernani stops petrified.*)
THE MASK: "Whatsoe'er
    May happen, what the place, or what the hour,
    Whenever to thy mind it seems the time
    Has come for me to die – blow on this horn
    And take no other care. All will be done."
    This compact had the dead for witnesses.
    Is it all done?
HERNANI: (*In a low voice.*) 'T is he!
THE MASK: Unto thy home
    I come, I tell thee that it is the time.
    It is my hour. I find thee hesitate.
HERNANI: Well, then, thy pleasure say.
    What wouldest thou
    Of me?
THE MASK: I give thee choice 'twixt poison draught
    And blade. I bear about me both. We shall
    Depart together.
HERNANI: Be it so.
THE MASK: Shall we
    First pray?

HERNANI: What matter?

THE MASK: Which of them wilt thou?

HERNANI: The poison.

THE MASK: Then hold out your hand.
> (*He gives a vial to Hernani, who pales at receiving it.*)
> Now drink,
> That I may finish
> (*Hernani lifts the vial to his lips, but recoils.*)

HERNANI: Oh, for pity's sake,
> Until to-morrow wait! If thou hast heart
> Or soul, if thou art not a specter just
> Escaped from flame, if thou art not a soul
> Accursed, forever lost; if on thy brow
> Not yet has God inscribed his "never."
> Oh,
> If thou hast ever known the bliss supreme
> Of loving, and at twenty years of age
> Of wedding the beloved; if ever thou
> Hast clasped the one thou lovedst in thine arms,
> Wait till to-morrow. Then thou canst come back!

THE MASK: Childish it is for you to jest this way!
> To-morrow! Why, the bell this morning toll'd
> Thy funeral! And I should die this night,
> And who would come and take thee after me!
> I will not to the tomb descend alone,
> Young man, 't is thou must go with me!

HERNANI: Well, then,
> I say thee nay; and, demon, I from thee
> Myself deliver. I will not obey.

THE MASK: As I expected. Very well. On what
> Then, didst thou swear? Ah, on a trifling thing,
> The mem'ry of thy father's head. With ease
> Such oath may be forgotten. Youthful oaths
> Are light affairs.

HERNANI: My father! – father! Oh
> My senses I shall lose!

THE MASK: Oh, no, – 't is but
> A perjury and treason.

HERNANI: Duke!

THE MASK: Since now

The heirs of Spanish houses make a jest
Of breaking promises, I'll say Adieu!
(*He moves as if to leave.*)

HERNANI: Stay!

THE MASK: Then –

HERNANI: Oh, cruel man. (*He raises the vial.*) Thus to return
Upon my path at heaven's door!
(*Reenter Doña Sol, without seeing The Mask, who is standing
erect near the balustrade of the stairway at the back of the stage.*)

DOÑA SOL: I've failed
To find that little box.

HERNANI: (*Aside.*) O God! 't is she!
At such a moment here!

DOÑA SOL: What is't that thus
I frighten him, – e'en at my voice he shakes!
What hold'st thou in thy hand? Reply to me.
(*The Domino unmasks; she utters a cry in recognizing Don Ruy.*)
'T is poison!

HERNANI: Oh, great Heaven!

DOÑA SOL: (*To Hernani.*) What is it
That I have done to thee? What mystery
Of horror? I'm deceived by thee, Don Juan!

HERNANI: Ah, I had thought to hide it all from thee.
My life I promised to the Duke that time
He saved it. Aragon must pay this debt
To Silva.

DOÑA SOL: Unto me you do belong,
Not him. What signify your other oaths?
(*To Don Ruy Gomez.*) My love it is which gives me strength, and,
Duke,
I will defend him against you and all
The world.

DON RUY GOMEZ: (*Unmoved.*) Defend him if you can against
An oath that's sworn.

DOÑA SOL: What oath?

HERNANI: Yes, I have sworn.

DOÑA SOL: No, no; naught binds thee; it would be a crime,
A madness, an atrocity – no, no,
It cannot be.

DON RUY GOMEZ: Come, Duke.

(*Hernani makes a gesture to obey. Doña Sol tries to stop him.*)
HERNANI: It must be done.

> Allow it, Doña Sol. My word was pledged
> To the Duke, and to my father now in heaven!

DOÑA SOL: (*To Don Ruy Gomez.*) Better that to a tigress you should go

> And snatch away her young, than take from me
> Him whom I love. Know you at all what is
> This Doña Sol? Long time I pitied you,
> And, in compassion for your age, I seemed
> The gentle girl, timid and innocent,
> But now see eyes made moist by tears of rage.
> (*She draws a dagger from her bosom.*)
> See you this dagger? Old man imbecile!
> Do you not fear the steel when eyes flash threat?
> Take care, Don Ruy! I'm of thy family.
> Listen, mine uncle! Had I been your child
> It had been ill for you, if you had laid
> A hand upon my husband!
> (*She throws away the dagger, and falls on her knees before him.*)
> At thy feet
> I fall! Mercy! Have pity on us both.
> Alas! my lord, I am but woman weak,
> My strength dies out within my soul, I fail
> So easily; 't is at your knees I plead,
> I supplicate – have mercy on us both!

DON RUY GOMEZ: Doña Sol!
DOÑA SOL: Oh, pardon! With us Spaniards

> Grief bursts forth in stormy words, you know it.
> Alas! you used not to be harsh! My uncle,
> Have pity, you are killing me indeed
> In touching him! Mercy, have pity now,
> So well I love him!

DON RUY GOMEZ: (*Gloomily.*) You love him too much!
HERNANI: Thou weepest!
DOÑA SOL: No, my love, no, no, it must

> Not be. I will not have you die.
> (*To Don Ruy.*) To-day
> Be merciful, and I will love you well,
> You also.

DON RUY GOMEZ: After him; the dregs you'd give,
The remnants of your love, and friendliness.
Still less and less. – Oh, think you thus to quench
The thirst that now devours me?
(*Pointing to Hernani.*) He alone
Is everything. For me kind pityings!
With such affection, what, pray, could I do?
Fury! 't is he would have your heart, your love,
And be enthroned, and grant a look from you
As alms; and if vouchsafed a kindly word
'T is he would tell you, – say so much, it is
Enough, – cursing in heart the greedy one
The beggar, unto whom he's forced to fling
The Drops remaining in the emptied glass.
Oh, shame! derision! No, we'll finish.
Drink!

HERNANI: He has my promise, and it must be kept.

DON RUY GOMEZ: Proceed.
(*Hernani raises the vial to his lips; Doña Sol throws herself on his arm.*)

DOÑA SOL: Not yet. Deign both of you to hear me.

DON RUY GOMEZ: The grave is open and I cannot wait.

DOÑA SOL: A moment, only, – Duke, and my Don Juan, –
Ah! both are cruel! What is it I ask?
An instant! That is all I beg from you.
Let a poor woman speak what's in her heart,
Oh, let me speak –

DON RUY GOMEZ: I cannot wait.

DOÑA SOL: My lord,
You make me tremble! What, then, have I done?

HERNANI: His crime is rending him.

DOÑA SOL: (*Still holding his arm.*) You see full well
I have a thousand things to say.

DON RUY GOMEZ: (*To Hernani.*) Die – die.
You must.

DOÑA SOL: (*Still hanging on his arm.*) Don Juan, when all's said,
indeed,
Thou shalt do what thou wilt.
(*She snatches the vial.*) I have it now!
(*She lifts the vial for Hernani and the old man to see.*)

DON RUY GOMEZ: Since with two women I have to deal,
It needs, Don Juan, that I elsewhere go
In search of souls. Grave oaths you took to me,
And by the race from which you sprang. I go
Unto your father, and to speak among
The dead. Adieu.

(*He moves as if to depart. Hernani holds him back.*)

HERNANI: Stay, Duke.

(*To Doña Sol.*) Alas! I do
Implore thee. Wouldst thou wish to see in me
A perjured felon only, and e'erwhere
I go "a traitor" written on my brow?
In pity give the poison back to me.
'T is by our love I ask it, and our souls
Immortal –

DOÑA SOL: (*Sadly.*) And thou wilt? (*She drinks.*) Not take the rest.

DON RUY GOMEZ: (*Aside.*) 'T was, then, for her!

DOÑA SOL: (*Returning the half-emptied vial to Hernani.*) I tell thee, take.

HERNANI: (*To Don Ruy.*) See'st thou, oh, miserable man!

DOÑA SOL: Grieve not for me,
I've left my share.

HERNANI: (*Taking the vial.*) O God!

DOÑA SOL: Not thus would'st thou
Have left me mine. But thou! Not thine the heart
Of Christian wife! Thou knowest not to love
As Silvas do – but I've drunk first – made sure.
Now, drink it, if thou wilt!

HERNANI: What hast thou done, unhappy one?

DOÑA SOL: 'T was thou who willed it so.

HERNANI: It is a frightful death!

DOÑA SOL: No – no – why so?

HERNANI: This philter leads unto the grave.

DOÑA SOL: And ought
We not this night to rest together? Does
It matter what bed?

HERNANI: My father, thou
Thyself avengest upon me, who did
Forget thee!

(*He lifts the vial to his mouth.*)

DOÑA SOL: (*Throwing herself on him.*) Heavens, what strange
    agony!
    Ah, throw this philter far from thee! My reason
    Is wand'ring. Stop! Alas! oh, my Don Juan,
    This drug is potent, in the heart it wakes
    A hydra with a thousand tearing teeth
    Devouring it. I knew not that such pangs
    Could be! What is the thing? 'T is liquid fire.
    Drink not! For much thou'dst suffer!

HERNANI: (*To Don Ruy.*) Ah, thy soul
    Is cruel! Could'st thou not have found for her
    Another drug? (*He drinks and throws the vial away.*)

DOÑA SOL: What dost thou?

HERNANI: What thyself hast done.

DOÑA SOL: Come to my arms, young lover, now.
    (*They sit down close to each other.*)
    Does not one suffer horribly?

HERNANI: No, no.

DOÑA SOL: These are our marriage rites! But for a bride
    I'm very pale, say am I not?

HERNANI: Ah me!

DON RUY GOMEZ: Fulfilled is now the fatal destiny!

HERNANI: Oh, misery and despair to know her pangs!

DOÑA SOL: Be calm. I'm better. Toward new brighter light
    We now together open out our wings
    Let us with even flight set out to reach
    A fairer world. Only a kiss – a kiss! (*They embrace.*)

DON RUY GOMEZ: Oh, agony supreme!

HERNANI: (*In a feeble voice.*) Oh, bless'd be Heav'n
    That will'd for me a life by specters followed,
    And by abysses yawning circled still,
    Yet grants, that weary of a road so rough,
    I fall asleep my lips upon they hand.

DON RUY GOMEZ: How happy are they!

HERNANI: (*In voice growing weaker and weaker.*) Come – come
    Doña Sol,
    All's dark. Dost thou not suffer?

DOÑA SOL: (*In a voice equally faint.*) Nothing now.
    Oh, nothing.

HERNANI: Seest thou not fires in the gloom?

DOÑA SOL: Not yet.

HERNANI: (*With a sigh.*) Behold – (*He falls.*)

DON RUY GOMEZ: (*Raising the head, which falls again.*) He's
dead!

DOÑA SOL: (*Disheveled and half raising herself on the seat.*) Oh,
no, we sleep.
He sleeps. It is my spouse that here you see.
We love each other – we are sleeping thus.
It is our bridal. (*In a failing voice.*)
I entreat you not
To wake him, my Lord Duke of Mcudocé,
For he is weary.
(*She turns round the face of Hernani.*)
Turn to me, my love.
More near – still closer – (*She falls back.*)

DON RUY GOMEZ: Dead! Oh, I am damn'd! (*He kills himself.*)

A FAMILY AFFAIR
Alexander Ostrovsky
1850

Serio-Comic / 2 Women

    Agrafena: the no-nonsense wife of a well-to-do merchant, 40-50
    Lipochka: her self-centered daughter, 16-20

The Setting: a merchant's home in Russia

Lipochka, a strong-willed and petulant young woman, here complains to her mother that she is not yet married.

LIPOCHKA: One, two, three. One, two, three.
    (*Enter Agrafena.*)
AGRAFENA: Caught you! In the act!
LIPOCHKA: I've got to practise!
AGRAFENA: Not before breakfast you haven't. You're shameless.
    Flouncing about like that in front of the window. And without
    even a bite of food inside you.
LIPOCHKA: Not true, Mama. I finished off the trifle and the last
    three cream meringues.
AGRAFENA: (*Following her around*) What's wrong with eating
    bread and tea for breakfast like ordinary Christians? Will you
    stand still when I'm talking to you!
LIPOCHKA: Why should I? One, two, three –
AGRAFENA: Lipochka! Come here, you minx! Oh, this twirling and
    whirling and showing your legs, it's sinful!
LIPOCHKA: Not sinful. Everybody does it.
AGRAFENA: Stop. Or I'll bash your head against that table just as if
    I was a peasant threshing wheat.
    (*Lipochka stops dancing and sits down.*)
LIPOCHKA: I'd finished anyway. Goodness, I'm perspiring like a
    horse. Give me your hankie, mummy.
AGRAFENA: I'll do it myself. (*Wipes Lipochka's brow.*) You've
    worn yourself out, my angel. I expect you feel giddy, do you?
    (*Lipochka nods.*) Sick? Feeling sick (*She nods, rubbing her
    tummy.*) Well don't say we never let you have your own way.

LIPOCHKA: You ignorant old bag.

AGRAFENA: If you have no respect for me, at least have respect for the walls of your father's house.

LIPOCHKA: All your ideas are completely out of date.

AGRAFENA: What a charming child you are. The way you treat your mother . . . !

LIPOCHKA: You are repulsive. Like a corpse.

AGRAFENA: Have you nothing in your head but filth, miss? Did I bring you into the world and suckle you at my own breast and teach you everything you know to be compared in the end to a dead person?

LIPOCHKA: You didn't teach me everything I know. Proper people did. The truth is, mama, you never got educated at all. You don't know a single thing. And when I popped out of you, what was I fit for? I hadn't the first idea about life. I behaved like a child. I couldn't dance. I didn't know what cutlery to use for the fish course. I was a completely pointless being. But when I got out on my own, I took a look around at the world of taste and sensibility, and I improved myself. And now I have to accept that I'm vastly better equipped for life than most people. So why should I listen to you?

AGRAFENA: One day you'll drive me mad.

LIPOCHKA: Only because you're a narrow-minded old bigot.

AGRAFENA: One day I shall throw myself to the ground in front of your father and say, 'Samson Bolshov, that daughter of ours is ruining my life.'

LIPOCHKA: Ruining *your* life? O ha ha. That's a good one. Very witty indeed.

AGRAFENA: Pardon?

LIPOCHKA: What about my life? What about the mess you've made of that? Why for instance did you send my last suitor packing? He was rather tasteful, he was. He was the best match I'm ever likely to make. Coming from a family like this. Well?

AGRAFENA: He had a filthy mouth.

LIPOCHKA: He never.

AGRAFENA: He swore!

LIPOCHKA: An oath of undying love. In French.

AGRAFENA: He minced around like a ballet dancer.

LIPOCHKA: He was a Grand Duke, mother! They walk like that!

AGRAFENA: Well I barely understood a word he spoke.

LIPOCHKA: He loved beauty. And style. And hunting bears. How dare you find fault with the higher things in life? He was a sight more refined than some scruffy merchant with a briefcase and inkstains on his cuff – ugh! (*Aside.*) Boris, my love, my angel, take me, I'm yours.

AGRAFENA: You most certainly are not!

LIPOCHKA: You don't want me to be happy.

AGRAFENA: You're so stubborn, I sometimes wish I'd given you away to the village idiot. Yes! Fedot down the road! But you're probably too old now.

LIPOCHKA: Find me a real husband, mama . . . !

AGRAFENA: We're doing our best. Your father and me worry ourselves sick over it.

LIPOCHKA: The whole of Moscow to choose from – and they can't dig up one decent man.

AGRAFENA: They're not the that thick on the ground to be honest.

LIPOCHKA: All my friends are married. Been married for years. I'm still hanging around. Look: find me a husband, and quick. Or else I'll take a lover.

AGRAFENA: No!

LIPOCHKA: Yes. I'll run off with a hussar. And marry him in secret.

AGRAFENA: You silly little slut. Hussars never have any money. I can see I'll have to call your father.

LIPOCHKA: Oh, the worst punishment – a conversation with father.

AGRAFENA: I may be simple, Lipochka, but I'm not daft. You know about as many hussars as I know archbishops. You've the devil in you, waggling your tongue. Little blue-eyes – why did you turn out like this? So naughty. So suspicious. And such a chubby baby. With such a turned-up nose. Put a stop to it, right now. Or you'll be down in the kitchen with your hands in the sink. I am your mother! – whilst I live. Lord have mercy on me. Any more cheek and you'll sleep with the pigs.

LIPOCHKA: That's right. You want to smother me in your own muck. You want to drive me to an early grave. And death is terribly unfashionable at the minute. – So I'm obnoxious. But what about you? You're absolutely vile! I'm your only daughter and you hate the sight of me. (*Coughs.*) You'll kill me with your silly superstitions, you see my lungs are weak already – (*Starts to weep.*) Life is a fragile thing you know – (*Weeps.*)

(*Agrafena stands and looks at her.*)

AGRAFENA: All right. That will do.

(*Lipochka just weeps louder.*)

There, there. Little baby . . . (*Lipochka weeps still.*) Stop, please stop . . . that's enough! Look I know it's my fault, I know we haven't done all we might, Lipochka, don't be cross with me . . . (*Agrafena starts to weep also.*) I'm only a stupid old woman, don't mind me . . . (*They cry together.*) Stop it, I'll buy you some earrings.

LIPOCHKA: Earrings? I've got a million earrings. I want emeralds. Buy me an emerald bracelet.

AGRAFENA: Anything you want, if you'll stop that wailing.

LIPOCHKA: The day I get married, I'll stop.

AGRAFENA: It will come soon, I promise. Kiss me. (*They kiss.*) God bless you. Come, let me dry your tears. All this talk about passing away, you're sounding like mad Fominishna.

LIPOCHKA: I'm warning you, mummy, if I don't get a husband soon I probably will turn out like her.

THE DEMI-MONDE
Alexandre Dumas Fils
1855

Serio-Comic / 1 Man, 1 Woman

Olivier: a handsome bon vivant, 20-30

Suzanne: a scheming woman, 20-30

The Setting: Paris

Suzanne has recently returned from the spa at Baden and here pays an enigmatic visit to her former lover.

OLIVIER: What! It's you!
  (*He offers his hand to her.*)
SUZANNE: (*Shaking hands and smiling.*) Yes it's I.
OLIVIER: I thought you were dead.
SUZANNE: I'm very well, you see.
OLIVIER: When did you come from Baden?
SUZANNE: A week ago.
OLIVIER: A week ago!
SUZANNE: Yes.
OLIVIER: And to-day I see you for the first time! There must be some news!
SUZANNE: Possibly. (*A pause.*) Are you as clever as ever?
OLIVIER: More so.
SUZANNE: Since when?
OLIVIER: Since your return.
SUZANNE: That's almost a compliment.
OLIVIER: Almost.
SUZANNE: So much the better.
OLIVIER: Why?
SUZANNE: Because on my return from Baden, I'm not at all sorry to talk over a number of things.
OLIVIER: Don't people talk at Baden?
SUZANNE: No – they just speak!
OLIVIER: Well, it seems that you weren't any too anxious to talk this last week. Otherwise you would have come to see me sooner.

SUZANNE: I've been in the country. I've come to Paris to-day for the first time, and no one knows I'm here. You were saying that you were as clever as ever?

OLIVIER: Yes.

SUZANNE: We'll see.

OLIVIER: What are you driving at?

SUZANNE: One point: a question. Will you marry me?

OLIVIER: You?

SUZANNE: Don't be too surprised; that would be most impolite.

OLIVIER: What an idea!

SUZANNE: Then you won't? Don't say any more about it. Well, my dear Olivier, I must now let you know that we shall never see each other again. I'm going away.

OLIVIER: For long?

SUZANNE: Yes.

OLIVIER: Where are you going?

SUZANNE: Far away.

OLIVIER: I'm puzzled.

SUZANNE: It's very simple. People talk; you find them everywhere. It was for such people that carriages and steamboats were invented.

OLIVIER: True. Well, what about me?

SUZANNE: You?

OLIVIER: Yes.

SUZANNE: You stay here at Paris, I imagine.

OLIVIER: Ah!

SUZANNE: At least — unless you want to go away, too?

OLIVIER: With you?

SUZANNE: Oh, no.

OLIVIER: Then – it's all over?

SUZANNE: What?

OLIVIER: We don't love each other any more?

SUZANNE: Have we ever done so?

OLIVIER: I once thought it.

SUZANNE: I did all in my power to believe it.

OLIVIER: Really?

SUZANNE: I have spent my life wanting to love. Up to now, it has been impossible.

OLIVIER: Thank you!

SUZANNE: I'm not referring to you alone.

OLIVIER: Thank you on *our* behalf, then!

SUZANNE: You must know that when I left for Baden, I went there less as a woman who wanted to be lazy than as one who wanted time to reflect – like a sensible woman. At a distance, one can better realize what one truly feels and thinks. Possibly you were of more importance to me than I had wanted to believe. I went away in order to see whether I could do without you.

OLIVIER: Well?

SUZANNE: I can. You did not follow me; and the most that can be said of your letters is that they were clever. Two weeks after I left, you were completely indifferent to me.

OLIVIER: Your words possess the inestimable advantage of being absolutely clear.

SUZANNE: My first idea on returning was not even to see you and have that explanation, but to wait until chance should bring us together. But then I knew we were both sensible people, and that in place of trying to escape that situation, it was a much more dignified proceeding to try to have it over with at once. And here I am, asking you whether you wish to make out of our false love a true friendship? (*Olivier smiles.*) Why do you smile?

OLIVIER: Because, except for the form, I said or rather wrote the same thing not two hours ago.

SUZANNE: To a woman?

OLIVIER: Yes.

SUZANNE: To the beautiful Charlotte de Lornan?

OLIVIER: I don't know the lady.

SUZANNE: Toward the end of my last stay in Paris you did not come to see me so regularly as you used to. I soon saw that the excuses you gave for not coming, or rather the pretexts you made before not coming, were hiding some mystery. That mystery could be nothing other than a woman. One day when you were leaving my home, after saying that you were to meet some man friend, I followed you to the house where you were going; I gave the porter twenty francs, and learned that Madame de Lornan lived there, and that you went to see her every day. That's how simple it was. Then I understood that I didn't love you: I did my best to be jealous, and failed.

OLIVIER: And how does it happen that you have not spoken to me before about Madame de Lornan?

SUZANNE: If I had, I should have had to ask you to choose between that woman and me. As she was more recent than I, I should have been sacrificed for her, and my pride would have suffered cruelly. I didn't want to speak to you.

OLIVIER: But you were mistaken. I did go to see Madame de Lornan, but I declare she has never been, is not, and never will be, other than a good friend of mine.

SUZANNE: That is nothing to me. You are free to love whom you like. All I ask is your friendship; may I have it?

OLIVIER: What is the use, since you are going away?

SUZANNE: Exactly. Friends are rare and more precious at a distance than near at hand.

OLIVIER: Tell me the whole truth.

SUZANNE: What truth?

OLIVIER: Why are you going away?

SUZANNE: Merely in order to – get away.

OLIVIER: Is there no other reason?

SUZANNE: No other.

OLIVIER: Then stay.

SUZANNE: There are reasons to prevent that.

OLIVIER: Don't you want to tell me?

SUZANNE: To ask for a secret in exchange for one's friendship is not friendship, but a venal transaction.

OLIVIER: You are logic incarnate. And what are you going to do before you leave?

SUZANNE: Stay in the country. I know you are bored to death with the country, that is why I am not asking you to come.

OLIVIER: Very well. Then this is a dismissal in good form. Well, my task as friend will not be difficult.

SUZANNE: It will be more difficult than you imagine. I don't mean by that word friendship one of those banal traditional affairs that every lover offers to every other when the two separate; that is nothing more than the mite of a reciprocal indifference. What I want is an intelligent friendship, a useful attachment, a form of devotion and protection, if need be, and above all, of discretion. You will doubtless have but one occasion, and that lasting five minutes, to prove your friendship. But that will be a sufficient proof. Do you accept?

OLIVIER: I do.

THE THUNDERSTORM
Alexander Ostrovsky
1860

Dramatic / 3 Women

Katerina: young woman trapped in an unhappy marriage, 20s
Varvara: her sympathetic sister-in-law, 20s
Old Lady: a wandering crazy woman, 70s

The Setting: the town of Kalinov, on the banks of the Volga

Passionate Katerina here confesses her love for a man other than her husband.

KATERINA: Are you sorry for me then, Varya?

VARVARA: (*Looking to one side.*) Of course I am.

KATERINA: Then you love me? (*Kisses her eagerly.*)

VARVARA: Why shouldn't I love you?

KATERINA: O, thank you! You're so good, I love you dearly. (*A pause.*) Do you know what came into my head?

VARVARA: What?

KATERINA: Why can't people fly?

VARVARA: I don't understand what you mean.

KATERINA: I tell you: I wonder why people can't fly like birds. You know, sometimes I imagine that I am a bird. When you stand on a hill, you just long to fly. You feel that you could take a run, raise your arms, and fly away. Do you want to try it now? (*She starts to run.*)

VARVARA: What notions you get!

KATERINA: (*Sighing.*) I used to be so lively! I have shriveled up completely in your house.

VARVARA: Don't you think I can see that?

KATERINA: I was so different. I just lived and didn't worry about anything; I was like an uncaged bird. My mother was so fond of me; she dressed me up like a doll and never made me work; I used to do just as I pleased. Do you know how I used to live before I was married? I'll tell you all about it. I used to get up early. In summer I would go to the spring and bathe; I would carry back water and sprinkle all the flowers in the house. I had lots and lots of flowers. Then mamma and I would go to church, and the pilgrims too – our house used to be full of pilgrims and holy women. When we came from church we would sit down to some work, usually gold thread on velvet, and the pilgrims would begin to tell about the places they had visited, what they had seen, and the lives of saints, or they would sing songs. So the time would pass till dinner. Then the older people would lie down to rest, and I would walk about the garden. Then I would go to vespers, and in the evening there would be more stories and songs. It was so nice!

VARVARA: But it is just the same at our house.

KATERINA: But everything here seems to be under restraint. I used to love dearly to go to church! It seemed as if I were in heaven. I could see no one, I didn't notice the time passing and I didn't hear when the service ended. It seemed all to have happened in a second. Mamma said that every one used to look at me and wonder what was happening to me. And you know, on sunny days a shining column came down from the dome and in it smoke hovered like clouds and I seemed to see angels flying and singing in the column. Or else I would get up at night – we, too, used to have lamps burning everywhere at night – and I would go into some corner and pray till morning. Or early in the morning I would go into the garden when the sun was hardly up; I would fall on my knees and pray and weep, and I would not know myself why I prayed or why I wept – and so they would find me. And what I prayed about then, and what I asked for, I cannot imagine; I didn't need anything. I had enough of everything. And such dreams as I used to have, Varenka, wonderful dreams! of golden temples, or marvelous gardens where unseen voices would sing and cypress trees wafted forth their fragrance. And the mountains and trees were not the ordinary kind, but like those that are painted on the sacred images. Or I would fly and fly away through the air. And sometimes I dream now, but rarely, and then it is not the same.

VARVARA: Why?

KATERINA: (*After a pause.*) I shall die soon.

VARVARA: Don't say that. What's the matter?

KATERINA: No, I'm sure that I am going to die. O, my dear, something evil is happening to me, something strange. I never was this way before. There is some strange feeling in my heart. It seems as if I were beginning to live again, or – I don't know.

VARVARA: What is the matter with you then?

KATERINA: (*Taking her by the hand.*) Varya, a misfortune will happen to someone. I am so afraid, so afraid! I seem to stand on a precipice and some one is pushing me toward it, and I have nothing to hold to. (*She clutches her head with her hand.*)

VARVARA: What is the matter? Are you well?

KATERINA: Yes, I am well. – It would be better if I were ill – but something is wrong. Such a fancy keeps flitting through my head and I cannot escape from it. I begin to think and I cannot collect my thoughts; I try to pray and I cannot: I murmur words with my lips but my mind is on something else. The evil one seems to be whispering in my ear, whispering about something wicked. Then I imagine things that make me ashamed of myself. What is the matter with me? Some misfortune is going to happen! At night, Varya, I cannot sleep; I keep hearing that whisper in my dreams; some one speaks so caressingly to me, speaks endearingly like a cooing dove. I no longer dream those old dreams, Varya, about the trees of paradise and the mountains, but some one seems to embrace me, fiercely, fiercely, and he leads me somewhere and I follow him, follow –

VARVARA: And then?

KATERINA: But why am I talking like this to you? You are an unmarried girl.

VARVARA: (*Glancing around.*) Go on! I am worse than you are.

KATERINA: How can I tell you? I am ashamed.

VARVARA: Go on. You needn't be.

KATERINA: It becomes so oppressive at home, so oppressive that I could run away. And such ideas come to me that, if I were free, I would drift along the Volga now, in a boat, singing, or in a fine troika, embracing –

VARVARA: But not your husband.

KATERINA: How do you know?

VARVARA: How can I help knowing?

KATERINA: O, Varya, I have evil thoughts in my mind. How I have cried and struggled with myself, wretched girl that I am! But the temptation will not leave me. I cannot escape it. It is not right. It is a dreadful sin to love another than my husband, is it not, Varenka?

VARVARA: I cannot judge you! I have my own sins on my conscience.

KATERINA: What can I do? I am not strong enough. Where can I go? I shall kill myself from this suffering.

VARVARA: What are you saying? What is the matter? Wait, tomorrow brother will be going away and we will think of something; perhaps you can see each other.

KATERINA: No, no, we must not. What do you mean, what do you mean? God forbid!

VARVARA: What are you so afraid of?

KATERINA: If I see him even once I shall flee from the house and not return home for anything on earth.

VARVARA: Just wait, we'll see.

KATERINA: No, no, don't talk to me; I don't even want to listen.

VARVARA: Well, what is the pleasure in withering away here? Even if you die of despair, will any one pity you? Don't expect it. Why are you forced to torture yourself!

(Enter an Old Lady with a stick, followed by two lackeys in three-cornered hats.)

OLD LADY: Well, my beauties! What are you doing here? Are you waiting for some young men, some gallants? Are you feeling happy? Are you? Does your beauty make you joyful? That is where beauty leads to. *(She points to the Volga.)* There, there into the deep flood. *(Varvara smiles.)* Why are you laughing? Don't feel joyful! *(She raps with her stick.)* All of you will burn in eternal fire. You will boil in the unquenchable pitch. *(Going out.)* That is where beauty leads to.

(Goes out.)

KATERINA: Oh, how she frightened me! I am trembling all over as if she had made me an evil prophecy.

VARVARA: May it fall on your own head, you old hag!

KATERINA: What was it she said? What did she say?

VARVARA: It was all nonsense. There is no use listening to her chatter. She always raves like that. She has led a wicked life from her youth up. Ask any one what people say about her! And now she is afraid to die and she tries to frighten others with what she fears herself. Even the little boys in the town hide from her. She shakes her stick at them and shouts: *(Mocking the old woman.)* "You will all be burned in the fire!"

KATERINA: *(Closing her eyes.)* O, be quiet! My heart has stopped beating.

VARVARA: What is there to be afraid of? An old fool –

KATERINA: But I am afraid. I am mortally afraid. She seems to be hovering before me all the time. (*A pause.*)

VARVARA: (*Looking around.*) I wonder why brother doesn't come. Here is a thunderstorm coming up.

KATERINA: (*Terrified.*) A thunderstorm! Let's run home! Hurry!

VARVARA: Have you gone crazy? How would you dare to show yourself at home without brother?

KATERINA: No, no, let's run home, home! Never mind him!

VARVARA: Why are you so afraid? The thunderstorm is still far away.

KATERINA: If it's far off we can wait a little while, but really it would be better to go. We'd better go.

VARVARA: Well, if anything is going to happen, you can't hide from it at home.

KATERINA: Yes, but it's better, it's more comfortable; at home I can pray to God before the holy images.

VARVARA: I didn't know that you were so afraid of a thunderstorm. I'm not afraid.

KATERINA: How can you help being afraid, girl? Everyone must be afraid. It is not so dreadful that you may be killed, as that death may come suddenly and find you just as you are, with all your sins and with all your evil thoughts. I am not afraid to die, but when I think that I shall appear suddenly before God just as I am here with you, after this conversation – that is what is so dreadful. What thoughts are in my mind! Such a sin! It is terrible to speak of it! (*A thunderclap.*) O! (*Kabanov comes in.*)

VARVARA: There comes brother. (*To Kabanov.*) Hurry! (*Thunder.*)

KATERINA: O, hurry, hurry!

PEER GYNT
Henrik Ibsen
1868

Serio-Comic / 1 Man, 1 Woman
    Peer Gynt: a strongly-built youth of 20
    Aase: his mother, small and frail, 40-50

The Setting: a wooded hillside near Aase's farm

Peer has returned empty-handed from a hunting expedition and lies to
Aase to cover his failure.

AASE: Peer, you're lying!
PEER GYNT: (*Without stopping.*) I am not!
AASE: Well, then swear it's true!
PEER GYNT: Why swear?
AASE: Ah, you daren't! It's all rubbish.
PEER GYNT: (*Stops.*) It's true, every word.
AASE: (*Squares up in front of him.*) Aren't you ashamed?
    First you sneak off into the mountains
    For weeks on end in the busy season
    To stalk reindeer in the snow –
    Come home with your coat torn,
    Without the gun, without the meat.
    And then you look me straight in the face
    And try to fool me with your hunter's lies!
    Well, where did you meet the buck?
PEER GYNT: West near Gjendin.
AASE: (*Laughs scornfully.*) Did you, now?
PEER GYNT: I suddenly smelt him on the wind.
    Hidden behind an elder-bush
    He was scratching in the snow for lichen –
AASE: (*Still scornfully.*) Oh, yes!
PEER GYNT: I held my breath
    And stood listening. I heard his hoof
    Crunch, and saw one branching antler.
    I wormed on my belly through the stones towards him.

Still hidden, I peered out.
Oh, mother, you never saw such a buck!
So sleek and fat –!

AASE: No, I'm sure!

PEER GYNT: I fired. Down he dropped, smack on the hill!
But the moment he fell, I straddled his back,
Seized his left ear, and was about
To plunge my knife into his neck –
Aah! The brute let out a scream,
Suddenly stood on all fours,
Hit the knife and sheath from my hand,
Forced its horns against my thigh,
Pinned me tight like a pair of tongs,
And shot right on to the Gjendin Edge!

AASE: (*Involuntarily.*) In the name of Christ!

PEER GYNT: Have you seen the Gjendin Edge?
Three miles long and sharp as a scythe.
Down over glacier, slide and cliff,
[Straight down over sheer grey scree],
You can see, on either side,
Straight into the lakes that sleep
Black and heavy, more than four thousand
Feet below. The length of the Edge
He and I cut our way through the air.
I never rode such a steed!
Before us as we thundered
It was as though there glittered suns.
Brown backs of eagles swam
In the huge and dizzy void halfway between us
And the lakes below – they fell behind
Like motes of dust. Ice-floes broke
And crashed on the shore, but we couldn't hear their thunder.
Only the spirits of dizziness leaped
As in dance. They sang, they swung in a ring
In my eyes and ears.

AASE: (*Dazed.*) Ah, God preserve me!

PEER GYNT: Suddenly, on a sheer impossible spot
A great cock-ptarmigan flew into the air
Flapping, cackling, terrified,
From the crevice where it lurked

Hidden at the buck's foot on the Edge.
He swung half round, gave a high leap to heaven,
And down we both plunged into the abyss!
(*Aase totters and gropes at the trunk of a tree. Peer continues.*)
Behind us the black walls of the mountain,
Beneath a bottomless void!
First we clove sheets of mist, then a flock of gulls,
Which turned in the air and fled to every side,
Screeching. Still we fell.
But in the abyss something gleamed
Whitish, like a reindeer's belly.
Mother, it was our reflection
In the calm water of the mountain lake,
Darting up towards the surface
With the same wild speed with which we fell.

AASE: (*Gasps for breath.*) Peer! God help me! Tell me quickly –!

PEER GYNT: Buck from air and buck from deep
In a moment smashed together,
So that the foam rose high about us.
We plunged, we gasped and choked.
At long last, mother, I don't know how,
We reached the northern shore.
The buck swam, and I hung behind him.
I ran home–

AASE: But the buck, Peer?

PEER GYNT: Oh, still there, I expect.
(*Snaps his fingers, turns on his heel, and adds:*)
If you find him, you can have him.

AASE: And you haven't broken your neck? Or both
Your legs? Not fractured your spine? Oh, Lord,
Praise and thanks be to Thee, who saved my son!
Your breeches are torn, but what's that
When one thinks what you might have suffered in such a fall –?
(*Stops suddenly, stars at him open-mouthed, wide-eyed, and
speechless. At length she explodes.*)
Oh, you bloody story-teller! How you can lie!
I remember now, I heard all this rubbish
Before, when I was a girl of twenty.
It happened to Gudbrand Glesne, not to you,
You –!

PEER GYNT: To both of us.

    Such a thing can happen twice.

AASE: (*Hotly.*) Yes, a lie can be stood on its head,

    Smartened up and put in new clothes,

    So its own mother wouldn't know its skinny carcass.

    [That's what you've done, letting on wild and great,

    Tricking it out with eagles' backs

    And all that humbug, lying right and left,

    Yarning away and searing me dumb

    So I couldn't recognize a story

    I'd heard in my mother's lap.]

PEER GYNT: If anyone else spoke to me like that

    I'd bash him senseless.

AASE: (*Weeps.*) Oh God, I wish I was dead.

    I wish I was asleep in the black ground.

    Prayers and tears don't touch him. Peer, you're lost,

    And always will be.

PEER GYNT: Dear, beautiful, little mother,

    Every word you say is the truth.

    Calm yourself. Be happy –

AASE: Shut up!

    How can I be happy with such a pig for a son?

    Isn't it bitter for a poor, helpless

    Widow like me to be always put to shame?

    (*Weeps again.*)

    What has the family left now from the days

    When your grandfather was a wealthy man?

    Where are the sacks of silver

    Left by old Rasmus Gynt? Your father

    Gave them feet, wasted them like sand,

    Bought land in every parish, drove

    In gilded carriages! Where's what he wasted

    At the great winter feast, when every guest

    Threw glass and bottle over his shoulder

    To splinter against the wall?

PEER GYNT: Where are the snows of yesteryear?

AASE: Shut up while your mother's speaking!

    Look at the house!

    Half the window-panes stuffed with rags,

    Hedge and fence fallen down,

Cows and chickens exposed to wind and weather,
Fields and meadows lying fallow,
Never a month but I have the bailiffs in –
PEER GYNT: Stop that old wives' tattle!
Many's the time our luck has failed –
[And sprung again to its feet as tall as ever.]
AASE: [There's salt strewn where that grew.] Lord, you're a fine one!
[As proud and uppish as ever, just as bold
As when the priest that came from Copenhagen,
Asked you your name, and swore it was one
That many a prince where he came from would envy you,
So that your father gave him a horse and bridle
In gratitude for his civil talk.
Oh, things were fine then. The Bishop and the Captain
And all the rest of them turning up every day,
Guzzling and boozing and stuffing themselves
Till they were nearly bursting. But
It's when times are hard that a man knows his neighbour.
Empty and silent it was here the day
John Moneybags set off to tramp the roads
With a pedlar's pack on his shoulder.
(*Dries her eyes with her handkerchief.*)
You're a fine, strong lad.] You ought to be a rod
And staff for your frail old mother, work the farm,
And guard the little you've left of your inheritance.
(*Weeps again.*)
God help me, it's little use I've had of you!
Lounging all day by the hearth, poking the embers,
Frightening the girls out of the barn on dance-nights,
Making me the game of the whole county
And swapping blows with every ruffian in the parish –
PEER GYNT: (*Walks away from her.*) Oh, let me be!
AASE: (*Follows him.*) Can you deny you were the ringleader
In that shindy at Lunde, when you fought
Like mad dogs. Wasn't it you who broke
The arm of Aslak the smith? Or at least
Put one of his fingers out of joint?
PEER GYNT: Who's been filling your head with such rubbish?
AASE: (*Heatedly.*) The crofter's wife heard him hollering.
PEER GYNT: (*Rubs his elbow.*) No, that was me.

AASE: You?

PEER GYNT: Yes, mother. I was the one that took the beating.

AASE: What!

PEER GYNT: He's a nimble man.

AASE: Who's nimble?

PEER GYNT: Aslak the smith. I'm telling you, I know.

AASE: Shame upon you, shame! Now I must spit!
That loafing sot, that swaggerer,
That boozing sponge! Did you let him beat you?
(*Weeps again.*)
Many's the shame I've suffered, but this is the worst.
Nimble, is he? Need you be weak?

PEER GYNT: Whether I bash a man or get bashed,
You start moaning. (*Laughs.*) Now cheer up, mother –

AASE: What! Have you been lying again?

PEER GYNT: Yes, just this once. So dry your tears.
(*Clenches his left fist.*)
This was my tongs. With this I held the smith
Bent double; my right fist was my hammer –

AASE: Oh, you ruffian! You'll send me to my grave!

PEER GYNT: No, you're worth better. Twenty thousand times
better.
Sweet, ugly little mother, you take my word.
The whole parish shall honour you. Just wait
Till I do something, something really big!

AASE: (*Snorts.*) You!

PEER GYNT: Who knows what will happen?

AASE: You'll learn to mend your breeches first!

PEER GYNT: (*Hotly.*) I'll be King! Emperor!

AASE: God help me!
Now he's losing the little wit he's got.

PEER GYNT: Yes, I will! Just give me time!

AASE: Oh, yes! I've heard that one before.

PEER GYNT: You'll see, mother!

AASE: Shut your gullet. You're out of your mind.
Oh, it's true enough something might have come to you
If you hadn't got lost in lies and twaddle.
The Heggstad girl fancied you.
You could have won her easily if you'd wanted –

PEER GYNT: Do you think so?

AASE: Her dad's a ninny, he'd not have argued with her.
He's a stubborn old fool, but she gets her way in the end,
And where she leads he'll follow, grumbling.
(*Begins to weep again.*)
Ah, Peer, my son, she's rich. The land's all hers.
Just think. If you'd only put your mind to it
You'd be wearing the bridegroom's coat,
Not standing here black and tattered.

PEER GYNT: (*Briskly.*) Come on, let's go wooing!

AASE: Where?

PEER GYNT: At Heggstad.

AASE: My poor boy, you'll find no bride there.

PEER GYNT: Why?

AASE: [Wait while I dry my eyes.]
You've lost your chance, you luck's ended –

PEER GYNT: How?

AASE: (*Gulps.*) While you were away
In the western mountains, riding stags through the air,
Mads Moen's got the girl.

PEER GYNT: What! That scarecrow?

AASE: Yes, now she's taking him to her bridal bed.

PEER GYNT: Wait here while I harness a horse to the cart –
(*Turns to go.*)

AASE: Save your pains. The wedding's tomorrow.

PEER GYNT: Good. I'll be there tonight.

AASE: Shame on you! Haven't I grief enough?
[Without your bringing a general scorn on our heads.]

PEER GYNT: Don't worry, it'll be all right.
(*Shouts and laughs at the same time.*)
Yippee, mother! We'll do without the cart.
I can't waste time running after the mare –
(*Lifts her high into the air.*)

AASE: Put me down!

PEER GYNT: No! I'm carrying you to my wedding in my arms!
(*Wades out into the stream.*)

AASE: Help! Lord save us! We'll be drowned!

PEER GYNT: I was born for a nobler death –

AASE: Yes! You'll end by being hanged!

GHOSTS
Henrik Ibsen
1881

Dramatic / 1 Man, 1 Woman
   Engstrand: an alcoholic laborer, 40-50
   Regine: a serving girl, 18-20

The Setting: Mrs. Alving's country estate by a large fjord in Western Norway

Engstrand, a coarse and unpleasant man, here tries to persuade his daughter to help him open a home for retired sailors, but the high-minded young lady clearly has other plans.

REGINE: (*Keeping her voice low.*) Well—what is it you want? No—stay where you are—you're dripping wet!

ENGSTRAND: It's only God's rain, my child.

REGINE: It's the Devil's rain, that's what it is!

ENGSTRAND: Lord, how you talk, Regine (*Limping a few steps into the room.*) But, here's what I want to tell you–

REGINE: Don't go clumping about with that foot of yours! The young master's upstairs asleep.

ENGSTRAND: Asleep at this hour—in broad daylight?

REGINE: It's none of your business.

ENGSTRAND: Now—look at *me*—I was on a bit of a spree last night—

REGINE: That's nothing new!

ENGSTRAND: Well—we're all frail creatures, my child—

REGINE: We are that!

ENGSTRAND: And temptations are manifold in this world, you see—but that didn't prevent me from going to work at half past five as usual!

REGINE: That's as it may be—and now, get out! I can't stand here having a rendezvous with you.

ENGSTRAND: What's that?

REGINE: I don't want anyone to see you here—so get out!

ENGSTRAND: (*Comes a few steps nearer.*) Damned if I go till I've had a talk with you. Listen—I'll be through with my work at the school-house this afternoon—then I'm going right back to town by the night boat—

REGINE: (*Mutters.*) A pleasant journey to you!

ENGSTRAND: Thank you, my child! Tomorrow's the opening of the Orphanage, they'll all be celebrating—sure to be a lot of drinking too—I'll prove to them that Jakob Engstrand can keep out of the way of temptation—

REGINE: Ha!...

ENGSTRAND: Lots of grand people'll be here—Pastor Manders is expected from town—

REGINE: He gets here today.

ENGSTRAND: There—you see! Damned if I give *him* a chance to say anything against me!

REGINE: So that's it, is it?

ENGSTRAND: That's what?

REGINE: (*Gives him a searching look.*) What are you going to try and put over on him this time?

ENGSTRAND: Are you crazy? As if I'd try and put anything over on *him*! No—Pastor Manders has been too good a friend to me—and that's just what I want to talk to you about. As I was saying, I'm going back home tonight—

REGINE: You can't go soon enough to please me!

ENGSTRAND: But I want you to come with me, Regine.

REGINE: (*Open-mouthed.*) *I*, go with *you*?

ENGSTRAND: Yes—I want you to come home with me.

REGINE: (*Scornfully.*) You'll never get me to do that!

ENGSTRAND: Well—we'll see.

REGINE: Yes! You'll see all right! After being brought up here by Mrs. Alving—treated almost like one of the family—do you suppose I'd go home with you—back to that kind of a house! You're crazy!

ENGSTRAND: What kind of talk's that! You'd defy your own father, would you?

REGINE: (*Mutters, without looking at him.*) You've said often enough I'm no concern of yours—

ENGSTRAND: Never mind about that—

REGINE: Many's the time you've cursed at me and called me a—*Fi donc*!

ENGSTRAND: When did I ever use a foul word like that?

REGINE: I know well enough what word you used!

ENGSTRAND: Well—maybe—when I wasn't feeling quite myself—hm. Temptations are manifold in this world, Regine!

REGINE: Pah!...

ENGSTRAND: And then your mother used to drive me crazy—I had to find some way to get back at her. She put on so many airs: (*Mimicking her.*) "Let me go Engstrand! Leave me alone! Don't forget I spent three years in Chamberlain Alving's house at Rosenvold!" (*Laughs.*) God almighty! She never got over the Captain being made Chamberlain while she was working here!

REGINE: Poor mother! You certainly hounded her into her grave!

ENGSTRAND: (*Shrugging his shoulders.*) Oh, of course! I'm to blame for everything!

REGINE: (*Under her breath as she turns away.*) Ugh! And then that leg of yours!

ENGSTRAND: What did you say, my child?

REGINE: *Pied de mouton!*

ENGSTRAND: What's that, English?

REGINE: Yes.

ENGSTRAND: Yes—well; you've certainly got educated here—and that may come in handy too.

REGINE: (*After a short silence.*) Why do you want me to go back with you?

ENGSTRAND: Why wouldn't a father want his only child with him? Aren't I a lonely, deserted widower?

REGINE: Oh, don't talk rubbish to me! why do you want me with you?

ENGSTRAND: Well—I'll tell you—I'm thinking of setting up in a new line of business—

REGINE: (*Whistles.*) What, again! What is it this time?

ENGSTRAND: You'll see—this time it'll be different. Christ Almighty—!

REGINE: Stop your swearing! (*She stamps her foot.*)

ENGSTRAND: Sh! You're right, my child. Well—what I wanted to say was—I've managed to save quite a bit of money—from this work on the Orphanage—

REGINE: You have, have you? So much the better for you.

ENGSTRAND: There's nothing to spend your money on in this God-forsaken hole—

REGINE: Well?

ENGSTRAND: So I thought I'd invest it in a paying concern. I thought of starting a sort of tavern—for seamen—

REGINE: Ugh!

ENGSTRAND: A really high-class tavern, you know—none of your cheap dives. No—by God! I'd cater to Captains and First-mates—really high-class people.

REGINE: And I suppose I'd be expected to—

ENGSTRAND: Oh, you could be a great help, Regine. You wouldn't have to do anything—it wouldn't be hard on you, my child—you'd have everything your own way!

REGINE: Oh yes, of course!

ENGSTRAND: After all there must be some women in the house—that goes without saying. We'd have to have a bit of fun in the evenings, singing and dancing—and that sort of thing. You've got to remember—these poor fellows are sailors—wanderers on the seas of the world. (*Comes nearer to her.*) Don't be a fool and stand in your own way. What future is there for you out here? What good's all this education the Mrs. has paid for? You're to look after the kids in the new Orphanage I hear—is that a job for you? Do you want to wear yourself to the bone looking after a lot of dirty brats?

REGINE: If things turn out as I hope—well—it could be—it could be—

ENGSTRAND: What "could be"?

REGINE: You keep your nose out of that! How much money did you save?

ENGSTRAND: I'd say—in all—close to two hundred dollars.

REGINE: Not so bad.

ENGSTRAND: Enough to get me started, my child.

REGINE: Do I get any of it?

ENGSTRAND: You do not!

REGINE: Not even enough to buy myself a new dress?

ENGSTRAND: You come with me—you'll get plenty of new dresses then!

REGINE: I can get them myself, if I set my mind to it.

ENGSTRAND: But a father's guiding hand is a good thing, Regine. There's a nice little house right on Harbor Street—not much money down either—it'd be like a kind of Seamen's Home, you know.

REGINE: But I don't want to live with you! I don't want to have anything to do with you! So now—get out!

ENGSTRAND: You wouldn't be with me for long, my child—I know that well enough. All you've got to do is use your wits—you've turned into a handsome wench—do you know that?

REGINE: Well—what of it?

ENGSTRAND: Before you know it, some First-mate'll come along—maybe even a Captain.

REGINE: I don't intend to marry any such trash. Sailors have no "*savoir vivre.*"

ENGSTRAND: Well—I couldn't say about that—

REGINE: I tell you I know all about sailors. I wouldn't think of marrying one of them!

ENGSTRAND: Who says you'd have to marry? You can make it pay just the same. (*More confidentially.*) That Englishman—the one with the yacht—he gave three hundred dollars, he did—and she wasn't any better looking than you are.

REGINE: (*Goes toward him.*) Get out of here!

ENGSTRAND: (*Retreating.*) Now, now! You wouldn't hit me, would you?

REGINE: You just say anything against Mother, and you'll see whether I'd hit you or not! Get out, I say! (*She pushes him toward the garden door.*) And don't bang the door; young Mister Alving—

ENGSTRAND: Is asleep—I know! Why should you be so worried about him? (*In a lower tone.*) God—Almighty! You don't mean to tell me that *he*—

REGINE: You must be out of your head—you fool! Go on now—get out this minute. No—not that way—here comes Pastor Manders; the back stairs for you!

ENGSTRAND: (*Goes toward door right.*) All right—I'll go. But listen—you have a talk with him—he'll tell you what you owe your father—for I am your father after all, you know; I can prove that by the Church Register.

Dramatic / 1 Man, 1 Woman

    Mrs. Alving: a woman haunted by the past, 50s
    Osvald: her ailing son, 20-30

The late Captain Alving lived a debauched life the details of which Mrs. Alving has finally revealed to her son. Osvald in turn confesses that he suffers from hereditary syphilis – his father's final legacy.

MRS. ALVING: (*Stands behind him and puts her hands on his shoulders.*) Osvald—my dear; has it been a very great shock to you?

OSVALD: (*Turns his face towards her.*) All that about Father, you mean?

MRS. ALVING: Yes, your poor father!—I'm afraid it's been too much for you.

OSVALD: Why do you say that? It was a great surprise to me, I admit; but after all, it doesn't really matter.

MRS. ALVING: (*Withdraws her hands.*) Not matter? That your father was so unspeakably unhappy?

OSVALD: I feel sorry for him of course—as I would for anyone who suffered.

MRS. ALVING: No more that than that?—But he was your *father*, Osvald.

OSVALD: (*Impatiently.*) Father, Father! I never knew my *father*. The only thing I remember about him is that he once made me sick!

MRS. ALVING: What a dreadful thought! But surely a child must have some love for his father, in spite of everything.

OSVALD: Even if he owes his father nothing? Even if he never knew him? Come now, Mother! You're too broadminded to believe in that superstitious nonsense!

MRS. ALVING: Superstitious nonsense—you think that's all it is?

OSVALD: Of course, Mother—you must see that. It's one of those old-fashioned illusions people go on clinging to—

MRS. ALVING: (*Shaken.*) Ghosts—

OSVALD: (*Paces up and down.*) Yes—call them ghosts if you like.

MRS. ALVING: (*In a burst of emotion.*) Osvald—Then you don't love me either!

OSVALD: Well, at least I know *you* –

MRS. ALVING: You know me, yes; but is that all?

OSVALD: I know how much you care for me; I should be grateful to you for that. And now that I'm ill, you can be of great help to me.

MRS. ALVING: I can, can't I, Osvald? I'm almost glad you're ill— since it's brought you home to me. I understand—you don't belong to me yet—I'll have to win you.

OSVALD: (*Impatiently.*) Oh, don't let's have a lot of phrases, Mother! You must remember I'm ill. I can't be bothered with other people; I've got to think about myself.

MRS. ALVING: (*Gently.*) I'll be very quiet and patient, Osvald.

OSVALD: And, for God's sake, *happy*, Mother!

MRS. ALVING: Yes, my darling—you're right. (*Goes to him.*) And you've no more doubts, no more remorse? I've freed you of all that?

OSVALD: Yes, Mother, you have. But who's to free me of the terror—?

MRS. ALVING: Terror!

OSVALD: (*Pacing up and down.*) Regine would have done it, if I'd asked her.

MRS. ALVING: I don't understand. What is this terror—and what has Regine to do with it?

OSVALD: Mother—is it very late?

MRS. ALVING: It's early morning. (*She goes to the conservatory and looks out.*) The dawn is just breaking. It's going to be a lovely day, Osvald! In a little while you'll see the sun!

OSVALD: I'll be glad of that. Perhaps after all there are lots of things I could be glad about, Mother—lots of things I'd like to live for—

MRS. ALVING: Of course there are!

OSVALD: And even if I'm not able to work –

MRS. ALVING: You'll soon be able to work again, you'll see. Now that you're rid of all those depressing, gloomy thoughts.

OSVALD: Yes—it's good that you were able to wipe out that obsession. Now, if I can just get over this other—(*Sits down on the sofa.*) Come here, Mother. I want to talk to you—

MRS. ALVING: Yes, Osvald. (*She pushes an armchair over near the sofa and sits close to him.*)

OSVALD: Meanwhile the sun is rising. And now that you know—I don't feel—so afraid any more.

MRS. ALVING: Now that I know—what?

OSVALD: (*Without listening to her.*) Mother—didn't you say a little while ago that there was nothing in this world you wouldn't do for me, if I asked you?

MRS. ALVING: Yes—of course I did.

OSVALD: And you stand by that, Mother?

MRS. ALVING: You can depend on me, my darling. You're the only thing on earth I have to live for.

OSVALD: Well then—listen, Mother; you have a strong, gallant spirit—I know that; I want you to sit quite still while I tell you something.

MRS. ALVING: What dreadful thing are you going to—?

OSVALD: Don't scream or get excited, do you hear? Promise me! We'll sit here and talk it over quietly. Promise!

MRS. ALVING: Yes, yes—I promise! Tell me what it is!

OSVALD: Well then—listen: this fatigue of mine—my inability to work—all of that is not the *essence* of my illness—

MRS. ALVING: How do you mean?

OSVALD: You see—my illness *is* hereditary—it—(*Touches his forehead and speaks very quietly.*) It is centered—*here.*

MRS. ALVING: (*Almost speechless.*) Osvald! No—No!

OSVALD: Don't scream, Mother—I can't stand it! It's lurking here— lying in wait—ready to spring at any moment.

MRS. ALVING: How horrible—!

OSVALD: Quiet, Mother!—Now you understand the state I'm in.

MRS. ALVING: (*Springing up.*) It's not true, Osvald—it's impossible!

OSVALD: I had one attack while I was abroad—it didn't last long. But when I realized the condition I'd been in, I was filled with unspeakable terror—and I could think of nothing but getting home to you.

MRS. ALVING: So that's what you mean by "the terror"!

OSVALD: Yes – unspeakable, sickening terror! If it had only been an ordinary illness—even a fatal one—I wouldn't have minded so much—I'm not afraid of death—though I should like to live as long as possible—

MRS. ALVING: You will, Osvald—you must!

OSVALD: But there's something so utterly revolting about this! To become a child again—a helpless child—to have to be fed—to have to be—oh! It's too ghastly to think of!

MRS. ALVING: I'll be here to look after you, Osvald.

OSVALD: (*Jumping up.*) No, never; I won't stand it! I can't endure the thought of lingering on like that—of growing old like that—old and gray-haired like that! And you might die and I should be left alone. (*Sits down in Mrs. Alving's chair.*) For the doctor said I might live for years, you see. He called it "Softening of the brain" or something of the sort. (*With a sad smile.*) Charming expression! It makes one think of cherry-colored velvet curtains—soft and delicate to stroke—

MRS. ALVING: (*Screams.*) Osvald!

OSVALD: (*Springs up and paces up and down.*) And now you've taken Regine away from me—if only I had her. She'd have been willing to help me, I know.

MRS. ALVING: (*Goes to him.*) What do you mean by that, my darling?—You know I'd give my life to help you—

OSVALD: I recovered from that attack abroad—but the doctor said that the next time—and there's bound to be a "next time"—it would be hopeless.

MRS. ALVING: How could he be so brutal—!

OSVALD: I insisted on the truth—I made him tell me. I explained that I had certain arrangements to make (*With a cunning smile.*) and so I had. (*Takes a small box from his breast pocket.*) Do you see this, Mother?

MRS. ALVING: What is it?

OSVALD: Morphine tablets.

MRS. ALVING: (*Looks at him in terror.*) Osvald—

OSVALD: I managed to save up twelve of them—

MRS. ALVING: (*Snatching at it.*) Give me the box, Osvald!

OSVALD: Not yet, Mother. (*Puts the box in his pocket.*)

MRS. ALVING: I can't endure this!

OSVALD: You must endure it, Mother. If only Regine were here—I'd have explained to her how matters stood; I'd have asked her to help me put an end to it; she'd have done it, I know.

MRS. ALVING: Never!

OSVALD: Oh yes she would! If she'd seen that ghastly thing take hold of me—if she'd seen me lying there like an imbecile child—beyond help—hopelessly, irrevocably lost—

MRS. ALVING: Regine would never have done it.

OSVALD: Oh yes! She'd have done it! Regine has such a magnificently light and buoyant nature. She wouldn't have put up long with an invalid like me!

MRS. ALVING: Then I can only thank God Regine is not here!

OSVALD: Yes, but then you'll have to help me, Mother.

MRS. ALVING: (*With a loud scream.*) I!

OSVALD: Who has a better right?

MRS. ALVING: I—your mother.

OSVALD: For that very reason.

MRS. ALVING: I, who gave you life!

OSVALD: I didn't ask you for life—and what kind of a life did you give me! I don't want it—take it back again!

MRS. ALVING: Help—help! (*She runs out into the hall.*)

OSVALD: (*Following her.*) Don't leave me! Where are you going?

MRS. ALVING: (*In the hall.*) I must fetch a doctor, Osvald—let me out!

OSVALD: (*In the hall.*) You shall not go out—and no one shall come in. (*Sound of a key turning in the lock.*)

MRS. ALVING: (*Re-entering the room.*) Osvald! Osvald—my little one!

OSVALD: (*Follows her in.*) Mother—if you love me—how can you bear to see me suffer this agony of fear!

MRS. ALVING: (*After a moment's silence, in a firm voice.*) I give you my word, Osvald.

OSVALD: Then, you will—?

MRS. ALVING: Yes—if it becomes necessary—but it won't become necessary! That's impossible!

OSVALD: Let us hope so—Meanwhile we'll live together as long as we can. Thank you, Mother. (*He sits in the armchair that Mrs. Alving has moved over to the sofa. Day breaks; the lamp is still burning on the table.*)

MRS. ALVING: (*Approaching him cautiously.*) Do you feel calmer now?

OSVALD: Yes.

MRS. ALVING: (*Bends over him.*) This has all been a nightmare, Osvald—just something you've imagined. It's been a dreadful strain, but now you're home with me and you'll be able to get some rest. I'll spoil you as I did when you were a tiny little boy— you shall have everything you want. There! The attack's over now—You see how easily it passed. It's not so serious—I was sure it couldn't be! And it's going to be such a lovely day, Osvald. Bright sunshine! Now you'll really be able to see your home. (*She goes to the table and puts out the lamp. The sun rises. The glaciers and peaks in the background are bathed in the bright* *morning light.*)

OSVALD: (*Immovable in his armchair with his back to the view outside, suddenly speaks.*) Mother—give me the sun.

MRS. ALVING: (*By the table, looks at him in amazement.*) What did you say?

OSVALD: (*Repeats dully and tonelessly.*) The sun—The sun.

MRS. ALVING: (*Goes to him.*) Osvald, what's the matter with you? (*Osvald seems to crumple up in the chair; all his muscles relax; his face is expressionless—his eyes vacant and staring.*)

MRS. ALVING: (*Trembling with terror.*) What is it? (*Screams.*) Osvald—what's the matter with you? (*Throws herself on her knees beside him and shakes him.*) Osvald! Osvald! Look at me! Don't you know me?

OSVALD: (*Tonelessly as before.*) The sun—The sun.

MRS. ALVING: (*Springs up in despair, tears at her hair with both hands and screams.*) I can't bear it! (*Whispers, paralyzed with fear.*) I can't bear it! Never! (*Suddenly.*) Where did he put them? (*Passes her hand rapidly over his breast.*) Here! (*Draws back a couple of steps and cries.*) No; no; no!—Yes! No; no! (*She stands a few steps away from him, her hands clutching her hair, and stares at him in speechless terror.*)

OSVALD: (*Immovable as before.*) The sun—The sun.

THE POWER OF DARKNESS
Leo Tolstoy
1886

Dramatic / 3 Women

Anisya:	a woman plotting to murder her husband, 32
Matriona:	the mother of the man Anisya loves, 50s
Mavra:	a friend, 30s

The Setting: a peasant village in 19th century Russia

Anisya is goaded into poisoning her wealthy husband by the greedy Matriona, who hopes the old man's money will pass on to her son. Here the three women discuss the mysterious "illness" which has befallen the master of the house.

MATRIONA: God be with you, my dear. How are you?

ANISYA: (*Throws her arms up in joy.*) You gave me such a start. What a surprise. God has sent you, in the nick of time.

MATRIONA: Why, what's the matter? What's happened?

ANISYA: I'm going out of my mind. It's terrible!

MATRIONA: Still alive then?

ANISYA: Only just. I can't tell you how terrible it's been. He won't die.

MATRIONA: What about the money?

ANISYA: He's just sent for his sister, Martha. I'm sure he'll give it to her –

MATRIONA: You're sure he hasn't given it to anyone else?

ANISYA: Positive. I've been watching him like a hawk.

MATRIONA: Where is it then?

ANISYA: He won't tell me. I don't know. He keeps moving it from one hiding place to another. And Akulina's always hovering about, which doesn't help. She may be an idiot, but she's watching me all the time. O-oh! My poor head! I'm at the end of my tether.

MATRIONA: My dear, if someone else gets that money, you'll weep the rest of your life. They'll throw you out of this house, with nothing. You've drudged my precious . . . drudged for a man you don't love . . . As a widow you'll walk with a beggar's pouch, if –

ANISYA: Don't! Don't even suggest such a fate! My heart aches. I don't know what to do. There's nobody to help me. I told Nikita. He flinched. He wouldn't have anything to do with it. The only thing he's done – Yesterday he told me the money was under the floorboards.

MATRIONA: And?

ANISYA: Well, I haven't had a chance to look, because the old man hasn't left the room. You see, the problem is that one minute he's got it on him and the next he's hidden it somewhere.

MATRIONA: Well my dear, if you let the money go, you'll never forgive yourself. Your life will never be the same. (*Whispers.*) Did you give him some of that strong tea?

ANISYA: O – oh!

(*She is about to reply when she catches sight of her neighbour. Mavra enters. She passes the cottage.*)

MAVRA: (*To Anisya.*) Anisya! Anisya! Good neighbour! Your husband's calling for you.

ANISYA: No, no, that's him coughing. It sounds like he's calling someone. He's in a terrible state.

MAVRA: (*To Matriona.*) Good day, old woman. Where've you come from?

MATRIONA: Home, dear, where else? I've come to see Nikita. He's my son. I've brought him some new shirts. One has to look after one's own.

MAVRA: Certainly one does. (*To Anisya.*) I want to start bleaching the linen, but I think I'm too early. Nobody else has started.

ANISYA: There's no hurry.

MATRIONA: Has he had communion?

ANISYA: Yes, the priest was here yesterday.

MAVRA: My dear, yesterday he was barely alive. When I saw him . . . I just can't believe how much he's wasted away. The other day he was so close to death, they laid him out under the icons. They started to keen, and were preparing to wash the body –

ANISYA: When he suddenly recovered. He got up and started creeping about again.

MATRIONA: Is he going to be given extreme unction?

ANISYA: I've been told it's important. If he's still alive we'll send for the priest tomorrow.

MAVRA: It's so hard on you, Anisya. But don't they always say, the one that does the looking after suffers the most.

ANISYA: You have no idea how difficult it's been.

MAVRA: I can imagine. He's been about to die for nearly a year. You've been bound, hand and foot.

MATRIONA: It won't be any easier for you as a widow. Ah, it'll be all right while you're young, but when you're old nobody could care less. Old age is a misery. Look at me, I haven't come far, and I'm exhausted. My feet are numb. Where's my son?

ANISYA: He's busy, ploughing the fields. You must come in, we'll start the samovar. Tea will revive you.

MATRIONA: I'm so tired, my dears. You know, I think he ought to have extreme unction, they say it frees the soul.

ANISYA: Don't worry, I'll get the priest tomorrow.

MATRIONA: Good. You know there's been a wedding in our district.

MAVRA: During Lent?

MATRIONA: Yes, you know what they say, "A poor man marries before the night is through." Semyen Matvycich has married Marina.

ANISYA: So she's got herself a husband.

MAVRA: He's a widower, isn't he? That means she's looking after the children.

MATRIONA: All four of them. No decent girl would have him. Still, he chose her. The wine may have overflowed, but you know what they say, never drink out of a cracked glass!

MAVRA: Well how's it going? He's rich isn't he?

MATRIONA: So far so good.

MAVRA: What sort of woman would marry a man with four children? There's our Mikhail, my dear. Now there's a man desperate to find –

VOICE OFF: Hey Mavra! Where the devil are you? Bring in the cow.

(*Mavra leaves.*)

MATRIONA: Well, my dear, that's Marina out of harm's way. My old man needn't give her another thought. (*Once Mavra is out of the way, whispers.*) She's gone. Where was I? Oh yes, did you give him some tea?

ANISYA: Don't talk about it. I'd prefer he died a natural death. Besides they don't work. He won't die. And I'm left with the sin on my conscience. Oh! My poor head! Why did you ever have to give them to me?

MATRIONA: What? The powders? Why shouldn't I sell you sleeping powders? There's nothing wrong with them.

ANISYA: Not the sleeping powders. The other powder, the white powder in the other packet.

MATRIONA: My dear, they were for medicinal use only.

ANISYA: (*Sighs.*) I know . . . I know . . . I'm so afraid . . . He's worn me out.

MATRIONA: How much have you given him?

ANISYA: I've given it to him twice.

MATRIONA: Did he suspect anything?

ANISYA: I tasted the powder myself. It's very bitter. He drank it down with his tea, and then said, "I'm so sick, this tea tastes revolting," I said, "Everything tastes bitter when you're ill." Matriona, I was terrified.

MATRIONA: Don't think about it. The more you think about it, the worse you'll feel.

ANISYA: I wish you hadn't given them to me, and led me to sin. You've scorched my soul. Why did you have to give me that powder?

MATRIONA: What d'you mean? Anisya, Christ have mercy on you. Why blame me? You'll see, it'll do you no good accusing the innocent. If something goes wrong . . . I know nothing about it. It's got nothing to do with me. I'll kiss the cross and swear that I never gave you the powder . . . that I never knew such powder existed. No, you'll have to think for yourself. But, my dear, I know how difficult it's been for you. Just the other day we were talking about you. "The poor thing . . . She has to suffer so much. Her stepdaughter's a fool. Her husband's nothing but skin and bone . . ." And someone said, "If I were in her situation, there's nothing I wouldn't do to make life more bearable!"

ANISYA: That's how I feel. I've had enough of this wretched life. I'm ready to hang myself. I could strangle him. This life isn't worth living!

MATRIONA: That's more like it. Now, don't just stand there – Find out where that money is, and make sure he has some more tea.

ANISYA: Poor me. I don't know what to do. I'm so scared. If only he'd die a natural death. I don't want to burden my soul.

MATRIONA: (*Angry.*) Why won't he show you where it is? Does he want it buried with him? To leave it to no one? I ask you, is it right? God forbid, that such a large sum of money should go to waste. It'd be a sin! What is he playing at? Let me see him!

ANISYA: I don't know any more. He's worn me out.

MATRIONA: What d'you mean, you don't know? It's as simple as this: if you give up now, you'll never forgive yourself. He'll give the money to his sister, and that'll be the last you see of it.

ANISYA: Oh, dear . . . That's right . . . He sent for her. I must go and fetch her.

MATRIONA: Not yet. First things first. Light the samovar. We'll give him some tea and then we'll both look for the money. Don't worry, I'm sure we'll find it.

ANISYA: O – oh! But what if something goes wrong?

MATRIONA: Look what's the matter with you? You've come this far, and now you decide to give up. It's within reach and you're prepared to let it go. Come on.

ANISYA: I'll light the samovar.

MATRIONA: That's more like it. You won't forget it.

LADY WINDERMERE'S FAN
Oscar Wilde
1891

Dramatic / 1 Man, 1 Woman
Lord and Lady Windermere: a couple facing a crisis in their
marriage, 20-30

The Setting: Lord Windermere's house, London

Lady Windermere suspects her husband of having an affair and here
confronts him on the matter.

LORD WINDERMERE: Well, dear, has the fan been sent home yet?
(*Going R.C. sees book.*) Margaret, you have cut open my bank
book. You have no right to do such a thing!

LADY WINDERMERE: You think it wrong that you are found out,
don't you?

LORD WINDERMERE: I think it wrong that a wife should spy on
her husband.

LADY WINDERMERE: I did not spy on you. I never knew of this
woman's existence till half an hour ago. Some one who pitied me
was kind enough to tell me what every one in London knows
already – your daily visits to Curzon Street, your mad infatuation,
the monstrous sums of money you squander on this infamous
woman! (*Crossing L.*)

LORD WINDERMERE: Margaret, don't talk like that of Mrs.
Erlynne, you don't know how unjust it is!

LADY WINDERMERE: (*Turning to him.*) You are very jealous of
Mrs. Erlynne's honor. I wish you had been as jealous of mine.

LORD WINDERMERE: Your honor is untouched. Margaret. You
don't think for a moment that – (*Puts book back into desk.*)

LADY WINDERMERE: I think that you spend your money
strangely. That is all. Oh, don't imagine I mind about the money.
As far as I am concerned, you may squander everything we have.
But what I *do* mind is that you who have loved me, you have
taught me to love you, should pass from the love that is given to

the love that is bought. Oh, it's horrible! (*Sits on sofa.*) And it is I who feel degraded. *You* don't feel anything. I feel stained, utterly stained. You can't realize how hideous the last six months seem to me now – every kiss you have given me is tainted in my memory.

LORD WINDERMERE: (*Crossing to her.*) Don't say that, Margaret. I never loved any one in the whole world but you.

LADY WINDERMERE: (*Rises.*) Who is this woman, then? Why do you take a house for her?

LORD WINDERMERE: I did not take a house for her.

LADY WINDERMERE: You gave her the money to do it, which is the same thing.

LORD WINDERMERE: Margaret, as far as I have known Mrs. Erlynne –

LADY WINDERMERE: Is there a Mr. Erlynne – or is he a myth?

LORD WINDERMERE: Her husband died many years ago. She is alone in the world.

LADY WINDERMERE: No relations? (*A pause.*)

LORD WINDERMERE: None.

LADY WINDERMERE: Rather curious, isn't it? (*L.*)

LORD WINDERMERE: (*L.C.*) Margaret, I was saying to you – and I beg you to listen to me – that as far as I have known Mrs. Erlynne, she has conducted herself well. If years ago –

LADY WINDERMERE: Oh! (*Crossing R.C.*) I don't want details about her life.

LORD WINDERMERE: I am not going to give any details about her life. I tell you simply this – Mrs. Erlynne was once honored, loved, respected. She was well born, she had a position – she lost everything – threw it away, if you like. That makes it all the more bitter. Misfortunes one can endure – they come from outside, they are accidents. But to suffer for one's faults – ah! there is the sting of life. It was twenty years ago, too. She was little more than a girl then. She had been a wife for even less time than you have.

LADY WINDERMERE: I am not interested in her – and – you should not mention this woman and me in the same breath. It is an error of taste. (*Sitting R. at desk.*)

LORD WINDERMERE: Margaret, you could save this woman. She wants to get back into society, and she wants you to help her. (*Crossing to her.*)

LADY WINDERMERE: Me!

LORD WINDERMERE: Yes, you.

LADY WINDERMERE: How impertinent of her! (*A pause.*)

LORD WINDERMERE: Margaret, I came to ask you a great favour, and I still ask it of you, though you have discovered what I had intended you should never have known, that I have given Mrs. Erlynne a large sum of money. I want you to send her an invitation for our party to-night. (*Standing L. of her.*)

LADY WINDERMERE: You are mad. (*Rises.*)

LORD WINDERMERE: I entreat you. People may chatter about her, do chatter about her, of course, but they don't know anything definite about her. She has been to several houses – not to houses where you should go, I admit, but still to houses where women who are in what is called Society now-a-days do go. That does not content her. She wants you to receive her once.

LADY WINDERMERE: As a triumph for her, I suppose?

LORD WINDERMERE: No; but because she knows that you are a good woman – and that if she comes here once she will have a chance of a happier, a surer life than she has had. She will make no further effort to know you. Won't you help a woman who is trying to get back?

LADY WINDERMERE: No! If a woman really repents, she never wishes to return to the society that has made or seen her ruin.

LORD WINDERMERE: I beg of you.

LADY WINDERMERE: (*Crossing to door R.*) I am going to dress for dinner, and don't mention the subject again this evening. Arthur (*Going to him C.*), you fancy because I have no father or mother that I am alone in the world and that you can treat me as you choose. You are wrong, I have friends, many friends.

LORD WINDERMERE: (*L.C.*) Margaret, you are talking foolishly, recklessly. I won't argue with you, but I insist upon your asking Mrs. Erlynne to-night.

LADY WINDERMERE: (*R.C.*) I shall do nothing of the kind. (*Crossing L.C.*)

LORD WINDERMERE: You refuse? (*C.*)

LADY WINDERMERE: Absolutely!

LORD WINDERMERE: Ah, Margaret, do this for my sake; it is her last chance.

LADY WINDERMERE: What has that to do with me?

LORD WINDERMERE: How hard good women are!

LADY WINDERMERE: How weak bad men are!

LORD WINDERMERE: Margaret, none of us men may be good

enough for the women we marry – that is quite true – but you don't imagine I would ever – oh, the suggestion is monstrous!

LADY WINDERMERE: Why should *you* be different from other men? I am told that there is hardly a husband in London who does not waste his life over *some* shameful passion.

LORD WINDERMERE: I am not one of them.

LADY WINDERMERE: I am not sure of that!

LORD WINDERMERE: You are sure in your heart. But don't make chasm after chasm between us. God knows the last few minutes have thrust us wide enough apart. Sit down and write the card.

LADY WINDERMERE: Nothing in the whole world would induce me.

LORD WINDERMERE: (*Crossing to the bureau.*) Then I will. (*Rings electric bell, sits and writes card.*)

LADY WINDERMERE: You are going to invite this woman? (*Crossing to him.*)

LORD WINDERMERE: Yes.

Dramatic / 1 Man, 1 Woman

Lady Windermere: a woman flirting with disaster, 20-30
Mrs. Erlynne: a woman with a questionable background, 30-40

Lady Windermere believes that Mrs. Erlynne has been having an affair with her husband. Here, Mrs. Erlynne does her best to save the Windermere's volatile marriage.

MRS. ERLYNNE: Lady Windermere! (*Lady Windermere starts and looks up. Then recoils in contempt.*) Thank Heaven I am in time. You must go back to your husband's house immediately.

LADY WINDERMERE: Must?

MRS. ERLYNNE: (*Authoritatively.*) Yes, you must! There is not a second to be lost. Lord Darlington may return at any moment.

LADY WINDERMERE: Don't come near me.

MRS. ERLYNNE: Oh, you are on the brink of ruin: you are on the brink of a hideous precipice. You must leave this place at once. My carriage is waiting at the corner of the street. You must come with me and drive straight home. (*Lady Windermere throws off her cloak and flings it on the sofa.*) What are you doing?

LADY WINDERMERE: Mrs. Erlynne – if you had not come here, I would have gone back. But now that I see you, I feel that nothing in the whole world would induce me to live under the same roof as Lord Windermere. You fill me with horror. There is something about you that stirs the wildest rage within me. And I know why you are here. My husband sent you to lure me back that I might serve as a blind to whatever relations exist between you and him.

MRS. ERLYNNE: Oh! you don't think that – you can't.

LADY WINDERMERE: Go back to my husband, Mrs. Erlynne. He belongs to you and not to me. I suppose he is afraid of scandal. Men are such cowards. They outrage every law of the world, and are afraid of the world's tongue. But he had better prepare himself. He shall have a scandal. He shall have the worst scandal there has been in London for years. He shall see his name in every vile paper, mine on every hideous placard.

MRS. ERLYNNE: No – no –

LADY WINDERMERE: Yes, he shall! Had he come himself, I admit I would have gone back to the life of degradation you and he had prepared for me – I was going back – but to stay himself at home, and to send you as his messenger – oh! it was infamous – infamous!

MRS. ERLYNNE: (*C.*) Lady Windermere, you wrong me horribly – you wrong your husband horribly. He doesn't know you are here – he thinks you are safe in your own house. He thinks you are asleep in your own room. He never read the mad letter you wrote to him!

LADY WINDERMERE: (*R.*) Never read it!

MRS. ERLYNNE: No – he knows nothing about it.

LADY WINDERMERE: How simple you think me! (*Going to her.*) You are lying to me!

MRS. ERLYNNE: (*Restraining herself.*) I am not. I am telling you the truth.

LADY WINDERMERE: If my husband didn't read my letter, how is it that you are here? Who told you I had left the house you were shameless enough to enter? Who told you where I had gone to? My husband told you, and sent you to decoy me back. (*Crosses L.*)

MRS. ERLYNNE: (*R.C.*) Your husband has never seen the letter. I – saw it, I opened it. I – read it.

LADY WINDERMERE: (*Turning to her.*) You opened a letter of mine to my husband? You wouldn't dare!

MRS. ERLYNNE: Dare! Oh! to save you from the abyss into which you are falling, there is nothing in the world I would not dare, nothing in the whole world. Here is the letter. Your husband has never read it. He never shall read it. (*Going to fireplace.*) It should never have been written. (*Tears it and throws it into the fire.*)

LADY WINDERMERE: (*With infinite contempt in her voice and look.*) How do I know that that was my letter after all? You seem to think the commonest device can take me in!

MRS. ERLYNNE: Oh! why do you disbelieve everything I tell you! What object do you think I have in coming here, except to save you from utter ruin, to save you from the consequence of a hideous mistake? That letter that is burning now *was* your letter. I swear it to you!

LADY WINDERMERE: (*Slowly.*) You took good care to burn it before I had examined it. I cannot trust you. You, whose whole life is a lie, how could you speak the truth about anything? (*Sits down.*)

MRS. ERLYNNE: (*Hurriedly.*) Think as you like about me – say what you choose against me, but go back, go back to the husband you love.

LADY WINDERMERE: (*Sullenly.*) I do *not* love him!

MRS. ERLYNNE: You do, and you know that he loves you.

LADY WINDERMERE: He does not understand what love is. He understands it as little as you do – but I see what you want. It would be a great advantage for you to get me back. Dear Heaven! what a life I would have then! Living at the mercy of a woman who has neither mercy nor pity in her, a woman whom it is an infamy to meet, a degradation to know, a vile woman, a woman who comes between husband and wife!

MRS. ERLYNNE: (*With a gesture of despair.*) Lady Windermere, Lady Windermere, don't say such terrible things. You don't know how terrible they are, how terrible and how unjust. Listen, you must listen! Only go back to your husband, and I promise you never to communicate with him again on any pretext – never to see him – never to have anything to do with his life or yours. The money that he gave me, he gave me not through love, but through hatred. Not in worship, but in contempt. The hold I have over him –

LADY WINDERMERE: (*Rising.*) Ah! you admit you have a hold!

MRS. ERLYNNE: Yes, and I will tell you what it is. It is his love for you, Lady Windermere.

LADY WINDERMERE: You expect me to believe that?

MRS. ERLYNNE: You must believe it! It is true. It is his love for you that has made him submit to – oh! call it what you like, tyranny, threats, anything you choose. But it is his love for you. His desire to spare you shame, yes, shame and disgrace.

LADY WINDERMERE: What do you mean? You are insolent! What have I to do with you?

MRS. ERLYNNE: (*Humbly.*) Nothing. I know it – but I tell you that your husband loves you – that you may never meet with such love again in your whole life – that such love you will never meet – and that if you throw it away, the day may come when you will starve for love and it will not be given to you, beg for love and it will be denied you – Oh! Arthur loves you!

LADY WINDERMERE: Arthur? And you tell me there is nothing between you?

MRS. ERLYNNE: Lady Windermere, before Heaven your husband is guiltless of all offense towards you! And I – I tell you that had it ever occurred to me that such a monstrous suspicion would have entered your mind, I would have died rather than have crossed your life or his – oh! died, gladly died! (*Moves away to sofa R.*)

LADY WINDERMERE: You talk as if you had a heart. Women like you have no hearts. Heart is not in you. You are bought and sold.

UNCLE VANYA
Anton Chekhov
1899

Serio-Comic / 1 Man, 1 Woman
Serebryakov: a retired professor, 60s
Yelyena: his younger wife, 27

The Setting: the Serebryakov estate

Here, the cranky professor complains of his age to his wife.

SEREBRYAKOV: (*Waking up.*) Who is it? Sonya?

YELYENA: It's me.

SEREBRYAKOV: Ah, Elyenochka. It's you. I'm having terrible pains.

YELYENA: Your blanket fell. (*She wraps up his legs.*) I'm going to close the window, Alyeksandr.

SEREBRYAKOV: No, don't, I'm suffocating. I dozed off. I dreamt my left leg wasn't my own . . . a terrible pain woke me. It's not gout. Maybe it's rheumatism. What time is it?

YELYENA: Twenty after midnight. (*A pause.*)

SEREBRYAKOV: We must have the works of Batyushkov in the library. Bring them to me tomorrow morning.

YELYENA: What?

SEREBRYAKOV: Tomorrow morning. Bring me the works of Batyushkov. I think I remember seeing them there. Why am I having such trouble breathing?

YELYENA: It's fatigue. You haven't slept for two nights.

SEREBRYAKOV: They say Turgenev's gout turned into angina. I think the same thing's happening to me. Damn old age! I hate it, the hell with it! I'm old now. I disgust myself. And everyone else finds me disgusting too. All of you. Don't you?

YELYENA: The way you talk about your age, you'd think it were our fault.

SEREBRYAKOV: And I disgust you most of all – don't I? (*Yelyena Andreyevna moves away, sits further from him.*) Obviously. And it's understandable. I'm not dumb. You're young and healthy, you're beautiful, you have your life to live, and I'm an old man, half dead. I know. Of course. I understand. Too bad I'm still alive, right? Well, don't worry – you won't have long to wait, just be patient.

YELYENA: For God's sake, stop it . . . I can't stand it any more . . . stop it.

SEREBRYAKOV: It is my fault, isn't it? None of you can stand it any more, can you? Your youth is going down the drain, you're bored, isn't that right? And I'm the only one who enjoys life, who's happy. That's it, isn't it?

YELYENA: Stop it! You're exhausting me.

SEREBRYAKOV: I exhaust all of you, obviously.

YELYENA: (*Through tears.*) I can't stand it! Tell me what you want me to do!

SEREBRYAKOV: Nothing. Nothing at all.

YELYENA: Then be quiet. Please.

SEREBRYAKOV: Isn't it funny that when Ivan Pyetrovyich opens his mouth, or that old fool Mariya Vasilyevna, it's fine, everybody listens, but when I say a single word, it's disaster. The very sound of my voice repels you, all of you. Well, so what if I am disagreeable and egotistical, a tyrant? Isn't that allowed at my age? Don't I deserve it? I ask you: don't I have any right to a quiet old age? To some respect?

YELYENA: No one's denying you anything. (*A window bangs in the wind.*) There's a wind. I'm going to close the window. (*She closes it.*) It's going to rain. No one's denying you anything. (*A pause. Outside, the night watchman taps and sings.*)

SEREBRYAKOV: To give one's whole life to literature, to be accustomed to one's desk, to the lecture room, to respectable colleagues, and then, suddenly, without knowing why, to end up here in this tomb, and each day to see only vulgar people and hear them speak inanities! What I want is success, fame, noise – that's what I want. I'm in exile here! Yearning for the past, reading about other people's success, afraid of death . . . I can't stand it any more! I don't have the strength. And now they won't even forgive me my age!

YELYENA: Wait a little, be patient: another five or six years and I'll be old too.

THE IMPORTANCE OF BEING EARNEST
Oscar Wilde
1899

Serio-Comic / 1 Man, 1 Woman
   Jack: a young man in love, 20-30
   Lady Bracknell: an opinionated dowager, 50-60

The Setting: a flat in London

Here, the pompous Lady Bracknell informs Jack that she doesn't consider him to be an eligible suitor for her daughter.

LADY BRACKNELL: (*Sitting down.*) You can take a seat, Mr. Worthing. (*Looks in her pocket for notebook and pencil.*)

JACK: Thank you, Lady Bracknell, I prefer standing.

LADY BRACKNELL: (*Pencil and notebook in hand.*) I feel bound to tell you that you are not down on my list of eligible young men, although I have the same lists as the dear Duchess of Bolton has. We work together, in fact. However, I am quite ready to enter your name, should your answers be what a really affectionate mother requires. Do you smoke?

JACK: Well, yes, I must admit I smoke.

LADY BRACKNELL: I am glad to hear it. A man should always have an occupation of some kind. There are far too many idle men in London as it is. How old are you?

JACK: Twenty-nine.

LADY BRACKNELL: A very good age to be married at. I have always been of opinion that a man who desires to get married should know either everything or nothing. Which do you know?

JACK: (*After some hesitation.*) I know nothing, Lady Bracknell.

LADY BRACKNELL: I am pleased to hear it. I do not approve of anything that tampers with natural ignorance. Ignorance is like a delicate exotic fruit; touch it and the bloom is gone. The whole theory of modern education is radically unsound. Fortunately in England, at any rate, education produces no effect whatsoever. If it did, it would prove a serious danger to the upper classes, and probably lead to acts of violence in Grosvenor Square. What is your income?

JACK: Between seven and eight thousand a year.

LADY BRACKNELL: (*Makes a note in her book.*) In land, or in investments?

JACK: In investments, chiefly.

LADY BRACKNELL: That is satisfactory. What between the duties expected of one during one's life-time, and the duties exacted from one after one's death, land has ceased to be either a profit or a pleasure. It gives one position, and prevents one from keeping it up. That's all that can be said about land.

JACK: I have a country house with some land, of course, attached to it, about fifteen hundred acres, I believe; but I don't depend on that for my real income. In fact, as far as I can make out, the poachers are the only people who make anything out of it.

LADY BRACKNELL: A country house! How many bedrooms? Well, that point can be cleared up afterwards. You have a town house, I hope? A girl with a simple, unspoiled nature, like Gwendolen, could hardly be expected to reside in the country.

JACK: Well, I own a house in Belgrave Square, but it is let by the year to Lady Bloxham. Of course, I can get it back whenever I like, at six months' notice.

LADY BRACKNELL: Lady Bloxham? I don't know her.

JACK: Oh, she goes about very little. She is a lady considerably advanced in years.

LADY BRACKNELL: Ah, now-a-days that is no guarantee of respectability of character. What number in Belgrave Square?

JACK: 149.

LADY BRACKNELL: (*Shaking her head.*) The unfashionable side. I thought there was something. However, that could easily be altered.

JACK: Do you mean the fashion, or the side?

LADY BRACKNELL: (*Sternly.*) Both, if necessary, I presume. What are your politics?

JACK: Well, I am afraid I really have none. I am a Liberal Unionist.

LADY BRACKNELL: Oh, they count as Tories. They dine with us. Or come in the evening, at any rate. Now to minor matters. Are your parents living?

JACK: I have lost both my parents.

LADY BRACKNELL: Both? . . . That seems like carelessness. Who was your father? He was evidently a man of some wealth. Was he born in what the Radical papers call the purple of commerce, or did he rise from the ranks of the aristocracy.

JACK: I am afraid I really don't know. The fact is, Lady Bracknell, I said I had lost my parents. It would be nearer the truth to say that my parents seem to have lost me . . . I don't actually know who I am by birth. I was . . . well, I was found.

LADY BRACKNELL: Found!

JACK: The late Mr. Thomas Cardew, an old gentleman of very charitable and kindly disposition, found me, and gave me the name of Worthing, because he happened to have a first-class ticket for Worthing in his pocket at the time. Worthing is a place in Sussex. It is a seaside resort.

LADY BRACKNELL: Where did the charitable gentleman who had a first-class ticket for this seaside resort find you?

JACK: (*Gravely.*) In a hand-bag.

LADY BRACKNELL: A hand-bag?

JACK: (*Very seriously.*) Yes, Lady Bracknell. I was in a hand-bag – a somewhat large, black leather hand-bag, with handles to it – an ordinary hand-bag in fact.

LADY BRACKNELL: In what locality did Mr. James, or Thomas, Cardew come across this ordinary hand-bag?

JACK: In the cloak-room at Victoria Station. It was given to him in mistake for his own.

LADY BRACKNELL: The cloak-room at Victoria Station?

JACK: Yes. The Brighton line.

LADY BRACKNELL: The line is immaterial, Mr. Worthing, I confess I feel somewhat bewildered by what you have just told me. To be born, or at any rate bred, in a hand-bag, whether it had handles or not, seems to me to display a contempt for the ordinary decencies of family life that remind one of the worst excesses of the French Revolution. And I presume you know what that unfortunate movement led to? As for the particular locality in which the hand-bag was found, a cloak-room at a railway station might serve to conceal a social indiscretion – has probably, indeed, been used for the purpose before now – but it could hardly be regarded as an assured basis for a recognized position in good society.

JACK: May I ask you then what you would advise me to do? I need hardly say I would do anything in the world to ensure Gwendolen's happiness.

LADY BRACKNELL: I would strongly advise you, Mr. Worthing, to try and acquire some relations as soon as possible, and to make a definite effort to produce at any rate one parent, of either sex, before the season is quite over.

JACK: Well, I don't see how I could possibly manage to do that. I can produce the hand-bag at any moment. It is in my dressing-room at home. I really think that should satisfy you, Lady Bracknell.

LADY BRACKNELL: Me, sir! What has it to do with me? You can hardly imagine that I and Lord Bracknell would dream of allowing our only daughter – a girl brought up with the utmost care– to marry into a cloak-room, and form an alliance with a parcel? Good morning, Mr. Worthing! (*Lady Bracknell sweeps out in majestic indignation.*)

MRS. WARREN'S PROFESSION
George Bernard Shaw
1902

Dramatic / 2 Women

Vivie: a highly educated young Englishwoman, 22

Mrs. Warren: her mother, 40-50

The Setting: a cottage in Surrcy

When Mrs. Warren attempts to assert authority over her willful daughter, she finds that Vivie has turned into quite the intellectual snob.

MRS. WARREN: (*Coming back to her place at the table, opposite Vivie, resigning herself to an evening of boredom now that the men are gone.*) Did you ever in your life hear anyone rattle on so? Isn't he a tease? (*She sits down.*) Now that I think of it, dearie, don't you go encouraging him. I'm sure he's a regular good-for-nothing.

VIVIE: Yes: I'm afraid poor Frank is a thorough good-for-nothing. I shall have to get rid of him; but I shall feel sorry for him, though he's not worth it, poor lad. That man Crofts does not seem to me to be good for much either, is he?

MRS. WARREN: (*Galled by Vivie's cool tone.*) What do you know of men, child, to talk that way about them? You'll have to make up your mind to see a good deal of Sir George Crofts, as he's a friend of mine.

VIVIE: (*Quite unmoved.*) Why? Do you expect that we shall be much together – you and I, I mean?

MRS. WARREN: (*Staring at her.*) Of course – until you're married. You're not going back to college again.

VIVIE: Do you think my way of life would suit you? I doubt it.

MRS. WARREN: Your way of life! What do you mean?

VIVIE: (*Cutting a page of her book with the paper knife on her chatelaine.*) Has it really never occurred to you, mother, that I have a way of life like other people?

MRS. WARREN: What nonsense is this you're trying to talk? Do you want to shew your independence, now that you're a great little person at school? Don't be a fool, child.

VIVIE: (*Indulgently.*) That's all you have to say on the subject, is it, Mother?

MRS. WARREN: (*Puzzled, then angry.*) Don't you keep on asking me questions like that. (*Violently.*) Hold your tongue. (*Vivie works on, losing no time, and saying nothing.*) You and your way of life, indeed! What next? (*She looks at Vivie again. No reply.*) Your way of life will be what I please, so it will. (*Another pause.*) I've been noticing these airs in you ever since you got that tripos or whatever you call it. If you think I'm going to put up with them you're mistaken; and the sooner you find it out, the better. (*Muttering.*) All I have to say on the subject, indeed! (*Again raising her voice angrily.*) Do you know who you're speaking to, Miss?

VIVIE: (*Looking across at her without raising her head from the book.*) No. Who are you? What are you?

MRS. WARREN: (*Rising breathless.*) You young imp!

VIVIE: Everybody knows my reputation, my social standing, and the profession I intend to pursue. I now nothing about you. What is that way of life which you invite me to share with you and Sir George Crofts, pray?

MRS. WARREN: Take care. I shall do something I'll be sorry for after, and you, too.

VIVIE: (*Putting aside her books with cool decision.*) Well, let us drop the subject until you are better able to face it. (*Looking critically at her mother.*) You want some good walks and a little lawn tennis so set you up. You are shockingly out of condition: you were not able to manage twenty yards uphill to-day without stopping to pant; and your wrists are mere rolls of fat. Look at mine. (*She holds out her wrists.*)

MRS. WARREN: (*After looking at her helplessly, begins to whimper.*) Vivie –

VIVIE: (*Springing up sharply.*) Now pray don't begin to cry. Anything but that. I really cannot stand whimpering. I will go out of the room if you do.

MRS. WARREN: (*Piteously.*) Oh, my darling, how can you be so hard on me? Have I no rights over you as your mother?

VIVIE: Are you my mother?

MRS. WARREN: (*Appalled.*) Am I your mother! Oh, Vivie!

VIVIE: Then where are our relatives – my father – our family friends? You claim the rights of a mother: the right to call me fool and child; to speak to me as no woman in authority over me at college dare speak to me; to dictate my way of life; and to force on me the acquaintance of a brute whom anyone can see to be the most vicious sort of London man about town. Before I give myself the trouble to resist such claims, I may as well find out whether they have any real existence.

MRS. WARREN: (*Distracted, throwing herself on her knees.*) Oh, no, no. Stop, stop. I am your mother: I swear it. Oh, you can't mean to turn on me – my own child: it's not natural. You believe me, don't you? Say you believe me.

VIVIE: Who was my father?

MRS. WARREN: You don't know what you're asking. I can't tell you.

VIVIE: (*Determinedly.*) Oh yes, you can, if you like. I have a right to know; and you know very well that I have that right. You can refuse to tell me, if you please; but if you do, you will see the last of me to-morrow morning.

MRS. WARREN: Oh, it's too horrible to hear you talk like that. You wouldn't – you couldn't leave me.

VIVIE: (*Ruthlessly.*) Yes, without a moment's hesitation, if you trifle with me about this. (*Shivering with disgust.*) How can I feel sure that I may not have the contaminated blood of that brutal waster in my veins?

MRS. WARREN: No, no. On my oath it's not he, nor any of the rest that you have ever met. I'm certain of that, at least. (*Vivie's eyes fasten sternly on her mother as the significance of this flashes on her.*)

VIVIE: (*Slowly.*) You are certain of that, at least. Ah! You mean that that is all you are certain of. (*Thoughtfully.*) I see. (*Mrs. Warren buries her face in her hands.*) Don't do that, mother: you know you don't feel it a bit. (*Mrs. Warren takes down her hands and looks up deplorably at Vivie, who takes out her watch and says:*) Well, that is enough for to-night. At what hour would you like breakfast? Is half-past eight too early for you?

MRS. WARREN: (*Wildly.*) My God, what sort of woman are you?

VIVIE: (*Coolly.*) The sort the world is mostly made of, I should hope. Otherwise I don't understand how it gets its business done. Come: (*Taking her mother by the wrist, and pulling her up pretty* *resolutely.*) pull yourself together. That's right.

MRS. WARREN: (*Querulously.*) You're very rough with me, Vivie.

VIVIE: Nonsense. What about bed? It's past ten.

MRS. WARREN: (*Passionately.*) What's the use of my going to bed? Do you think I could sleep?

VIVIE: Why not? I shall.

MRS. WARREN: You! you've no heart. (*She suddenly breaks out vehemently in her natural tongue – the dialect of a woman of the people – with all her affectations of maternal authority and conventional manners gone, and an overwhelming inspiration of true conviction and corn in her.*) Oh, I won't bear it: I won't put up with the injustice of it. What right have you to set yourself up above me like this? You boast of what you are to me – to me, who gave you the chance of being what you are. What chance had I? Shame on you for a bad daughter and a stuck-up prude!

VIVIE: (*Cool and determined, but no longer confident; for her replies, which have sounded convincingly sensible and strong to her so far, now begin to ring rather woodenly and even priggishly against the new tone of her mother.*) Don't think for a moment I set myself above you in any way. You attacked me with the conventional authority of a mother: I defended myself with the conventional authority of a respectable woman. Frankly, I am not going to stand any of your nonsense; and when you drop it I shall not expect you to stand any of mine. I shall always respect your right to your own opinions and your own way of life.

MRS. WARREN: My own opinions and my own way of life! Listen to her talking! Do you think I was brought up like you – able to pick and choose my own way of life? Do you think I did what I did because I liked it, or thought it right, or wouldn't rather have gone to college and been a lady if I'd had the chance?

VIVIE: Everybody has some choice, mother. The poorest girl alive may not be able to choose between being Queen of England or Principal of Newnham; but she can choose between ragpicking and flowerselling, according to her taste. People are always blaming their circumstances. The people who get on in this world are the people who get up and look for the circumstances they want, and, if they can't find them, make them.

THE PLAYBOY OF THE WESTERN WORLD
John Millington Synge
1907

Serio-Comic / 1 Man, 1 Woman
Pegeen Mike: a wild-looking but fine girl, 20
Shawn Keogh: her cousin, a fat and fair young man, 20s

The Setting: a country public house, the West coast of Ireland

When her father, a pub owner, leaves Pegeen Mike alone at the bar to attend a wake, her shy cousin stops by for a visit.

PEGEEN: (*Slowly as she writes.*) Six yards of stuff for to make a yellow gown. A pair of lace boots with lengthy heels on them and brassy eyes. A hat is suited for a wedding day. A fine tooth comb. To be sent with three barrels of porter in Jimmy Farrell's creel cart on the evening of the coming Fair to Mister Michael James Flaherty. With the best compliments of this season. Margaret Flaherty.

SHAWN: (*Comes in as she signs, looks round awkwardly, when he sees she is alone.*) Where's himself?

PEGEEN: (*Without looking at him.*) He's coming. (*She directs the letter.*) To Mister Sheamus Mulroy, Wine and Spirit Dealer, Castlebar.

SHAWN: (*Uneasily.*) I didn't see him on the road.

PEGEEN: How would you see him (*Licks stamp and puts it on letter.*) and it dark night this half hour gone by?

SHAWN: (*Turning towards the door again.*) I stood a while outside wondering would I have a right to pass on or to walk in and see you, Pegeen Mike, (*Comes to fire.*) and I could hear the cows breathing, and sighing in the stillness of the air, and not a step moving any place from this gate to the bridge.

PEGEEN: (*Putting letter in envelope.*) It's above at the crossroads he is, meeting Philly Cullen; and a couple more are going along with him to Kate Cassidy's wake.

SHAWN: (*Looking at her blankly.*) And he's going that length in the dark night?

PEGEEN: (*Impatiently.*) He is surely, and leaving me lonesome on the scruff of the hill. (*She gets up and puts envelope on dresser, then winds clock.*) Isn't it long the nights are now, Shawn Keogh, to be leaving a poor girl with her own self counting the hours to the dawn of day?

SHAWN: (*With awkward humour.*) If it is, when we're wedded in a short while you'll have no call to complain, for I've little will to be walking off to wakes or weddings in the darkness of the night.

PEGEEN: (*With rather scornful good humour.*) You're making mighty certain, Shaneen, that I'll wed you now.

SHAWN: Aren't we after making a good bargain, the way we're only waiting these days on Father Reilly's dispensation from the bishops, or the Court of Rome.

PEGEEN: (*Looking at him teasingly, washing up at dresser.*) It's a wonder, Shaneen, the Holy Father'd be taking notice of the likes of you; for if I was him I wouldn't bother with this place where you'll meet none but Red Linahan, has a squint in his eye, and Patcheen is lame in his heel, or the mad Mulrannies were driven from California and they lost in their wits. We're a queer lot these times to go troubling the Holy Father on his sacred seat.

SHAWN: (*Scandalized.*) If we are, we're as good this place as another, maybe, and as good these times as we were for ever.

PEGEEN: (*With scorn.*) As good, is it? Where now will you meet the like of Daneen Sullivan knocked the eye from a peeler, or Marcus Quin, God rest him, got six months for maiming ewes, and he a great warrant to tell stories of holy Ireland till he'd have the old women shedding down tears about their feet. Where will you find the likes of them, I'm saying?

SHAWN: (*Timidly.*) If you don't, it's a good job, maybe; for (*With peculiar emphasis on the words.*) Father Reilly has small conceit to have that kind walking around and talking to the girls.

PEGEEN: (*Impatiently, throwing water from basin out of the door.*) Stop tormenting me with Father Reilly (*Imitating his voice.*) when I'm asking only what way I'll pass these twelve hours of dark, and not take my death with the fear. (*Looking out the door.*)

SHAWN: (*Timidly*) Would I fetch you the Widow Quin, maybe?

PEGEEN: Is it the like of that murderer? You'll not, surely.

SHAWN: (*Going to her, soothingly.*) Then I'm thinking himself will stop along with you when he sees you taking on, for it'll be a long night-time with great darkness, and I'm after feeling a kind of fellow above in the furzy ditch, groaning wicked like a maddening dog, the way it's good cause you have, maybe, to be fearing now.

PEGEEN: (*Turning on him sharply.*) What's that? Is it a man you seen?

SHAWN: (*Retreating.*) I couldn't see him at all; but I heard him groaning out, and breaking his heart. It should have been a young man from his words speaking.

PEGEEN: (*Going after him.*) And you never went near to see was he hurted or what ailed him at all?

SHAWN: I did not, Pegeen Mike. It was a dark, lonesome place to be hearing the like of him.

PEGEEN: Well, you're a daring fellow, and if they find his corpse stretched above in the dew of dawn, what'll you say then to the peelers, or the Justice of the Peace?

SHAWN: (*Thunderstruck.*) I wasn't thinking of that. For the love of God, Pegeen Mike, don't let on I was speaking of him. Don't tell your father and the men is coming above; for if they heard that story, they'd have great blabbing this night at the wake.

PEGEEN: I'll maybe tell them, and I'll maybe not.

SHAWN: They are coming at the door. Will you whisht, I'm saying?

PEGEEN: Whisht yourself.

THUNDER IN THE AIR
August Strindberg
1907

Dramatic / 1 Man, 1 Woman

    The Man: a man made bitter by the past, 50s
    Gerda: his ex-wife, 30s

The Setting: an apartment

Several years after their divorce, Gerda visits her ex-husband and discovers that he remains as bitter as the day they parted.

GERDA: I am sorry . . I just happened to walk past and I longed to see my old home again. The windows were open and . . . (*Pause.*)

THE MAN: Well, do you think it has changed much?

GERDA: No, it is just the same, but something has come between . . .

THE MAN: (*Ill-at-ease.*) Are you happy . . . in your new life?

GERDA: Yes, it is as I expected.

THE MAN: And our daughter?

GERDA: She is growing and she is happy.

THE MAN: Then I won't ask any more questions. (*Pause.*) Do you want anything from me, can I help in any way?

GERDA: Thank you for asking, but . . . I don't need anything. I can see that you are well, too. (*Pause.*) Do you want to see Ann-Charlotte? (*Pause.*)

THE MAN: I don't think so. Now that I know she is alright. It is difficult to go back and start again. Like when you had to do your homework over again even though you knew it so well. I am so far removed from all that now. I can't go back to the past. It is not in my nature to be discourteous, but I won't ask you to sit down . . . you belong to another man now and you are not the same person I was married to once.

GERDA: Have I changed so much?

THE MAN: Your voice, your eyes, your movements are those of a stranger.

GERDA: Have I aged so much?

THE MAN: I don't know. They say that every atom in your body is renewed every three years and every five years you are a completely new person. So to me you are now a totally different person from the one who used to sit here, bored. I can hardly bring myself to call you by your first name; you are like a stranger. And I expect I'd feel the same about my daughter.

GERDA: Don't talk like that. I'd rather you were angry.

THE MAN: Why should I be angry?

GERDA: After all the terrible things I have done to you.

THE MAN: Have you? I don't recall any.

GERDA: Didn't you see the writ?

THE MAN: No, I passed it on to my solicitor. (*Sits down.*)

GERDA: And the verdict?

THE MAN: I didn't read that, either. I have no intention of marrying again so I don't need papers like that.

(*Pause. Gerda sits down.*)

What was the verdict, then? That I was too old for you, sexually? (*Gerda nods in the affirmative.*)

Well, it was the truth, so why are you embarrassed? I said the very same thing in my counter-writ and I asked the court to release you from your marriage bond.

GERDA: Did you really ask that?

THE MAN: I didn't put it in writing that I was too old, but I said I was getting too old for YOU.

GERDA: (*Hurt.*) For ME?

THE MAN: Yes. I couldn't very well say that I was too old for you when we got married because then the arrival of our child might have caused some suspicions, and it was our child after all, wasn't it?

GERDA: You know it is. But . . .

THE MAN: Am I to be condemned because I am growing old? If I should suddenly decide to dance "the Boston" at my age or play cards all through the night I wouldn't have the stamina any more. I would probably collapse with exhaustion and surely that would be more undignified, don't you think?

GERDA: You don't look your age . . .

THE MAN: Did you think the divorce would finish me? (*Gerda doesn't show what she feels.*)

Some people thought you'd be the end of me. Do I look like a finished man, do you think?

(*Gerda is embarrassed.*)
Your friends have drawn caricatures of me in some papers, I've been told. But I don't want you to have a bad conscience about me.

GERDA: Why did you marry me in the first place?

THE MAN: Surely you know why a man wants to get married? You also know that I didn't exactly have to beg for your love. And don't you remember how we both smiled at all those busy-bodies who advised against our union. But why did you tempt me? I have never understood that. Soon after the wedding you didn't even look at me. And even at the reception you behaved as if you were attending someone else's wedding. I thought you might have conspired with my enemies to kill me. At work, all my subordinates hated me because I was their superior but they soon made friends with you. Every new enemy of mine became a friend of yours. That caused me to say: One must not hate one's enemies, true, but you shouldn't *love* my enemies either. However, when I became aware of your true nature, I started to be on my guard. But first I wanted proof that you had told lies and that is why I waited until the baby was born.

GERDA: I never knew that you could be so deceitful.

THE MAN: I kept quiet, but I never lied. You gradually turned my former friends into spies and you lured my brother into deceiving me as well. But the worst of all was that you made me doubt the legitimacy of my own child.

GERDA: I take it all back.

THE MAN: A word once airborne cannot be recalled. But the worst thing of all is that this false rumour has now reached the ears of our daughter and she thinks that her mother is a . . .

GERDA: Oh, no!

THE MAN: Yes, that is so. You built a whole tower on a foundation of lies, and now this tower of lies will fall on top of you.

GERDA: It is not true.

THE MAN: Oh yes, I saw Ann-Charlotte a minute ago.

GERDA: Have you met her?

THE MAN: We met on the stairs and she called me "uncle." Do you know what an uncle is? It is an old friend of the family, especially of the wife. I am known as her "uncle" at her school as well. It is horrible for the child.

GERDA: So you've met her, then?

THE MAN: Yes. But I didn't want to talk about it. The meeting was so upsetting that I erased it from my mind.

GERDA: What can I do to make up for everything?

THE MAN: There is nothing you can do. It is entirely up to me. (*They regard each other in silence.*) And I have already done something about it.

GERDA: Everything I do seems to go wrong. Can I ask you to forget and forgive . . .

THE MAN: What do you mean?

GERDA: Restore, repair . . .

THE MAN: Do you mean to tie the knot again? To resume your old role as mistress of my house? No thank you, I don't want you.

GERDA: I never thought I'd hear you say that!

THE MAN: I am sure it does you good.

GERDA: That is a very pretty table runner.

THE MAN: Yes, it is pretty.

GERDA: Where did it come from?

WILD HONEY
Anton Chekhov
1920

Serio-Comic / 1 Man, 1 Woman
  Anna Petrovna: a wealthy widow, 30-40
  Platanov: the local school master, 40s

The Setting: the Voynitzev family estate in a Southern province of Russia

On a summer's eve, Anna Petrovna searches out Platanov and confesses her desire for him all the while not knowing that he loves another.

ANNA PETROVNA: And here he is. Our philosopher. Shunning us all. Pacing the garden and thinking his own thoughts. But what a perfect summer's night! Cool air at last. And the first star . . . What a pity ladies aren't supposed to sleep outside under the open sky. When I was a little girl I always slept in the garden in summer. (*Pause.*) you've got a new tie.

PLATANOV: Yes.

ANNA PETROVNA: I'm in such an odd mood today . . . I feel pleased with everything . . . Say something, Platanov!

PLATANOV: What do you want me to say?

ANNA PETROVNA: I want to hear the sound of your voice. I want to hear it saying – I don't know – something new, something sharp, something sweet. Because you're being terribly clever today, and you're looking terribly handsome, and I'm more in love with you than ever. And you're being so nice! You're causing scarcely any trouble at all.

PLATANOV: I've never seen you looking more lovely.

ANNA PETROVNA: Are we friends, Platanov?

PLATANOV: Of course. If we're not friends, who is?

ANNA PETROVNA: Real friends? Great friends?

PLATANOV: What is this? We're friends, we're friends! You're behaving like a schoolgirl!

ANNA PETROVNA: So, we're friends. But you know, do you, my dear sir, that from friendship between a man and a woman it's only a short step to love?

PLATANOV: Is it indeed? You and I shall not be taking that one step to perdition, however short it may be.

ANNA PETROVNA: So you see love as perdition, do you? I see it as something noble. Why should we be ashamed of it? Why shouldn't we take that one short step?

PLATANOV: (*Stares at her.*) Let's go inside and dance, shall we?

ANNA PETROVNA: You can't dance! I think it's time you and I had a little talk. I don't know quite where to begin, though. You're such a difficult man! Now try to listen for once, and not to philosophize . . . (*She sits.*) Sit down . . . Look, he's quite embarrassed! It's all right, my dear – your wife can't hear us!

PLATANOV: Perhaps I should say something first.

ANNA PETROVNA: Perhaps you should.

PLATANOV: It's not worth it. I promise you, Anna Petrovna – it's simply not worth it.

ANNA PETROVNA: Isn't it? Now you listen to me. Sit down . . . Sit down!

(*He sits beside her.*)

Look, if you were free, I shouldn't think twice – I'd make myself your wife. I'd bestow my rank and station on you. But as it is . . .(*Pause.*) I think in the circumstances it is a little ungentlemanly of you not to say *something*.

PLATANOV: (*Jumps to his feet.*) Let's forget this conversation! Let's pretend it never took place!

ANNA PETROVNA: You are a clown, Misha.

PLATANOV: I respect you! And I respect in myself the respect I have for you! I'm not against harmless diversion . . .

ANNA PETROVNA: I know, Platanov.

PLATANOV: But not with a beautiful, intelligent, untrammeled woman like you! What – a month or two of foolishness, and then to go our ways in shame? I couldn't do it!

ANNA PETROVNA: I wasn't talking about foolishness. I was talking about love.

PLATANOV: And do you think I don't love you? I love you for your goodness, for your generous heart. I love you desperately – I love you to distraction! I'll lay down my life for you, if that's what you want! Does every love have to be reduced to the same common denominator? I love you as a woman, yes, but I also love you as a person. On top of which, my dear, I am just a tiny bit married.

ANNA PETROVNA: (*Rises.*) You've also had just a tiny bit too much to drink, and you're being just a tiny bit hypocritical. Go on, then. When your head's clear we'll have another talk.

PLATANOV: No, the trouble is, I can't hide my true feelings from you. (*Quietly and intimately.*) If I could, my precious, I should long since have been your lover.

(*Exit Platanov.*)

ANNA PETROVNA: (*To herself.*) Intolerable man! (*She calls.*) Come back here! Misha! Misha . . .

THE PLAYER QUEEN
William Butler Yeats
1922

Serio-Comic / 2 Women

Nona:	a player, 35
Decima:	the beautiful and vain young wife of the leading player, 20s

The Setting: a throne room

A play has been commissioned by the Prime Minister, but the leading lady, Decima, refuses to perform in a role older than 30. The prime minister threatens to jail her husband if the play isn't performed and Nona here does her best to convince Decima to perform.

DECIMA: (*Comes cautiously out of her hiding-place singing.*)
"He went away," my mother sang,
"When I was brought to bed."
And all the while her needle pulled
The gold and silver thread.

She pulled the thread and bit the thread
And made a golden gown,
She wept because she had dreamt that I
Was born to wear a crown.
(*She is just reaching her hand for the lobster when Nona comes forward holding out towards her the dress and mask of Noah's wife which she has been carrying over her left arm.*)
NONA: Thank God you are found! (*Getting between her and the lobster.*) No, not until you have put on this dress and mask. I have caught you now, and you are not going to hide again.
DECIMA: Very well, when I have had my breakfast.
NONA: Not a mouthful till you are dressed ready for rehearsal.
DECIMA: Do you know what song I was singing just now?
NONA: It is that song you're always singing. Septimus made it up.
DECIMA: It is the song of the mad singing daughter of a harlot. The only song she had. Her father was a drunken sailor waiting for the

full tide, and yet she thought her mother had foretold that she
would marry a prince and become a great queen. (*Singing.*)

"When she was got," my mother sang,
"I heard a seamew cry,
I saw a flake of yellow foam
That dropped upon my thigh."

How therefore could she help but braid
The gold upon my hair,
And dream that I should carry
The golden top of care?

The moment ago as I lay here I thought I could play a queen's
part, a great queen's part; the only part in the world I can play is a
queen's part.

NONA: You play a queen's part? You that were born in a ditch
between two towns and wrapped in a sheet that was stolen from a
hedge.

DECIMA: The Queen cannot play at all, but I could play so well. I
could bow with my whole body down to my ankles and could be
stern when hard looks were in season. O, I would know how to put
all summer in a look and after that all winter in a voice.

NONA: Low comedy is what you are fit for.

DECIMA: I understood all this in a wink of the eye, and then just
when I am saying to myself that I was born to sit up there with
soldiers and courtiers, you come shaking in front of me that mask
and that dress. I am not to eat my breakfast unless I play an old
peaky-chinned, drop-nosed harridan that a foul husband beats with
a stock because she won't clamber among the other brutes into his
cattle-boat. (*She makes a dart at the lobster.*)

NONA: No, no, not a drop, not a mouthful till you have put these on.
Remember that if there is no play Septimus must go to prison.

DECIMA: Would they give him dry bread to eat?

NONA: They would.

DECIMA: And water to drink and nothing in the water?

NONA: They would.

DECIMA: And a straw bed?

NONA: They would, and only a little straw maybe.

DECIMA: And iron chains that clanked.

NONA: They would.

DECIMA: And keep him there for a whole week?

NONA: A month maybe.

DECIMA: And he would say to the turnkey, "I am here because of my beautiful cruel wife, my beautiful flighty wife"?

NONA: He might not, he'd be sober.

DECIMA: But he'd think it, and every time he was hungry, every time he was thirsty, every time he felt the hardness of the stone floor, every time he heard the chains clank, he would think it, and every time he thought it I would become more beautiful in his eyes.

NONA: No, he would hate you.

DECIMA: Little do you know what the love of man is. If that Holy Image of the church where you put all those candles at Easter was pleasant and affable, why did you come home with the skin worn off your two knees?

NONA: (*In tears.*) I understand – you cruel, bad woman! – you won't play the part at all, and all that Septimus may go to prison, and he a great genius that can't take care of himself.

(*Seeing Nona distracted with tears, Decima makes a dart and almost gets the lobster.*)

No, no! Not a mouthful, not a drop. I will break the bottle if you go near it. There is not another woman in the world would treat a man like that, and you were sworn to him in church – yes, you were, there is no good denying it. (*Decima makes another dart, but Nona, who is still in tears, puts the lobster in her pocket.*)

Leave the food alone; not one mouthful will you get. I have never sworn to a man in church, but if I did swear, I would not treat him like a tinker's donkey – before God I would not – I was properly brought up; my mother always told me it was no light thing to take a man in church.

DECIMA: You are in love with my husband.

NONA: Because I don't want to see him gaoled you say I am in love with him. Only a woman with no heart would think one can't be sorry for a man without being in love with him – a woman who has never been sorry for anybody! But I won't have him gaoled; if you won't play the part I'll play it myself.

DECIMA: When I married him, I made him swear never to play with anybody but me, and well you know it.

NONA: Only this once, and in a part nobody can do anything with.

DECIMA: That is the way it begins, and all the time you would be saying things the audience couldn't hear.

NONA: Septimus will break his oath, and I have learnt the part. Every line of it.

DECIMA: Septimus would not break his oath for anybody in the world.

NONA: There is one person in the world for whom he will break his oath.

DECIMA: What have you in your head now?

NONA: He will break it for me.

DECIMA: You are crazy.

NONA: Maybe I have my secrets.

DECIMA: What are you keeping back? Have you been sitting in corners with Septimus? giving him sympathy because of the bad wife he has, and all the while he has sat there to have the pleasure of talking about me?

NONA: You think that you have his every thought because you are a devil.

DECIMA: Because I am a devil I have his every thought. You know how his own song runs. The man speaks first – (*Singing.*)

> Put off that mask of burning gold
> With emerald eyes,

and then the woman answers –

> O no, my dear, you make so bold
> To find if hearts be wild and wise
> And yet not cold.

NONA: His every thought – that is a lie. He forgets all about you the moment you're out of his sight.

DECIMA: Then look what I carry under my bodice. This is a poem praising me, all my beauties one after the other – eyes, hair, complexion, shape, disposition, mind – everything. And there are a great many verses to it. And here is a little one he gave me yesterday morning. I had turned him out of bed and he had to lie alone by himself.

NONA: Alone by himself!

DECIMA: And as he lay there alone, unable to sleep, he made it up, wishing that he were blind so as not to be troubled by looking at my beauty. Hear how it goes! (*Sings again.*)

> O would that I were an old beggar
> Without a friend on this earth
> But a thieving rascally cur,
> A beggar blind from his birth;

Or anything else but a man
Lying alone on a bed
Remembering a woman's beauty,
Alone with a crazy head.

NONA: Alone in his bed indeed. I know that long poem, that one with all the verses; I know it to my hurt, though I haven't read a word of it. Four lines in every verse, four beats in every line, and fourteen verses – my curse upon it!

DECIMA: (*Taking out a manuscript from her bodice.*) Yes, fourteen verses. There are numbers to them.

NONA: You have another there – ten verses all in fours and threes.

DECIMA: (*Looking at another manuscript.*) Yes, the verses are in fours and threes. But how do you know all this? I carry them here. They are a secret between him and me, and nobody can see them till they have lain a long while upon my heart.

NONA: They have lain upon your heart, but they were made upon my shoulder. Ay, and down along my spine in the small hours of the morning; so many beats a line, and for every beat a tap of the fingers.

DECIMA: My God!

NONA: That one with the fourteen verses kept me from my sleep two hours, and when the lines were finished he lay upon his back another hour waving one arm in the air, making up the music. I liked him well enough to seem to be asleep through it all, and many another poem too – but when he made up that short one you sang he was so pleased that he muttered the words all about his lying alone in his bed thinking of you, and that made me mad. So I said to him, "Am I not beautiful? Turn round and look." O, I cut it short, for even I can please a man when there is but one candle. (*She takes a pair of scissors that are hanging round her neck and begins snipping at the dress for Noah's wife.*) And now you know why I can play the part in spite of you and not be driven out. Work upon Septimus if you have a mind for it. Little need I care. I will clip this a trifle and re-stitch it again – I have a needle and thread ready.

THE ADDING MACHINE
Elmer Rice
1923

Serio-Comic / 1 Man, 1 Woman

Zero: a clerk, 40s

Daisy: his co-worker, 40s

The Setting: an office in a department store, 1920s

The alienation and dehumanization brought about by the industrial age can be seen in the two very separate dialogues of these department store clerks.

DAISY: (*Reading aloud.*) Three ninety-eight. Forty-two cents. A dollar fifty. A dollar fifty. A dollar twenty-five. Two dollars. Thirty-nine cents. Twenty-seven fifty.

ZERO: (*Petulantly.*) Speed it up a little, cancha?

DAISY: What's the rush? Tomorrow's another day.

ZERO: Aw, you make me sick.

DAISY: An' you make me sicker.

ZERO: Go on. Go on. We're losin' time.

DAISY: Then quit bein' so bossy. (*She reads.*) Three dollars. Two sixty-nine. Eighty-one fifty. Forty dollars. Eight seventy-five. Who do you think you are, anyhow?

ZERO: Never mind who I think I am. You tend to your work.

DAISY: Aw, don't be givin' me so many orders. Sixty cents. Twenty-four cents. Seventy-five cents. A dollar fifty. Two fifty. One fifty. One fifty. Two fifty. I don't have to take it from you and what's more I won't.

ZERO: Aw, quit talkin'.

DAISY: I'll talk if I want. Three dollars. Fifty cents. Fifty cents. Seven dollars. Fifty cents. Two fifty. Three fifty. Fifty cents. One fifty. Fifty cents. (*She goes bending over the slips and transferring them from one pile to another. Zero bends over his desk, busily entering the figures.*)

ZERO: (*Without looking up.*) You make me sick. Always shootin' off your face about somethin'. Talk, talk, talk. Just like all the other women. Women make me sick.

DAISY: (*Busily fingering the slips.*) Who do you think you are, anyhow? Bossin' me around. I don't have to take it from you, and what's more, I won't. (*They both attend closely to their work, neither looking up.*)

ZERO: Women make me sick. They're all alike. The judge gave her six months. I wonder what they do in the work-house. Peel potatoes. I'll bet she's sore at me. Maybe she'll try to kill me when she gets out. I better be careful. Hello, Girl Slays Betrayer. Jealous Wife Slays Rival. You can't tell what a woman's liable to do. I better be careful.

DAISY: I'm gettin' sick of it. Always pickin' on me about somethin'. Never a decent word out of you. Not even the time o' day.

ZERO: I guess she wouldn't have the nerve at that. Maybe she don't even know it's me. They didn't even put my name in the paper, the big bums. Maybe she's been in the work-house before. A bum like that. She didn't have nothin' on that one time – nothin' but a shirt. (*He glances up quickly, then bends over again.*) You make me sick. I'm sick of lookin' at your face.

DAISY: Gee, ain't that whistle ever goin' to blow? You didn't used to be like that. Not even good mornin' or good evenin'. I ain't done nothin' to you. It's the young girls. Goin' around without corsets.

ZERO: You face is gettin' all yeller. Why don't you put some paint on it? She was puttin' on paint that time. On her cheeks and on her lips. And that blue stuff on her eyes. Just sittin' there in a shimmy puttin' on the paint. An' walkin' around the room with her legs all bare.

DAISY: I wish I was dead.

ZERO: I was a goddam fool to let the wife get on to me. She oughta get six months at that. The dirty bum. Livin' in a house with respectable people. She'd be livin' there yet, if the wife hadn't o' got on to me. Damn her!

DAISY: I wish I was dead.

ZERO: Maybe another one'll move in. Gee, that would be great. But the wife's got her eye on me now.

DAISY: I'm scared to do it, though.

ZERO: You oughta move into that room. It's cheaper than where you're livin' now. I better tell you about it. I don't mean to be always pickin' on you.

DAISY: Gas. The smell of it makes me sick. (*Zero looks up and* *clears his throat.*)

DAISY: (*Looking up startled.*) Whadja say?

ZERO: I didn't say nothin'.

DAISY: I thought you did.

ZERO: You thought wrong. (*They bend over their work again.*)

DAISY: A dollar sixty. A dollar fifty. Two ninety. One sixty-two.

ZERO: Why the hell should I tell you? Fat chance of you forgettin' to pull down the shade!

DAISY: If I asked for carbolic they might get on to me.

ZERO: You hair's gettin' gray. You don't wear them shirt waists any more with the low collars. When you'd bend down to pick somethin' up –

DAISY: I wish I knew what to ask for. Girl Takes Mercury After All-Night Party. Woman In Ten-Story Death Leap.

ZERO: I wonder where'll she go when she gets out. Gee, I'd like to make a date with her. Why didn't I go over there the night my wife went to Brooklyn? She never woulda found out.

DAISY: I seen Pauline Frederick do it once. Where could I get a pistol though?

ZERO: I guess I didn't have the nerve.

DAISY: I'll bet you'd be sorry then that you been so mean to me. How do I know, though? Maybe you wouldn't.

ZERO: Nerve! I got as much nerve as anybody. I'm on the level, that's all. I'm a married man and I'm on the level.

DAISY: Anyhow, why ain't I got a right to live? I'm as good as anybody else. I'm too refined, I guess. That's the whole trouble.

ZERO: The time the wife had pneumonia I thought she was goin' to pass out. But she didn't. The doctor's bill was eighty-seven dollars. (*Looking up.*) Hey, wait a minute! Didn't you say eighty-seven dollars?

DAISY: (*Looking up.*) What?

ZERO: Was the last you said eighty-seven dollars?

DAISY: (*Consulting the slip.*) Forty-two fifty.

ZERO: Well, I made a mistake. Wait a minute. (*He busies himself with an eraser.*) All right. Shoot.

DAISY: Six dollars. Three fifteen. Two twenty-five. Sixty-five cents. A dollar twenty. You talk to me as if I was dirt.

ZERO: I wonder if I could kill my wife without anybody findin' out. In bed some night. With a pillow.

DAISY: I used to think you was stuck on me.

ZERO: I'd get found out, though. They always have ways.

DAISY: We used to be so nice and friendly together when I first came here. You used to talk to me then.

ZERO: Maybe she'll die soon. I noticed she was coughin' this mornin'.

DAISY: You used to tell me all kinds o' things. You were goin' to show them all. Just the same, you're still sittin' here.

ZERO: Then I could do what I damn please. Oh, boy!

DAISY: Maybe it ain't all your fault neither. Maybe if you'd had the right kind o' wife – somebody with a lot of common-sense, somebody refined – me!

ZERO: At that, I guess I'd get tired of bummin' around. A feller wants a place to hang his hat.

DAISY: I wish she would die.

ZERO: And when you start goin' with women you're liable to get into trouble. And lose your job maybe.

DAISY: Maybe you'd marry me.

ZERO: Gee, I wish I'd gone over there that night.

DAISY: Then I could quit workin'.

ZERO: Lots o' women would be glad to get me.

DAISY: You could look a long time before you'd find a sensible, refined girl like me.

ZERO: Yes, sir, they could look a long time before they'd find a steady meal-ticket like me.

DAISY: I guess I'd be too old to have any kids. They say it ain't safe after thirty-five.

ZERO: Maybe I'd marry you. You might be all right, at that.

DAISY: I wonder – if you don't want kids – whether – if there's any way –

ZERO: (Looking up.) Hey! Hey! Can't you slow up? What do you think I am – a machine?

DAISY: (Looking up.) Say, what do you want, anyhow? First it's too slow an' then it's too fast. I guess you don't know what you want.

ZERO: Well, never mind about that. Just you slow up.

DAISY: I'm gettin' sick o' this. I'm goin' to ask to be transferred.

ZERO: Go ahead. You can't make me mad.

DAISY: Aw, keep quiet. (She reads.) Two forty-five. A dollar twenty. A dollar fifty. Ninety cents. Sixty-three cents.

ZERO: Marry you! I guess not! You'd be as bad as the one I got.

DAISY: You wouldn't care if I did ask. I got a good mind to ask.

ZERO: I was a fool to get married.

DAISY: Then I'd never see you at all.

ZERO: What chance has a guy got with a woman tied around his neck?

DAISY: That time at the store picnic – the year the wife couldn't come – you were nice to me then.

ZERO: Twenty-five years holdin' down the same job!

DAISY: We were together all day – just sittin' around under the trees.

ZERO: I wonder if the boss remembers about it bein' twenty-five years.

DAISY: And comin' home that night – you sat next to me in the big delivery wagon.

ZERO: I got a hunch there's a big raise comin' to me.

DAISY: I wonder what it feels like to be really kissed. Men – dirty pigs! They want the bold ones.

ZERO: If he don't come across I'm goin' right up to the front office and tell him where he gets off.

DAISY: I wish I was dead.

ZERO: "Boss," I'll say, "I want to have a talk with you." "Sure," he'll say, "sit down. Have a Corona Corona." "No," I'll say, "I don't smoke." "How's that?" he'll say. "Well, boss," I'll say, "it's this way. Every time I feel like smokin' I just take a nickel and put it in the old sock. A penny saved is a penny earned, that's the way I look at it." "Damn sensible," he'll say. "You got a wise head on you, Zero."

DAISY: I can't stand the smell of gas. It makes me sick. You coulda kissed me if you wanted to.

ZERO: "Boss," I'll say, "I ain't quite satisfied. I been on the job twenty-five years now and if I'm gonna stay I gotta see a future ahead of me." "Zero," he'll say, "I'm glad you came in. I've had my eye on you, Zero. Nothin' gets by me." "Oh, I know that, boss," I'll say. That'll hand him a good laugh, that will. "You're a valuable man, Zero," he'll say, "and I want you right up here with me in the front office. You're done addin' figgers. Monday mornin' you move up here."

DAISY: Them kisses in the movies – them long ones – right on the mouth –

ZERO: I'll keep a-goin' right on up after that. I'll show some of them birds where they get off.

DAISY: That one the other night – "The Devil's Alibi" – he put his arms around her – and her head fell back and her eyes closed – like she was in a daze.

ZERO: Just give me about two years and I'll show them birds where they get off.

DAISY: I guess that's what it's like – a kinda daze – when I see them like that, I just seem to forget everything.

ZERO: Then me for a place in Jersey. And maybe a little Buick. No tin Lizzie for mine. Wait till I get started – I'll show 'em.

DAISY: I can see it now when I kinda half-close my eyes. The way her head fell back. And his mouth pressed right up against hers. Oh, Gawd! it must be grand! (*There is a sudden shrill blast from a steam whistle.*)

DAISY and **ZERO:** (*Together.*) The whistle!

(*With great agility they get off their stools, remove their eye shades and sleeve protectors and put them on the desks. Then each produces from behind the desk a hat – Zero, a dusty derby, Daisy a frowzy straw . . . Daisy puts on her hat and turns toward Zero as though she were about to speak to him. But he is busy cleaning his pen and pays no attention to her. She sighs and goes toward the door at the left.*)

ZERO: (*Looking up.*) G'night, Miss Devore.

DESIRE UNDER THE ELMS
Eugene O'Neill
1924

Dramatic / 3 Men
Simeon, Peter and Eben: the hardworking sons of Ephraim
Cabot, 20s

The Setting: a farm in New England

The sons of the tyrannical Ephraim Cabot have labored long and hard
on the family farm in hopes of inheriting the old man's wealth. A
monkey wrench is thrown into the works when Ephraim brings home a
young bride with whom he expects to produce a new heir. Here, the
three sons discuss the new marriage.

EBEN: The cussed old miser! (*He can be heard going in the front
door. There is a pause as he goes upstairs, then a loud knock on
the bedroom door of the brothers.*) Wake up!
SIMEON: (*Startedly.*) Who's that?
EBEN: (*Pushing open the door and coming in, a lighted candle in his
hand. The bedroom of the brothers is revealed. Its ceiling is the
sloping roof. They can stand upright only close to the center
dividing wall of the upstairs. Simeon and Peter are in a double
bed, front. Eben's cot is to the rear. Eben has a mixture of silly
grin and vicious scowl on his face.*) I be!
PETER: (*Angrily.*) What in hell's-fire . . . ?
EBEN: I got news fur ye! Ha! (*He gives one abrupt sardonic guffaw.*)
SIMEON: (*Angrily.*) Couldn't ye hold it 'til we'd got our sleep?
EBEN: It's nigh sunup. (*Then explosively.*) He's gone an' married
agen!
SIMEON and **PETER:** (*Explosively.*) Paw?
EBEN: Got himself hitched to a female 'bout thirty-five – an' purty,
they says . . .
SIMEON: (*Aghast.*) It's a durn lie!
PETER: Who says?
SIMEON: They been stringin' ye!
EBEN: Think I'm a dunce, do ye? The hull village says. The preacher

from New Dover, he brung the news – told it t'our preacher – New Dover, that's whar the old loon got himself hitched – that's what the woman lived –

PETER: (*No longer doubting – stunned.*) Waal . . . !

SIMEON: (*The same.*) Waal . . . !

EBEN: (*Sitting down on a bed – with vicious hatred.*) Ain't he a devil out o' hell? It's just t' spite us – the damned old mule!

PETER: (*After a pause.*) Everythin'll go t' her now.

SIMEON: Ay-eh. (*A pause - dully.*) Waal – if it's done –

PETER: It's done us. (*Pause – then persuasively.*) They's gold in the fields o' Californi-a, Sim. No good a-stayin' here now.

SIMEON: Jest what I was a-thinkin'. (*Then with decision.*) S'well fust's last! Let's light out and git this mornin'.

PETER: Suits me.

EBEN: Ye must like walkin'.

SIMEON: (*Sardonically.*) If ye'd grow wings on us we'd fly that!

EBEN: Ye'd like ridin' better – on a boat, wouldn't ye? (*Fumbles in his pocket and takes out a crumpled piece of fools-cap.*) Waal, if ye sign this ye kin ride on a boat. I've had it writ out an' ready in case ye'd ever go. It says fur three hundred dollars t' each ye agree yewr shares o' the farm is sold t' me. (*They look suspiciously at the paper. A pause.*)

SIMEON: (*Wonderingly.*) But if he's hitched agen –

PETER: An' whar'd yew git that sum o' money, anyways?

EBEN: (*Cunningly.*) I know whar it's hid. I been waitin' – Maw told me. She knew whar it lay fur years, but she was waitin' . . . It's her'n – the money he hoarded from her farm an' hid from Maw. It's my money by rights now.

PETER: Whar's it hid?

EBEN: (*Cunningly.*) Whar yew won't never find it without me. Maw spied on him – 'r she'd never knowed. (*A pause. They look at him suspiciously, and he at them.*) Wall, is it fa'r trade?

SIMEON: Dunno.

PETER: Dunno.

SIMEON: (*Looking at window.*) Sky's grayin'.

PETER: Ye better start the fire, Eben.

SIMEON: An' fix some vittles.

EBEN: Ay-eh. (*Then with a forced jocular heartiness.*) I'll git ye a good one. If ye're startin' t' hoof it t' Californi-a ye'll need somethin' that'll stick t' yer ribs. (*He turns to the door, adding meaningly.*) But ye kin ride on a boat if ye'll swap. (*He stops at the door and pauses. They stare at him.*)

SIMEON: (*Suspiciously.*) Whar was ye all night?

EBEN: (*Defiantly.*) Up t' Min's. (*Then slowly.*) Walkin' thar, fust I felt 's if I'd kiss her; then I got a-thinkin' o' what ye'd said o' him an' her an' I says, I'll bust her nose fur that! Then I got t' the village an' heerd the news an' I got madder'n hell an' run all the way t' Min's not knowin' what I'd do – (*He pauses – then sheepishly but more defiantly.*) Waal – when I seen her, I didn't hit her – nor I didn't kiss her nuther – I begun t' beller like a calf an' cuss at the same time, I was so durn mad – an' she got scared – an' I jest grabbed holt an' tuk her! (*Proudly.*) Yes, sirree! I tuk her. She may've been his'n – an' your'n, too – but she's mine now!

SIMEON: (*Dryly.*) In love, air yew?

EBEN: (*With lofty scorn.*) Love! I don't take no stock in sech slop!

PETER: (*Winking at Simeon.*) Mebbe Eben's aimin' t' marry, too.

SIMEON: Min'd make a true faithful he'pmeet! (*They snicker.*)

EBEN: What do I care fur her – 'ceptin' she's round an' wa'm? The p'int is she was his'n – an' now she belongs t' me! (*He goes to the door – then turns – rebelliously.*) An' Min hain't sech a bad un. They's worse'n Min in the world, I'll bet ye! Wait'll we see this cow the Old Man's hitched t'! She'll beat Min, I got a notion! (*He starts to go out.*)

SIMEON: (*Suddenly.*) Mebbe ye'll try t' make her your'n, too?

PETER: Ha! (*He gives a sardonic laugh of relish at this idea.*)

EBEN: (*Spitting with disgust.*) Her – here – sleepin' with him – stealin' my Maw's farm! I'd as soon pet a skunk 'r kiss a snake! (*He goes out. The two stare after him suspiciously. A pause. They listen to his steps receding.*)

PETER: He's startin' the fire.

SIMEON: I'd like t' ride t' Californi-a – but –

PETER: Min might o' put some scheme in his head.

SIMEON: Mebbe it's all a lie 'bout Paw marryin'. We'd best wait an' see the bride.

PETER: An' don't sign nothin' till we does!

SIMEON: Nor till we've tested it's good money! (*Then with a grin.*) But if Paw's hitched we'd be sellin' Eben somethin' we'd never git nohow!

PETER: We'll wait an' see. (*Then with sudden vindictive anger.*) An' till he comes, let's yew 'n' me not wuk a lick, let Eben tend to thin's if he's a mind t', let's us jest sleep an' eat an' drink likker, an' let the hull damned farm go t' blazes!

SIMEON: (*Excitedly.*) By God, we've 'arned a rest! We'll play rich fur a change. I hain't a-goin' to stir outa bed till breakfast's ready.

PETER: An' on the table!

SIMEON: (*After a pause – thoughtfully.*) What d'ye calc'late she'll be like – our new Maw? Like Eben thinks?

PETER: More'n likely.

SIMEON: (*Vindictively.*) Waal – I hope she's a she-devil that'll make him wish he was dead an' living in the pit o' hell fur comfort!

PETER: (*Fervently.*) Amen!

SIMEON: (*Imitating his father's voice.*) "I'm ridin' out t' learn God's message t' me in the spring like the prophets done,' he says. I'll bet right then an' thar he knew plumb well he was goin' whorin', the stinkin' old hypocrite!

WAITING FOR LEFTY
Clifford Odets
1935

Serio-Comic / 1 Man, 1 Woman
  Joe: a hack driver, 40s
  Edna: his wife, 30-40

The Setting: an apartment in New York City, 1935

Lack of money is making life tough for Joe and Edna. Here, Edna threatens to leave if things don't change for the better.

JOE: Where's all the furniture, honey?

EDNA: They took it away. No installments paid.

JOE: When?

EDNA: Three o'clock.

JOE: They can't do that.

EDNA: Can't? They took it.

JOE: Why, the palookas, we paid three-quarters.

EDNA: The man said read the contract.

JOE: We must have signed a phoney . . .

EDNA: It's a regular contract and you signed it.

JOE: Don't be so sour, Edna . . . (*Tries to embrace her.*)

EDNA: Do it in the movies, Joe – they pay Clark Gable big money for it.

JOE: This is a helluva house to come home to. Take my word!

EDNA: Take MY word! Whose fault is it?

JOE: Must you start that stuff again?

EDNA: Maybe you'd like to talk about books?

JOE: I'd like to slap you in the mouth!

EDNA: No you won't.

JOE: (*Sheepish.*) Jeez, Edna, you get me sore some time . . .

EDNA: But just look at me – I'm laughing all over!

JOE: Don't insult me. Can I help it if times are bad? What the hell do you want me to do, jump off a bridge or something?

EDNA: Don't yell. I just put the kids to bed so they won't know they missed a meal. If I don't have Emmy's shoes soled tomorrow, she can't go to school. In the meantime let her sleep.

JOE: Honey, I rode the wheels off the chariot today. I cruised around five hours without a call. It's conditions.

EDNA: Tell it to the A & P!

JOE: I booked two-twenty on the clock. A lady with a dog was lit . . . she gave me a quarter tip by mistake. If you'd only listen to me – we're rolling in wealth.

EDNA: Yeah? How much?

JOE: I had "coffee and – " in a beanery. (*Hands her silver coins.*) A buck four.

EDNA: The second month's rent is due tomorrow.

JOE: Don't look at me that way, Edna.

EDNA: I'm looking through you, not at you . . . Everything was gonna be so ducky! A cottage by the waterfall, roses in Picardy. You're a four-star-bust! If you think I'm standing for it much longer, you're crazy as a bedbug.

JOE: I'd get another job if I could. There's no work – you know it.

EDNA: I only know we're at the bottom of the ocean.

JOE: What can I do?

EDNA: Who's the man in the family, you or me?

JOE: That's no answer. Get down to brass tacks. Christ, gimme a break, too! A coffee cake and java all day. I'm hungry, too, Babe. I'd work my fingers to the bone if –

EDNA: I'll open a can of salmon.

JOE: Not now. Tell me what to do!

EDNA: I'm not God!

JOE: Jeez, I wish I was a kid again and didn't have to think about the next minute.

EDNA: But you're not a kid and you do have to think about the next minute. You got two blondie kids sleeping in the next room. They need food and clothes. I'm not mentioning anything else – But we're stalled like a flivver in the snow. For five years I laid awake at night listening to my heart pound. For God's sake, do something, Joe, get wise. Maybe get your buddies together, maybe go on strike for better money. Poppa did it during the war and they won out. I'm turning into a sour old nag.

JOE: (*Defending himself.*) Strikes don't work!

EDNA: Who told you?

JOE: Besides that means not a nickel a week while we're out. Then when it's over they don't take you back.

EDNA: Suppose they don't. What's to lose?

JOE: Well, we're averaging six-seven dollars a week now.

EDNA: That just pays for the rent.

JOE: That is something, Edna.

EDNA: It isn't. They'll push you down to three and four a week before you know it. Then you'll say, "That's somethin'," too!

JOE: There's too many cabs on the street, that's the whole damn trouble.

EDNA: Let the company worry about that, you big fool! If their cabs didn't make a profit, they'd take them off the streets. Or maybe you think they're in business just to pay Joe Mitchell's rent!

JOE: You don't know a-b-c, Edna.

EDNA: I know this – your boss is making suckers outa you boys every minute. Yes, and suckers out of all the wives and the poor innocent kids who'll grow up with crooked spines and sick bones. Sure, I see it in the papers, how good orange juice is for kids. But dammit, our kids get colds one on top of the other. They look like little ghosts. Betty never saw a grapefruit. I took her to the store last week and she pointed to a stack of grapefruits. "What's that!" she said. My God, Joe – the world is supposed to be for all of us.

JOE: You'll wake them up.

EDNA: I don't care, as long as I can maybe wake you up.

JOE: Don't insult me. One man can't make a strike.

EDNA: Who says one? You got hundreds in your rotten union!

JOE: The Union ain't rotten.

EDNA: No? Then what are they doing? Collecting dues and patting your back?

JOE: They're making plans.

EDNA: What kind?

JOE: They don't tell us.

EDNA: It's too damn bad about you. They don't tell little Joey what's happening in his bitsie witsie union. What do you think it is – a ping pong game?

JOE: You know they're racketeers. The guys at the top would shoot you for a nickel.

EDNA: Why do you stand for that stuff?

JOE: Don't you wanna see me alive?

EDNA: (*After a deep pause.*) No . . . I don't think I do, Joe. Not if you can lift a finger to do something about it, and don't. No, I don't care.

JOE: Honey, you don't understand what –

EDNA: And any other hackie that won't fight . . . let them all be ground to hamburger!

JOE: It's one thing to –

EDNA: Take your hand away! Only they don't grind me to little pieces! I got different plans. (*Starts to take off her apron.*)

JOE: Where are you going?

EDNA: None of your business.

JOE: What's up your sleeve?

EDNA: My arm'd be up my sleeve, darling, if I had a sleeve to wear. (*Puts neatly folded apron on back of chair.*)

JOE: Tell me!

EDNA: Tell you what?

JOE: Where are you going?

EDNA: Don't you remember my old boy friend?

JOE: Who?

EDNA: Bud Haas. He still has my picture in his watch. He earns a living.

JOE: What the hell are you talking about?

EDNA: I heard worse than I'm talking about.

JOE: Have you seen Bud since we got married?

EDNA: Maybe.

JOE: If I thought . . . (*He stands looking at her.*)

EDNA: See much? Listen, boy friend, if you think I won't do this it just means you can't see straight.

JOE: Stop talking bull!

EDNA: This isn't five years ago, Joe.

JOE: You mean you'd leave me and the kids?

EDNA: I'd leave *you* like a shot!

JOE: No . . .

EDNA: Yes!

(*Joe turns away, sitting in a chair with his back to her. Outside the lighted circle of the playing stage we hear the other seated members of the strike committee. "She will . . . she will . . . it happens that way," etc. This group should be used throughout for various comments, political, emotional and as general chorus. Whispering . . . The fat boss now blows a heavy cloud of smoke into the scene.*)

JOE: (*Finally.*) Well, I guess I ain't got a leg to stand on.

EDNA: No?

JOE: (*Suddenly mad.*) No, you lousy tart, no! Get the hell out of here. Go pick up that bull-thrower on the corner and stop at some cushy hotel downtown. He's probably been coming here every morning and laying with you while I hacked my guts out!

EDNA: You're crawling like a worm!

JOE: You'll be crawling in a minute.

EDNA: You don't scare me that much! (*Indicates a half inch on her finger.*)

JOE: This is what I slaved for!

EDNA: Tell it to your boss!

JOE: He don't give a damn for you or me!

EDNA: That's what I say.

JOE: Don't change the subject!

EDNA: This is the subject, the EXACT SUBJECT! Your boss makes this subject. I never saw him in my life, but he's putting ideas in my head a mile a minute. He's giving your kids that fancy disease called the rickets. He's making a jelly-fish outa you and putting wrinkles in my face. This is the subject every inch of the way! He's throwing me into Bud Haas' lap. When in hell will you get wise –

JOE: I'm not so dumb as you think! But you are talking like a Red.

EDNA: I don't know what that means. But when a man knocks you down you get up and kiss his fist! You gutless piece of baloney.

JOE: One man can't –

EDNA: (*With great joy.*) I don't say one man! I say a hundred, a thousand, a whole million, I say. But start in your own union. Get those hack boys together! Sweep out those racketeers like a pile of dirt! Stand up like men and fight for the crying kids and wives. Goddammit! I'm tired of slavery and sleepless nights.

JOE: (*With her.*) Sure, sure! . . .

EDNA: Yes. Get brass toes on your shoes and know where to kick!

JOE: (*Suddenly jumping up and kissing his wife full on the mouth.*) Listen, Edna. I'm goin' down to 174th Street to look up Lefty Costello. Lefty was saying the other day . . . (*He suddenly stops.*) How about this Haas guy?

EDNA: Get out of here!

JOE: I'll be back! (*Runs out.*)

MOTHER COURAGE AND HER CHILDREN
Bertolt Brecht
1939

Dramatic / 1 Man, 1 Woman
> Mother Courage: a woman determined to make her fortune during
>   the 30 Years War, 40s
> The Chaplain: Her fellow camp-follower, 40-50

The Setting: outside the city of Ingolstadt, Bavaria, 1632

During a quiet moment, Mother Courage and the Chaplain trade
philosophies.

CHAPLAIN: You don't mind her going with the clerk?

MOTHER COURAGE: She's not so pretty anyone would want to
ruin her.

CHAPLAIN: The way you run your business and always come
through is highly commendable, Mother Courage – I see how you
got your name.

MOTHER COURAGE: The poor need courage. Why? They're lost.
That they even get up in the morning is something – in *their*
plight. Or that they plough a field – in war time. Even their
bringing children into the world shows they have courage, for they
have no prospects. They have to hang each other one by one and
slaughter each other in the lump, so if they want to look each other
in the face once in a while, well, it takes courage. That they put up
with an Emperor and a Pope, that takes an unnatural amount of
courage, for *they* cost you your life. (*She sits, takes a small pipe
from her pocket and smokes it.*) You might chop me a bit of
firewood.

CHAPLAIN: (*Reluctantly taking his coat off and preparing to chop
wood.*) Properly speaking, I'm a pastor of souls, not a woodcutter.

MOTHER COURAGE: But I don't have a soul. And I do need
wood.

CHAPLAIN: What's that little pipe you've got there?

MOTHER COURAGE: Just a pipe.

CHAPLAIN: I think it's a very particular pipe.

MOTHER COURAGE: Oh?

CHAPLAIN: The cook's pipe in fact. The cook from the Oxenstierna Regiment.

MOTHER COURAGE: If you know, why beat about the bush?

CHAPLAIN: Because I don't know if you've been *aware* that's what you've been smoking. It was possible you just rummaged among your belongings and your fingers just lit on a pipe and you just took it. In pure absent-mindedness.

MOTHER COURAGE: How do you know that's not it?

CHAPLAIN: It isn't. You *are* aware of it. (*He brings the ax down on the block with a crash.*)

MOTHER COURAGE: What if I was?

CHAPLAIN: I must give you a warning, Mother Courage, it's my duty. You are unlikely to see the gentleman again but that's no pity, you're in luck. Mother Courage, he did not impress me as trustworthy. On the contrary.

MOTHER COURAGE: Really? He was such a nice man.

CHAPLAIN: Well! So that's what you call a nice man. I do not. (*The ax falls again.*) Far be it from me to wish him ill, but I cannot – cannot – describe him as nice. No, no, he's a Don Juan, a cunning Don Juan. Just look at that pipe if you don't believe me. You must admit it tells all.

MOTHER COURAGE: I see nothing special in it. It's been used, of course.

CHAPLAIN: It's bitten halfway through! He's a man of great violence! It is the pipe of a man of great violence, you can see *that* if you've any judgment left! (*He deals the block a tremendous blow.*)

MOTHER COURAGE: Don't bite my chopping block halfway through!

CHAPLAIN: I told you I had no training as a woodcutter. The care of souls was my field. Around here my gifts and capabilities are grossly misused. In physical labor my God-given talents find no – um – adequate expression – which *is* a sin. You haven't heard me preach. Why, I can put such spirit into a regiment with a single sermon that the enemy's a mere flock of sheep to them and their own lives no more than smelly old shoes to be thrown away at the thought of final victory! God has given me the gift of tongues. I can preach you out of your senses!

MOTHER COURAGE: I need my senses. What would I do without them?

CHAPLAIN: Mother Courage, I have often thought that – under a veil of plain speech – you conceal a heart. You are human, you need warmth.

MOTHER COURAGE: The best way of warming this tent is to chop plenty of firewood.

CHAPLAIN: You're changing the subject. Seriously, my dear Courage, I sometimes ask myself how it would be if our relationship should be somewhat more firmly cemented. I mean, now the wild wind of war has whirled us so strangely together.

MOTHER COURAGE: The cement's pretty firm already. I cook your meals. And you lend a hand – chopping firewood, for instance.

CHAPLAIN: (*Going over to her, gesturing with the ax.*) You know what I mean by a close relationship. It has nothing to do with eating and woodcutting and such base necessities. Let your heart speak!

MOTHER COURAGE: Don't come at me like that with your ax, that'd be *too* close a relationship!

CHAPLAIN: This is no laughing matter, I am in earnest. I've thought it all over.

MOTHER COURAGE: Dear Chaplain, be a sensible fellow. I like you, and I don't want to heap coals of fire on your head. All I want is to bring me and my children through in that wagon. It isn't just mine, the wagon, and anyway I've no mind to start any adventures. At the moment I'm taking quite a risk buying these things when the Commander's fallen and there's all this talk of peace. Where would you go, if I was ruined? See? You don't even know. Now chop some firewood and it'll be warm of an evening, which is quite a lot in times like these. What was that? (*She stands up. Kattrin enters, breathless, with a wound across the eye and forehead. She is dragging all sorts of articles, parcels, leather goods, a drum, etc.*) What is it, were you attacked? On the way back? She was attacked on the way back! I'll bet it was that soldier who got drunk on my liquor. I should never have let you go. Dump all that stuff! It's not bad, the wound is only a flesh wound. I'll bandage it for you, it'll all be healed up in a week. They're worse than animals. (*She bandages the wound.*)

CHAPLAIN: I reproach them with nothing. At home they never did these shameful things. The men who start the wars are responsible, they bring out the worst in people.

MOTHER COURAGE: Didn't the clerk walk you back home? That's because you're a respectable girl, he thought they'd leave you alone. The wound's not at all deep, it will never show. There: all bandaged up. Now, I've got something for you, rest easy. I've been keeping them secret. (*She digs Yvette's red boots out of a bag.*) Well, what do you see? You always wanted them. Now you have them. (*She helps to put the boots on.*) Put them on quick, before I change my mind. It will never show, though it wouldn't bother *me* if it did. The ones they like fare worst. They drag them around till they're finished. Those they don't care for they leave alone. I've seen so many girls, pretty as they come in the beginning, then all of a sudden they're so ugly they'd scare a wolf. They can't even go behind a tree on the street without having something to fear from it. They lead a frightful life. Like with trees: the tall, straight ones are cut down for roof timber, and the crooked ones can enjoy life. So this wound here is really a piece of luck. The boots have kept well. I gave them a good cleaning before I put them away.

(*Kattrin leaves the boots and creeps into the wagon.*)

CHAPLAIN: (*When she's gone.*) I hope she won't be disfigured?

MOTHER COURAGE: There'll be a scar. She needn't wait for peace now.

CHAPLAIN: She didn't let them get any of the stuff.

MOTHER COURAGE: Maybe I shouldn't have made such a point of it. If only I ever knew what went on inside her head. Once she stayed out all night, once in all the years. Afterward she seemed much the same, except that she worked harder. I could never get out of her what happened. I worried about it for quite a while. (*She picks up the things Kattrin spilled and sorts them angrily.*) This is war. A nice source of income, I must say!

(*Cannon shots.*)

CHAPLAIN: Now they're lowering the Commander into his grave! A historic moment.

MOTHER COURAGE: It's a historic moment to me when they hit my daughter over the eye. She's all but finished now, she'll never get a husband, and she's so mad about children! Even her dumbness comes from the war. A soldier stuck something in her mouth when she was little. I'll never see Swiss Cheese again, and where my Eilif is the Good Lord knows. Curse the war!

BLITHE SPIRIT
Noel Coward
1941

Serio-Comic / 1 Man, 2 Women

Charles Condomine: an author; somewhat stuffy and
               pretentious, 30-40
Ruth Condomine: his somewhat stuffy and pretentious wife, 30s
Elvira: Charles' first wife; a ghost, 30s

The Setting: the country home of Ruth and Charles Condomine

During a séance, Elvira is mistakenly summoned back to the world of
the living. She wastes no time in wreaking havoc upon her husband
and his new wife.

RUTH: Well, darling?

CHARLES: (*L. end of the sofa. Absently.*) Well?

RUTH: Would you say the evening had been profitable?

CHARLES: Yes – I suppose so.

RUTH: I must say it was extremely funny at moments.

CHARLES: Yes – it certainly was.

RUTH: What's the matter?

CHARLES: The matter?

RUTH: Yes. You seem old, somehow. Do you feel quite well?

CHARLES: Perfectly. I think I'll have a drink. Do you want one?

RUTH: No, thank you, dear.

CHARLES: (*Moving to the drinks table and pouring out a whisky
and soda.*) It's rather chilly in this room.

RUTH: Come over by the fire.

CHARLES: I don't think I'll make any notes tonight, I'll start fresh
in the morning.
(*Charles turns, the glass in his hand. He sees Elvira and drops the
glass on the floor.*)
My God!

RUTH: Charles!

ELVIRA: That was very clumsy, Charles dear.

CHARLES: Elvira! – then it's true – it was you!

ELVIRA: Of course it was.

RUTH: (*Starts to go to Charles.*) Charles – darling Charles – what are you talking about?

CHARLES: (*To Elvira.*) Are you a ghost?

ELVIRA: (*Crossing below the sofa to the fire.*) I suppose I must be. It's all very confusing.

RUTH: (*Moving to r. of Charles and becoming agitated.*) Charles – what do you keep looking over there for? Look at me. What's happened?

CHARLES: Don't you see?

RUTH: See what?

CHARLES: Elvira.

RUTH: (*Staring at him incredulously.*) Elvira!!

CHARLES: (*With an effort at social grace.*) Yes. Elvira dear, this is Ruth. Ruth, this is Elvira.

(*Ruth tries to take his arm. Charles retreats down stage l.*)

RUTH: (*With forced calmness.*) Come and sit down, darling.

CHARLES: Do you mean to say you can't see her?

RUTH: Listen, Charles – you just sit down quietly by the fire and I'll mix you another drink. Don't worry about the mess on the carpet, Edith can clean it up in the morning. (*She takes him by the arm.*)

CHARLES: (*Breaking away.*) But you must be able to see her – she's there – look – right in front of you . . . there!

RUTH: Are you mad? What's happened to you?

CHARLES: You can't see her?

RUTH: If this is a joke, dear, it's gone quite far enough. Sit down, for God's sake, and don't be idiotic.

CHARLES: (*Clutching his head.*) What am I to do! What the hell am I to do!

ELVIRA: I think you might at least be a little more pleased to see me. After all, you conjured me up.

CHARLES: I didn't do any such thing.

ELVIRA: Nonsense; of course you did. That awful child with the cold came and told me you wanted to see me urgently.

CHARLES: It was all a mistake, a horrible mistake.

RUTH: Stop talking like that, Charles. As I told you before the joke's gone far enough.

CHARLES: I've gone mad, that's what it is, I've just gone raving mad.

RUTH: (*Pouring out some brandy and bringing it to Charles below* *the piano.*) Here – drink this.

CHARLES: (*Mechanically – taking it.*) This is appalling!

RUTH: Relax.

CHARLES: How can I relax? I shall never be able to relax again as long as I live.

RUTH: Drink some brandy.

CHARLES: (*Drinking it at a gulp.*) There! Now are you satisfied?

RUTH: Now sit down.

CHARLES: Why are you so anxious for me to sit down? What good will that do?

RUTH: I want you to relax. You can't relax standing up.

ELVIRA: African natives can. They can stand on one leg for hours.

CHARLES: I don't happen to be an African native.

RUTH: You don't happen to be a *what?*

CHARLES: (*Savagely.*) An African native!

RUTH: What's that got to do with it?

CHARLES: It doesn't matter, Ruth; really it doesn't matter.
(*Charles sits in the armchair. Ruth moves above him.*)
We'll say no more about it. See, I've sat down.

RUTH: Would you like some more brandy?

CHARLES: Yes, please.
(*Ruth goes up to the drinks table with the glass.*)

ELVIRA: Very unwise. You always had a weak head.

CHARLES: I could drink you under the table.

RUTH: There's no need to be aggressive, Charles. I'm doing my best to help you.

CHARLES: I'm sorry.

RUTH: (*Coming to Charles with the brandy.*) Here, drink this; and then we'll go to bed.

ELVIRA: Get rid of her, Charles; then we can talk in peace.

CHARLES: That's a thoroughly immoral suggestion. You ought to be ashamed of yourself.

RUTH: What is there immoral in that?

CHARLES: I wasn't talking to you.

RUTH: Who were you talking to, then?

CHARLES: Elvira, of course.

RUTH: To hell with Elvira!

ELVIRA: There now – she's getting cross.

CHARLES: I don't blame her.

RUTH: What don't you blame her for?

CHARLES: (*Rising and backing downstage l. a pace.*) Oh, God!

RUTH: Now, look here, Charles, I gather you've got some sort of plan behind all this. I'm not quite a fool. I suspected you when we were doing that idiotic séance.

CHARLES: Don't be so silly. What plan could I have?

RUTH: I don't know. It's probably something to do with the characters in your book – how they, or one of them, would react to a certain situation. I refuse to be used as a guinea-pig unless I'm warned beforehand what it's all about.

CHARLES: (*Moving a couple of paces towards Ruth.*) Elvira is here, Ruth – she's standing a few yards away from you.

RUTH: (*Sarcastically.*) Yes, dear, I can see her distinctly – under the piano with a zebra!

CHARLES: But Ruth –

RUTH: I am not going to stay here arguing any longer.

ELVIRA: Hurray!

CHARLES: Shut up!

RUTH: (*Incensed.*) How dare you speak to me like that?

CHARLES: Listen, Ruth. Please listen –

RUTH: I will not listen to any more of this nonsense. I am going up to bed now; I'll leave you to turn out the lights. I shan't be asleep, I'm too upset. So you can come in and say good night to me if you feel like it.

ELVIRA: That's big of her, I must say.

CHARLES: Be quiet. You're behaving like a guttersnipe.

RUTH: (*Icily.*) That is all I have to say. Good night, Charles.
(*Ruth walks swiftly out of the room without looking at him again.*)

CHARLES: (*Following Ruth to the door.*) Ruth –

ELVIRA: That was one of the most enjoyable half-hours I have ever spent.

CHARLES: (*Putting down his glass on the drinks table.*) Oh, Elvira – how could you!

ELVIRA: Poor Ruth!

CHARLES: (*Staring at her.*) This is obviously an hallucination, isn't it?

ELVIRA: I'm afraid I don't know the technical term for it.

CHARLES: (*Coming down c.*) What am I to do?

ELVIRA: What Ruth suggested – relax.

CHARLES: (*Moving below the chair to the sofa.*) Where have you come from?

ELVIRA: Do you know, it's very peculiar, but I've sort of forgotten.

CHARLES: Are you to be here indefinitely?

ELVIRA: I don't know that either.

CHARLES: Oh, my God!

ELVIRA: Why? Would you hate it so much if I was?

CHARLES: Well, you must admit it would be embarrassing?

ELVIRA: I don't see why, really. It's all a question of adjusting yourself. Anyhow, I think it's horrid of you to be so unwelcoming and disagreeable.

CHARLES: Now look here, Elvira –

ELVIRA: (*Near tears.*) I do. I think you're mean.

CHARLES: Try to see my point, dear. I've been married to Ruth for five years, and you've been dead for seven . . .

ELVIRA: Not dead, Charles. 'Passed over.' It's considered vulgar to say 'dead' where I come from.

CHARLES: Passed over, then.

ELVIRA: At any rate, now that I'm here, the least you can do is to make a pretence of being amiable about it.

CHARLES: Of course, my dear, I'm delighted in one way.

ELVIRA: I don't believe you love me any more.

CHARLES: I shall always love the memory of you.

ELVIRA: (*Crossing slowly above the sofa by the armchair to downstage l.*) You mustn't think me unreasonable, but I really am a little hurt. You called me back; and at great inconvenience I came – and you've been thoroughly churlish ever since I arrived.

CHARLES: (*Gently.*) Believe me, Elvira, I most emphatically did not send for you. There's been some mistake.

ELVIRA: (*Irritably.*) Well, somebody did – and that child said it was you. I remember I was playing backgammon with a very sweet old Oriental gentleman, I think his name was Genghiz Khan, and I'd just thrown double sixes, and then the child paged me and the next thing I knew I was in this room. Perhaps it was your subconscious . . . .

CHARLES: You must find out whether you are going to stay or not, and we can make arrangements accordingly.

ELVIRA: I don't see how I can.

CHARLES: Well, try to think. Isn't there anyone that you know, that you can get in touch with over there – on the other side, or whatever it's called – who could advise you?

ELVIRA: I can't think – it seems so far away – as though I'd dreamed it . . .

CHARLES: You must know somebody else besides Genghiz Khan.

ELVIRA: (*Moving to the armchair.*) Oh, Charles . . .

CHARLES: What is it?

ELVIRA: I want to cry, but I don't think I'm able to.

CHARLES: What do you want to cry for?

ELVIRA: It's seeing you again – and you being so irascible, like you always used to be.

CHARLES: I don't mean to be irascible, Elvira.

ELVIRA: Darling. I don't mind really – I never did.

CHARLES: Is it cold – being a ghost?

ELVIRA: No – I don't think so.

CHARLES: What happens if I touch you?

ELVIRA: I doubt if you can. Do you want to?

CHARLES: (*Sitting at the l. end of the sofa.*) Oh, Elvira . . . (*He buries his face in his hands.*)

ELVIRA: (*Moving to the l. arm of the sofa.*) What is it, darling?

CHARLES: I really do feel strange, seeing you again.

ELVIRA: (*Moving to r. below the sofa and round above it again to the l. arm.*) That's better.

CHARLES: (*Looking up.*) What's better?

ELVIRA: Your voice was kinder.

CHARLES: Was I ever unkind to you when you were alive?

ELVIRA: Often.

CHARLES: Oh, how can you! I'm sure that's an expression.

ELVIRA: Not at all. You were an absolute pig that time we went to Cornwall and stayed in that awful hotel. You hit me with a billiard cue.

(*Light cue.*)

CHARLES: Only very, very gently.

ELVIRA: I loved you very much.

CHARLES: I loved you too . . . (*He puts his hand to her and then pulls it away.*) No, I can't touch you. Isn't that horrible?

ELVIRA: Perhaps it's as well if I'm going to stay for any length of time. (*She sits on the l. arm of the sofa.*)

CHARLES: I suppose I shall wake up eventually . . . but I feel strangely peaceful now.

(*Light cue.*)

ELVIRA: That's right. Put your head back.

CHARLES: (*Doing so.*) Like that?

ELVIRA: (*Stroking his hair.*) Can you feel anything?

CHARLES: Only a very little breeze through my hair . . .

ELVIRA: Well, that's better than nothing.

CHARLES: (*Drowsily.*) I suppose if I'm really out of my mind they'll put me in an asylum.

ELVIRA: Don't worry about that – just relax.

CHARLES: (*Very drowsily indeed.*) Poor Ruth.

ELVIRA: (*Gently and sweetly.*) To hell with Ruth.

    (*By now the blackout is complete.*)

    (*The curtain falls.*)

THE SKIN OF OUR TEETH
Thornton Wilder
1942

Serio-Comic / 2 Women
   Mrs. Antrobus: a mother, 30-50
   Sabina: her maid, 20-30

The Setting: home, Excelsior, New Jersey

The eternal struggle between faithful wife and temptress is illustrated in the following scene in which Mrs. Antrobus chides Sabina for having let the fire go out.

MRS. ANTROBUS: Sabina, you've let the fire go out.
SABINA: (*In a lather.*) One-thing-and-another; don't-know-whether-my-wits-are-upside-or-down; might-as-well-be-dead-as-alive-in-a-house-all-sixes-and-sevens.
MRS. ANTROBUS: You've let the fire go out. Here it is the coldest day of the year in the middle of August and you've let the fire go out.
SABINA: Mrs. Antrobus, I'd like to give my two weeks' notice, Mrs. Antrobus. A girl like I can get a situation in a home where they're rich enough to have a fire in every room, Mrs. Antrobus, and a girl don't have to carry the responsibility of the whole house on her two shoulders. And a home without children, Mrs. Antrobus, because children are a thing only a parent can stand, and a truer word was never said; and a home, Mrs. Antrobus, where the master of the house don't pinch decent, self-respecting girls when he meets them in a dark corridor. I mention no names and make no charges. So you have my notice, Mrs. Antrobus. I hope that's perfectly clear.
MRS. ANTROBUS: You've let the fire go out! – Have you milked the mammoth?
SABINA: I don't understand a word of this play. – Yes, I've milked the mammoth.
MRS. ANTROBUS: Until Mr. Antrobus comes home we have no food and we have no fire. You'd better go over to the neighbors

and borrow some fire.

SABINA: Mrs. Antrobus! I can't! I'd die on the way, you know I would. It's worse than January. The dogs are sticking to the sidewalks. I'd die.

MRS. ANTROBUS: Very well, I'll go.

SABINA: (*Even more distraught, coming forward and sinking on her knees.*) You'd never come back alive; we'd all perish; if you weren't here, we'd just perish. How do we know Mr. Antrobus'll be back? We don't know. If you go out, I'll just kill myself.

MRS. ANTROBUS: Get up, Sabina.

SABINA: Every night it's the same thing. Will he come back safe, or won't he? Will we starve to death or will we be killed by burglars? I don't know why we go on living. I don't know why we go on living at all. It's easier being dead.

(*She flings her arms on the table and buries her head in them. In each of the succeeding speeches she flings her head up – and sometimes her hands – then quickly buries her head again.*)

MRS. ANTROBUS: The same thing! Always throwing up the sponge, Sabina. Always announcing your own death. But give you a new hat – or a plate of ice cream – or a ticket to the movies, and you want to live forever.

SABINA: You don't care whether we live or die; all you care about is those children. If it would be any benefit to them you'd be glad to see us all stretched out dead.

MRS. ANTROBUS: Well, maybe I would.

SABINA: And what do they care about? Themselves – that's all they care about.

(*Shrilly.*)

They make fun of you behind your back. Don't tell me: they're ashamed of you. Half the time, they pretend they're someone else's children. Little thanks you get from them.

MRS. ANTROBUS: I'm not asking for any thanks.

SABINA: And Mr. Antrobus – you don't understand *him*. All that work he does – trying to discover the alphabet and the multiplication table. Whenever he tries to learn anything you fight against it.

MRS. ANTROBUS: Oh, Sabina, I know you.

When Mr. Antrobus raped you home from your Sabine hills, he did it to insult me.

He did it for your pretty face, and to insult me.

You were the new wife, weren't you?

For a year or two you lay on your bed all day and polished the nails on your hands and feet:

You made puff-balls of the combings of your hair and you blew them up to the ceiling.

And I washed your underclothes and I made you chicken broths.

I bore children and between my very groans I stirred the cream that

you'd put on your face.

But I knew you wouldn't last.

You didn't last.

SABINA: But it was I who encouraged Mr. Antrobus to make the alphabet. I'm sorry to say it, Mrs. Antrobus, but you're not a beautiful woman, and you can never know what a man could do if he tried. It's girls like I who inspire the multiplication table. I'm sorry to say it, but you're not a beautiful woman, Mrs. Antrobus, and that's the God's truth.

MRS. ANTROBUS: And you didn't last – you sank to the kitchen. And what do you do there? *You let the fire go out!*

No wonder to you it seems easier being dead.

Reading and writing and counting on your fingers is all very well in their way – but I keep the home going.

HOME OF THE BRAVE
Arthur Laurents
1946

Dramatic / 2 Men

Capt. Harold Bitterger: a doctor, 43
Coney: a wounded vet, 20s

The Setting: a hospital room on a Pacific base during WWII

Coney has experienced something so horrible in battle that it has left
him unable to walk. Here, a dedicated physician gets to the bottom of
Coney's trauma.

(*Before the lights come up, we hear Coney counting.*)
CONEY: 85 - 84 - 83 - 82 - 81 - 80 - 79 -
DOCTOR: 78.
CONEY: 78 - 77 - 76 - 75. (*The lights are up now. Coney is on the
bed, the doctor sitting by him watching the needle.*) 74 - 73 - 72 -
73 - 7 –
(*The doctor withdraws the needle and gets up.*)
DOCTOR: Coney, do you remember how you got off that island?
CONEY: I think – Mingo. Something about Mingo.
DOCTOR: Yes. Mingo picked you up and carried you out.
CONEY: I – I remember water. Being in the canoe on water. There
were bullets.
DOCTOR: Some of the Japs fired machine guns when they realized
what was happening.
CONEY: I think maybe I passed out because – it's all kind of dark.
Then I'm in the plane.
DOCTOR: T.J. lifted you in.
CONEY: T.J.?
DOCTOR: Yes.
CONEY: But Mingo.
DOCTOR: Mingo couldn't lift you in alone. His right arm was no
good.
CONEY: Oh yeah . . . yeah.
DOCTOR: That's all you remember, though?

CONEY: I remember being taken off the plane.

DOCTOR: I mean on the island. That's all you remember of what happened on the island.

CONEY: Yes.

DOCTOR: Then why can't you walk, Coney?

CONEY: What?

DOCTOR: You weren't shot, were you?

CONEY: No.

DOCTOR: You didn't break your legs, did you?

CONEY: No.

DOCTOR: Then why can't you walk, Coney?

CONEY: I don't know. I don't know.

DOCTOR: But you said you remember everything that happened.

CONEY: I – yes. Yes.

DOCTOR: Do you remember waking up in the hospital? Do you remember waking up with that bad feeling?

CONEY: Yes.

(*Slight pause. The Doctor walks next to the bed.*)

DOCTOR: Coney, when did you first get that bad feeling?

CONEY: It was – I don't know.

DOCTOR: Coney – (*He sits down.*) Coney, did you first get it right after Finch was shot?

CONEY: No.

DOCTOR: What did you think of when Finch was shot?

CONEY: I don't know.

DOCTOR: You said you remember everything that happened. And you do. You remember that, too. You remember how you felt when Finch was shot, don't you, Coney? Don't you?

CONEY: (*Sitting bolt upright.*) Yes. (*A long pause. His hands twist his robe and then lay still. With dead, flat tones.*) When we were looking for the map case, he said – he started to say: You lousy yellow Jew bastard. He only said you lousy yellow jerk, but he started to say you lousy yellow Jew bastard. So I knew. I knew.

DOCTOR: You knew what?

CONEY: I knew he'd lied when – when he said he didn't care. When he said people were people to him. I knew he lied. I knew he hated me because I was a Jew so – I was glad when he was shot.

(*The Doctor straightens up.*)

DOCTOR: Did you leave him there because you were glad?

CONEY: Oh, no!

DOCTOR: You got over it.

CONEY: I was – I was sorry I felt glad. I was ashamed.

DOCTOR: Did you leave him because you were ashamed?

CONEY: No.

DOCTOR: Because you were afraid?

CONEY: No.

DOCTOR: No. You left him because that was what you had to do. Because you were a good soldier. (*Pause.*) You left him and you ran through the jungle, didn't you?

CONEY: Yes.

DOCTOR: And you walked around in the clearing by the beach, didn't you?

CONEY: Yes.

DOCTOR: So your legs were all right.

CONEY: Yes.

DOCTOR: Then if anything did happen to your legs, it happened when Finch crawled back. And you say nothing happened to you then.

CONEY: I don't know.

DOCTOR: Did anything happen?

CONEY: I don't know. Maybe – maybe.

DOCTOR: But if anything did happen, you'd remember?

CONEY: I don't know.

DOCTOR: You *do* remember what happened when Finch crawled back, don't you? Don't you, Coney?

CONEY: (*Covers his face.*) Finch . . . Finch . . .

DOCTOR: Remember that. Think back to that, Coney. You were alone in the clearing and Finch crawled in.

CONEY: O God . . . O dear God . . .

DOCTOR: Remember. (*He gets up quickly, moves across the room and in a cracked voice calls:*) Coney!

CONEY: (*Plaintively – he turns sharply.*) Finch? . . . Finch?

DOCTOR: (*A cracked whisper.*) Coney . . .

CONEY: Oh, Finch, Finch! Is that you, Finch? (*He cradles an imaginary head in his lap and begins to rock back and forth.*) I'm so glad. I'm so glad, Finch! I'm so . . . . (*He stops short, waits, then ducks his head down as though to listen to Finch's heart. A moment, then he straightens up and then, with the same decisive, brutal gesture as before, shoves the imaginary body of Finch so that it rolls over. He looks at it in horror and then the Doctor calls* *out:*)

DOCTOR: Hey, Yank! Come out and fight!

CONEY: They won't get you, Finch. I won't leave you this time, I promise! (*He begins to pantomime digging feverishly.*)

DOCTOR: Come out and fight, Yank.

CONEY: I won't leave you this time!
(*The Doctor walks over deliberately and grabs Coney's hand, stopping it in the middle of a digging motion.*)

DOCTOR: (*Curtly.*) What are you trying to bury him in, Coney? (*Coney stops and stares up at him.*) This isn't earth, Coney. This is a bed. Feel it. It's a bed. Underneath is a floor, a wooden floor. Hear? (*He stamps.*) You can't bury Finch, Coney, because he isn't here. You're not on that island. You're in a hospital. You're in a hospital, Coney, and I'm your doctor. I'm your doctor!
(*Pause.*)

CONEY: Yes, sir.

DOCTOR: And you remember now, you remember that nothing happened to your legs at all, did it?

CONEY: No, sir.

DOCTOR: But you had to be carried here.

CONEY: Yes, sir.

DOCTOR: Why?

CONEY: Because I can't walk.

DOCTOR: Why can't you walk?

CONEY: I don't know.

DOCTOR: *I do.* It's because you didn't want to, isn't it, Coney? Because you knew if you couldn't walk, then you couldn't leave Finch. That's it, isn't it?

CONEY: I don't know.

DOCTOR: That must be it. Because there's nothing wrong with your legs. They're fine, healthy legs and you can walk. You can walk. You had a shock and you didn't want to walk But you're over the shock and now you do want to walk, don't you? You do want to walk, don't you, Coney?

CONEY: Yes. Yes.

DOCTOR: Then get up and walk.

CONEY: I – can't.

DOCTOR: Yes, you can.

CONEY: No.

DOCTOR: Try.

CONEY: I can't.

DOCTOR: Try.

CONEY: I can't.

DOCTOR: Get up and walk! (*Pause.*) Coney, get up and walk!
(*Pause.*) You lousy, yellow Jew bastard, get up and walk!
(*At that, Coney straightens up in rage. He is shaking but he grips
the edge of the bed and swings his feet over. He is in a white fury
and out of his anger comes this tremendous effort. Still shaking, he
stands up; holds for a moment; and glares at the Doctor. Then,
with his hands outstretched before him as though he is going to
kill the Doctor, he starts to walk. First one foot, then the other,
left, right, left – but he begins to cry violently and as he sinks to
the floor, the Doctor moves forward swiftly and grabs him.*)

DOCTOR: (*Triumphantly.*) All right, son! All right!

WAITING FOR GODOT
Samuel Beckett
1952

Serio-Comic / 2 Men

Vladimir and Estragon: two tramps waiting for Godot.

The Setting: a country road. A tree. Evening.

Here, two friends reunite and discuss various things while waiting for a third friend to join them.

ESTRAGON: (*Giving up again.*) Nothing to be done.

VLADIMIR: (*Advancing with short, stiff strides, legs wide apart.*) I'm beginning to come round to that opinion. All my life I've tried to put it from me, saying, Vladimir, be reasonable, you haven't yet tried everything. And I resumed the struggle. (*He broods, musing on the struggle. Turning to Estragon.*) So there you are again.

ESTRAGON: Am I?

VLADIMIR: I'm glad to see you back. I thought you were gone forever.

ESTRAGON: Me too.

VLADIMIR: Together again at last! We'll have to celebrate this. But how? (*He reflects.*) Get up till I embrace you.

ESTRAGON: (*Irritably.*) Not now, not now.

VLADIMIR: (*Hurt, coldly.*) May one inquire where His Highness spent the night?

ESTRAGON: In a ditch.

VLADIMIR: (*Admiringly.*) A ditch! Where?

ESTRAGON: (*Without gesture.*) Over there.

VLADIMIR: And they didn't beat you?

ESTRAGON: Beat me? Certainly they beat me.

VLADIMIR: The same lot as usual?

ESTRAGON: The same? I don't know.

VLADIMIR: When I think of it . . . all these years . . . but for me . . . where would you be . . . (*Decisively.*) You'd be nothing more than a little heap of bones at the present minute, no doubt about it.

ESTRAGON: And what of it?

VLADIMIR: (*Gloomily.*) It's too much for one man. (*Pause. Cheerfully.*) On the other hand what's the good of losing heart now, that's what I say. We should have thought of it a million years ago, in the nineties.

ESTRAGON: Ah stop blathering and help me off with this bloody thing.

VLADIMIR: Hand in hand from the top of the Eiffel Tower, among the first. We were respectable in those days. Now it's too late. They wouldn't even let us up. (*Estragon tears at his boot.*) What are you doing?

ESTRAGON: Taking off my boot. Did that never happen to you?

VLADIMIR: Boots must be taken off every day, I'm tired telling you that. Why don't you listen to me?

ESTRAGON: (*Feebly.*) Help me!

VLADIMIR: It hurts?

ESTRAGON: (*Angrily.*) Hurts! He wants to know if it hurts!

VLADIMIR: (*Angrily.*) No one ever suffers but you. I don't count. I'd like to hear what you'd say if you had what I have.

ESTRAGON: It hurts?

VLADIMIR: (*Angrily.*) Hurts! He wants to know if it hurts!

ESTRAGON: (*Pointing.*) You might button it all the same.

VLADIMIR: (*Stooping.*) True. (*He buttons his fly.*) Never neglect the little things of life.

ESTRAGON: What do you expect, you always wait till the last moment.

VLADIMIR: (*Musingly.*) The last moment . . . (*He meditates.*) Hope deferred maketh the something sick, who said that?

ESTRAGON: Why don't you help me?

VLADIMIR: Sometimes I feel it coming all the same. Then I go all queer. (*He takes off his hat, peers inside it, feels about inside it, shakes it, puts it on again.*) How shall I say? Relieved and at the same time . . . (*He searches for the word.*) . . . appalled. (*With emphasis.*) AP-PALLED. (*He takes off his hat, peers inside it.*) Funny. (*He knocks on the crown as though to dislodge a foreign body, peers into it again, puts it on again.*) Nothing to be done. (*Estragon with a supreme effort succeeds in pulling off his boot. He peers inside it, feels about inside it, turns it upside down, shakes it, looks on the ground to see if anything has fallen out, finds nothing, feels inside it again, staring sightlessly before him.*) Well?

ESTRAGON: Nothing.

VLADIMIR: Show.

ESTRAGON: There's nothing to show.

VLADIMIR: Try and put it on again.

ESTRAGON: (*Examining his foot.*) I'll air it for a bit.

VLADIMIR: There's man all over for you, blaming on his boots the faults of his feet. (*He takes off his hat again, peers inside it, feels about inside it, knocks on the crown, blows into it, puts it on again.*) This is getting alarming. (*Silence. Vladimir deep in thought, Estragon pulling at his toes.*) One of the thieves was saved. (*Pause.*) It's a reasonable percentage. (*Pause.*) Gogo.

ESTRAGON: What?

VLADIMIR: Suppose we repented.

ESTRAGON: Repented what?

VLADIMIR: Oh . . . (*He reflects.*) We wouldn't have to go into the details.

ESTRAGON: Our being born?

(*Vladimir breaks into a hearty laugh which he immediately stifles, his hand pressed to his pubis, his face contorted.*)

VLADIMIR: One daren't even laugh any more.

ESTRAGON: Dreadful privation.

VLADIMIR: Merely smile. (*He smiles suddenly from ear to ear, keeps smiling, ceases as suddenly.*) It's not the same thing. Nothing to be done. (*Pause.*) Gogo.

ESTRAGON: (*Irritably.*) What is it?

VLADIMIR: Did you ever read the Bible?

ESTRAGON: The Bible . . . (*He reflects.*) I must have taken a look at it.

VLADIMIR: Do you remember the Gospels?

ESTRAGON: I remember the maps of the Holy Land. Coloured they were. Very pretty. The Dead Sea was pale blue. The very look of it made me thirsty. That's where we'll go, I used to say, that's where we'll go for our honeymoon. We'll swim. We'll be happy.

VLADIMIR: You should have been a poet.

ESTRAGON: I was. (*Gesture towards his rags.*) Isn't that obvious? (*Silence.*)

VLADIMIR: Where was I . . . How's your foot?

ESTRAGON: Swelling visibly.

VLADIMIR: Ah yes, the two thieves. Do you remember the story?

ESTRAGON: No.

VLADIMIR: Shall I tell it to you?

ESTRAGON: No.

VLADIMIR: It'll pass the time. (*Pause.*) One is supposed to have been saved and the other ... (*He searches for the contrary of saved.*) ... damned.

ESTRAGON: Saved from what?

VLADIMIR: Hell.

ESTRAGON: I'm going.

(*He does not move.*)

VLADIMIR: And yet ... (*Pause.*) ... how is it – this is not boring you I hope – how is it that of the four Evangelists only one speaks of a thief being saved. The four of them were there – or thereabouts – and only one speaks of a thief being saved. (*Pause.*) Come on, Gogo, return the ball, can't you, once in a way?

ESTRAGON: (*With exaggerated enthusiasm.*) I find this really most extraordinarily interesting.

VLADIMIR: One out of four. Of the other three two don't mention any thieves at all and the third says that both of them abused him.

ESTRAGON: Who?

VLADIMIR: What?

ESTRAGON: What's all this about? Abused who?

VLADIMIR: The Saviour.

ESTRAGON: Why?

VLADIMIR: Because he wouldn't save them.

ESTRAGON: From hell?

VLADIMIR: Imbecile! From death.

ESTRAGON: I thought you said hell.

VLADIMIR: From death, from death.

ESTRAGON: Well what if it?

VLADIMIR: Then the two of them must have been damned.

ESTRAGON: And why not?

VLADIMIR: But one of the four says that one of the two was saved.

ESTRAGON: Well? They don't agree and that's all there is to it.

VLADIMIR: But all four were there. And only one speaks of a thief being saved. Why believe him rather than the others?

ESTRAGON: Who believes him?

VLADIMIR: Everybody. It's the only version they know.

ESTRAGON: People are bloody ignorant apes.

THE VISIT
Friedrich Durrenmatt
1956

Dramatic / 1 Man, 1 Woman
    Claire: a woman seeking vengeance, 50s
    Schill: the man who once rejected her love, 50s

The Setting: a small town in Central Europe

Claire returns to her destitute home with the intention of buying revenge with her great wealth. She offers a vast sum of money for the life of the man who once wronged her. Here, they say goodbye.

SCHILL: Clara.

CLARA: How pleasant to see you here. I was visiting my forest. May I sit by you?

SCHILL: Oh, yes. Please do. (*She sits next to him.*) I've just been saying good-bye to my family. They've gone to the cinema. Karl has bought himself a car.

CLARA: How nice.

SCHILL: Ottilie is taking French lessons. And a course in English literature.

CLARA: You see? They're beginning to take an interest in higher things.

SCHILL: Listen. A finch. You hear?

CLARA: Yes. It's a finch. And a cuckoo in the distance. Would you like some music?

SCHILL: Oh, yes. That would be very nice.

CLARA: Anything special?

SCHILL: "Deep in the Forest."

CLARA: Your favorite song. They know it. (*She raises her hand. Offstage, the mandolin and guitar play the tune softly.*)

SCHILL: We had a child?

CLARA: Yes.

SCHILL: Boy or girl?

CLARA: Girl.

SCHILL: What name did you give her?

CLARA: I called her Genevieve.

SCHILL: That's a very pretty name.

CLARA: Yes.

SCHILL: What was she like?

CLARA: I saw her only once. When she was born. Then they took her away from me.

SCHILL: Her eyes?

CLARA: They weren't open yet.

SCHILL: And her hair?

CLARA: Black, I think. It's usually black at first.

SCHILL: Yes, of course. Where did she die, Clara?

CLARA: In some family. I've forgotten their name. Meningitis, they said. The officials wrote me a letter.

SCHILL: Oh, I'm so very sorry, Clara.

CLARA: I've told you about our child. Now tell me about myself.

SCHILL: About yourself?

CLARA: Yes. How I was when I was seventeen in the days when you loved me.

SCHILL: I remember one day you waited for me in the great barn. I had to look all over the place for you. At last I found you lying in the haycart with nothing on and a long straw between your lips . . .

CLARA: Yes. I was pretty in those days.

SCHILL: You were beautiful, Clara.

CLARA: You were strong. The time you fought with those two railway men who were following me, I wiped the blood from your face with my red petticoat. (*The music ends.*) They've stopped.

SCHILL: Tell them to play "Thoughts of Home."

CLARA: They know that too. (*The music plays.*)

SCHILL: Here we are, Clara, sitting together in our forest for the last time. The town council meets tonight. They will condemn me to death, and one of them will kill me. I don't know who and I don't know where. Clara, I only know that in a little while a useless life will come to an end. (*He bows his head on her bosom. She takes him in her arms.*)

CLARA: (*Tenderly.*) I shall take you in your coffin to Capri. You will have your tomb in the park of my villa, where I can see you from my bedroom window. White marble and onyx in a grove of green cypress. With a beautiful view of the Mediterranean.

SCHILL: I've always wanted to see it.

CLARA: Your love for me died years ago, Anton. But my love for you would not die. It turned into something strong, like the hidden roots of the forest; something evil, like white mushrooms that grow unseen in the darkness. And slowly it reached out for your life. Now I have you. You are mine. Alone. At last, and forever, a peaceful ghost in a silent house. (*The music ends.*)

SCHILL: The song is over.

CLARA: Adieu, Anton. (*Claire kisses Anton, a long kiss. Then she rises.*)

SCHILL: Adieu.

WHO'S AFRAID OF VIRGINIA WOOLF?
Edward Albee
1962

Dramatic / 1 Man, 1 Woman

George: a disillusioned college professor, 46
Martha: his boisterous wife, 52

The Setting: a house on the campus of a small New England college

Following a night of heavy drinking, George and Martha wage a monstrous battle that threatens to destroy their crumbling marriage.

MARTHA: Very good, George.

GEORGE: Thank you, Martha.

MARTHA: Really good.

GEORGE: I'm glad you liked it.

MARTHA: I mean . . . You did a good job . . . you really fixed it.

GEORGE: Unh-hunh.

MARTHA: It's the most . . . life you've shown in a long time.

GEORGE: You bring out the best in me, baby.

MARTHA: Yeah . . . pigmy hunting!

GEORGE: PIGMY!

MARTHA: You're really a bastard.

GEORGE: I? I?

MARTHA: Yeah . . . you.

GEORGE: Baby, if quarterback there is a pigmy, you've certainly changed your style. What are you after now . . . giants?

MARTHA: You make me sick.

GEORGE: It's perfectly all right for you . . . I mean, you can make your own rules . . . you can go around like a hopped-up Arab, slashing away at everything in sight, scarring up half the world if you want to. But somebody else try it . . . no sir!

MARTHA: You miserable . . .

GEORGE: (*Mocking.*) Why baby, I did it all for you. I thought you'd like it, sweetheart . . . . it's sort of to your taste . . . blood, carnage and all. Why, I thought you'd get all excited . . . sort of heave and pant and come running at me, your melons bobbling.

MARTHA: You've really screwed up, George.

GEORGE: (*Spitting it out.*) Oh, for God's sake, Martha!

MARTHA: I mean it . . . you really have.

GEORGE: (*Barely containing anger now.*) You can sit there in that chair of yours, you can sit there with the gin running out of your mouth, and you can humiliate me, you can tear me apart . . . ALL NIGHT . . . and that's perfectly all right . . . that's O.K. . . .

MARTHA: YOU CAN STAND IT!

GEORGE: I CANNOT STAND IT!

MARTHA: YOU CAN STAND IT!! YOU MARRIED ME FOR IT!!
(*A silence.*)

GEORGE: (*Quietly.*) That is a desperately sick lie.

MARTHA: DON'T YOU KNOW IT, EVEN YET?

GEORGE: (*Shaking his head.*) Oh . . . Martha.

MARTHA: My arm has gotten tired whipping you.

GEORGE: (*Stares at her in disbelief.*) You're mad.

MARTHA: For twenty-three years!

GEORGE: You're deluded . . . Martha, you're deluded.

MARTHA: IT'S NOT WHAT I'VE WANTED!

GEORGE: I thought at least you were . . . on to yourself. I didn't know. I . . . didn't know.

MARTHA: (*Anger taking over.*) I'm on to myself.

GEORGE: (*As if she were some sort of bug.*) No . . . no . . . you're . . . sick.

MARTHA: (*Rises – screams.*) I'LL SHOW YOU WHO'S SICK!

GEORGE: All right, Martha . . . you're going too far.

MARTHA: (*Screams again.*) I'LL SHOW YOU WHO'S SICK. I'LL SHOW YOU.

GEORGE: (*He shakes her.*) Stop it! (*Pushes her back in her chair.*) Now, stop it!

MARTHA: (*Calmer.*) I'll show you who's sick. (*Calmer.*) Boy, you're really having a field day, hunh? Well, I'm going to finish you . . . before I'm through with you . . .

GEORGE: . . . you and the quarterback . . . you both gonna finish me . . .?

MARTHA: . . . . before I'm through with you you'll wish you'd died in that automobile, you bastard.

GEORGE: (*Emphasizing with his forefinger.*) And you'll wish you'd never mentioned our son!

MARTHA: (*Dripping contempt.*) You . . .

GEORGE: Now, I said I warned you.

MARTHA: I'm impressed.

GEORGE: I warned you not to go too far.

MARTHA: I'm just beginning.

GEORGE: (*Calmly, matter-of-factly.*) I'm numbed enough . . . and I don't mean by liquor, though maybe that's been part of the process – a gradual, over-the-years going to sleep of the brain cells – I'm numbed enough, now, to be able to take you when we're alone. I don't listen to you . . . or when I *do* listen to you, I sift everything, I bring everything down to reflex response, so I don't really *hear* you, which is the only way to manage it. But you've taken a new tack, Martha, over the past couple of centuries – or however long it's been I've lived in this house with you – that makes it just too much . . . too much. I don't mind your dirty underthings in public . . . well, I *do* mind, but I've reconciled myself to that . . . but you've moved bag and baggage into your own fantasy world now, and you've started playing variations on your own distortions, and, as a result . . .

MARTHA: Nuts!

GEORGE: Yes . . . you have.

MARTHA: Nuts!

GEORGE: Well, you can go on like that as long as you want to. And, when you're done . . .

MARTHA: Have you listened to your sentences, George? Have you ever listened to the way you talk? You're so frigging . . . convoluted . . . that's what you are. You talk like you were writing one of your stupid papers.

GEORGE: Actually, I'm rather worried about you. About your mind.

MARTHA: Don't you worry about my mind, sweetheart!

GEORGE: I think I'll have you committed.

MARTHA: You what?

GEORGE: (*Quietly . . . distinctly.*) I think I'll have you committed.

MARTHA: (*Breaks into long laughter.*) Oh babe, aren't you something!

GEORGE: I've got to find some way to really get at you.

MARTHA: You've got at me, George . . . you don't have to do anything. Twenty-three years of you has been quite enough.

GEORGE: Will you go quietly, then?

MARTHA: You know what's happened, George? You want to know what's *really happened?* (*Snaps her fingers.*) It's snapped, finally.

Not me . . . *it*. The whole arrangement. You can go along . . .
forever, and everything's . . . manageable. You make all sorts of
excuses to yourself . . . *you* know . . . this is life . . . the hell with it
. . . .maybe tomorrow he'll be dead . . maybe tomorrow *you'll* be
dead . . . all sorts of excuses. But then, one day, one night,
something happens . . . and SNAP! It breaks. and you just don't
give a damn anymore. I've tried with you, baby . . . really, I've
tried.

GEORGE: Come off it, Martha.

MARTHA: I've tried . . . I've really tried.

GEORGE: (*With some awe.*) You're a monster . . . you *are*.

MARTHA: I'm loud, and I'm vulgar, and I wear the pants in this
house because somebody's got to, but I am *not* a monster. I am
not.

GEORGE: You're a spoiled, self-indulgent, willful, dirty-minded,
liquor-ridden . . .

MARTHA: SNAP! It went snap. Look, I'm not going to try to get
through to you any more . . . I'm not going to try. There was a
second back there, maybe, there was a second, just a second, when
I could have gotten through to you, when maybe we could have
cut through all this crap. But that's past, and now I'm not going to
try.

GEORGE: Once a month, Martha! I've gotten used to it . . . once a
month and we get misunderstood Martha, the good-hearted girl
underneath the barnacles, the little Miss that the touch of
kindness'd bring to bloom again. And I've believed it more times
than I want to remember, because I don't want to think I'm that
much of a sucker. I don't believe you . . . I just don't believe you.
There is no moment . . . there is no moment any more when we
could . . . come together.

MARTHA: (*Armed again.*) Well, maybe you're right, baby. You
can't come together with nothing, and you're nothing! SNAP! It
went snap tonight at Daddy's party. (*Dripping contempt, but there
is fury and loss under it.*) I sat there at Daddy's party, and I
watched you . . . I watched you sitting there, and I watched the
younger men around you, the men who were going to go
somewhere. And I sat there and I watched you, and *you* weren't
there! And it snapped! It finally snapped! And I'm going to howl
it out, and I'm not going to give a damn what I do, and I'm going
to make the damned biggest explosion you ever heard.

GEORGE: (*Very pointedly.*) You try it and I'll beat you at your own game.

MARTHA: (*Hopefully.*) Is that a threat, George? Hunh?

GEORGE: That's a threat, Martha.

MARTHA: (*Fake-spits at him.*) You're going to get it, baby.

GEORGE: Be careful, Martha . . . I'll rip you to pieces.

MARTHA: You aren't man enough . . . you haven't got the guts.

GEORGE: Total war?

MARTHA: Total.

(*Silence. They both seem relieved . . . elated.*)

SMALL CRAFT WARNINGS
Tennessee Williams
1970

Serio-Comic / 2 Men, 1 Woman

Monk:	owner of the bar, 40-50
Steve:	a short order cook, 20-30
Leona:	a powerhouse, 30-40

The Setting: a bar along the Southern California coast

It's just another night at Monk's Place. Ball-busting Leona has arrived in search of her man only to discover him cozied up with Violet. Enraged, Leona takes Violet into the ladies' room for a chat and a fracas ensues.

LEONA: If that fink is howling out the ladies' room window, I'm going out back and throw a brick in at her.

MONK: Leona, now cool it, Leona.

LEONA: I'll pay the damage, I'll pay the hospital expenses.

MONK: Leona, why don't you play your violin number on the box and settle down at a table and . . .

LEONA: When I been insulted by someone, I don't settle down at a table, or nowhere, NOWHERE!
(Violet sobs and wails as Steve comes into the bar. Steve is wearing a floral-patterned sports shirt under a tan jacket and the greasy white trousers of a short-order cook.)

STEVE: Is that Violet in there?

LEONA: Who else do you think would be howling out the ladies' room window but her, and you better keep out of this, this is between her and me.

STEVE: What happened? Did you hit Violet?

LEONA: You're Goddam right I busted that filthy bitch in the kisser, and when she comes out of the ladies', if she ever comes out, I'm gonna bust her in the kisser again, and kiss my ass, I'm just the one that can do it! MONK! DRINK! BOURBON SWEET!

MONK: Leona, you're on a mean drunk, and I don't serve liquor to no one on a mean drunk.

LEONA: Well, you can kiss it, too, you monkey-faced mother. (*She slaps the bar top with her sailor hat.*)

STEVE: Hey, did you hit Violet?

(*Bill laughs at this anticlimactic question.*)

LEONA: Have you gone deaf, have you got wax in your ears, can't you hear her howling in there? Did I hit Violet? The answer is yes, and I'm not through with her yet. (*Leona approaches the door of the ladies' room.*) COME ON OUT OF THERE, VIOLET, OR I'LL BREAK IN THE DOOR! (*She bangs her fist on the door, then slaps it contemptuously with her cap, and resumes her pacing. Bill keeps grinning and chuckling.*)

STEVE: Why did she hit Violet?

LEONA: Why don't you ask *me* why?

STEVE: Why did you hit Violet?

LEONA: I hit Violet because she acted indecent with that son of a bitch I been supporting for six months in my trailer.

STEVE: What do you mean "indecent"?

LEONA: Jesus, don't you know her habits? Are you unconscious ev'ry night in this bar and in her rathole over the amusement arcade? I mean she acted indecent with her dirty paws under the table. I came in here tonight and saw her hands on the table. The red enamel had nearly chipped off the nails and the fingernails, black, I mean *black*, like she'd spent every day for a month without washing her hands after making mud-pies with filthy motherless kids, and I thought to myself, it's awful, the degradation a woman can sink down into without respect for herself, so I said to her, Violet, will you look at your hands, will you look at your fingernails, Violet?

STEVE: Is that why you hit Violet?

LEONA: Goddam it, NO! Will you listen? I told her to look at her nails and she said, oh, the enamel is peeling, I know. I mean the dirtiness of the nails was not a thing she could notice, just the chipped red enamel.

STEVE: Is that why you hit Violet?

LEONA: Shit, will you shut up till I tell you why I hit her? I wouldn't hit her just for being unclean, unsanitary. I wouldn't hit her for nothing that affected just her. And now, if you'll pay attention, I'm going to tell you exactly why I did hit her. I got up from the table to play "Souvenir."

STEVE: What is she talking about? What are you talking about?

LEONA: When I come back to the table her hands had disappeared off it. I thought to myself, I'm sorry, I made her ashamed of her hands and she's hiding them now.

STEVE: Is that why you hit Violet?

LEONA: Why do you come in a bar when you're already drunk? No! Listen! It wasn't embarrassment over her filthy nails that had made her take her hands off the table top, it was her old habit, as filthy as her nails. The reason her pitiful hands had disappeared off the table was because under the table she was acting indecent with her hands in the lap of that ape that moved himself into my trailer and tonight will move himself out as fast as he moved himself in. And now do you know why I hit her? If you had balls, which it doesn't look like you do, you would've hit her yourself instead of making me do it.

STEVE: I wasn't there when it happened, but that's the reason you hit her?

LEONA: Yeah, now the reason has got through the fog in your head, which is thick as the fog on the beach.

(*Violet wails from the ladies' room.*)

STEVE: I'm not married to Violet, I never was or will be. I just wanted to know who hit her and why you hit her.

LEONA: (*Slapping at him with her cap.*) Annhh!

STEVE: Don't slap at me with that cap. What do I have to do with what she done or she does?

LEONA: No responsibility? No affection? No pity? You stand there hearing her wailing in the ladies' and deny there's any connection between you? Well, now I feel sorry for her. I regret that I hit her. She can come back out now and I won't hit her again. I see her life, the awfulness of her hands reaching out under a table, automatically creeping under a table into the lap of anything with a thing that she can catch hold of. Let her out of the ladies', I'll never hit her again. I feel too much pity for her, but I'm going out for a minute to breathe some clean air and to get me a drink where a barman's willing to serve me, and then I'll come back to pay up whatever I owe here and say good-bye to the sailfish, hooked and shellacked and strung up like a flag over . . . over . . . lesser, much lesser . . . creatures that never, ever sailed an inch in their . . . lives . . . (*The pauses at the end of this speech are due to a shift of her attention toward a young man and a boy who have entered the bar. Her eyes have followed them as they walked past her to a*

table in the front. She continues speaking, but now as if to herself.)
... When I leave here tonight, none of you will ever see me again.
I'm going to stop by the shop, let myself in with my passkey and
collect my own equipment, which is enough to open a shop of my
own, write a good-bye note to Flo, she isn't a bad old bitch, I
doubled her trade since I been there, she's going to miss me, poor
Flo, then leave my passkey and cut back to my trailer and pack
like lightning and move on to . . .

BILL: Where?

LEONA: Where I go next. You won't know, but you'll know I went
fast.

PERMISSIONS ACKNOWLEDGMENTS

PROMETHEUS BOUND by Aeschylus. Reprinted by permission of Dover Publications, 180 Varrick Street, New York, New York.

ANTIGONE by Sophocles. Reprinted by permission of Dover Publications, 180 Varrick Street, New York, New York.

OEDIPUS REX by Sophocles. Reprinted by permission of Samuel French, Inc., 45 West 25th Street, New York , NY 10010-2751. CAUTION: Professionals and amateurs are hereby warned that OEDIPUS REX is subject to a royalty. It is fully protected under the copyright laws of the United States of America, the British Commonwealth, including Canada, and all other countries of the Copyright Union. All rights, including professional, amateur, motion picture, recitation, lecturing, public reading, radio broadcasting, television, and the rights of translation into foreign languages are strictly reserved. In its present form the play is dedicated to the reading public only. The amateur live stage performance rights to OEDIPUS REX are controlled exclusively by Samuel French, Inc., and royalty arrangements and licenses must be secured well in advance of presentation. PLEASE NOTE that amateur royalty fees are set upon application in accordance with your producing circumstances. When applying for a royalty quotation and license please give us the number of performances intended, dates of production, your seating capacity and admission fee. Royalties are payable one week before the opening performance of the play to Samuel French, Inc., 45 West 25th Street, New York , NY 10010-2751; or at 7623 Sunset Blvd., Hollywood, CA 90046-2795; or to Samuel French (Canada), Ltd., 80 Richmond Street East, Toronto, Ontario, Canada MAC 1P1.

THE CLOUDS by Aristophanes. Reprinted by permission of Dover Publications, 180 Varrick Street, New York , New York.

MILES GLORIOSUS by Plautus. Reprinted from Plautus: THREE COMEDIES: "MILES GLORIOSUS," "PSEUDOLUS," "RUDENS." Translated by Peter L. Smith. Copyright ©1991 by Cornell University. Used by permission of the publisher, Cornell University Press.

PSEUDOLUS by Plautus. Reprinted from Plautus: THREE COMEDIES: "MILES GLORIOSUS," "PSEUDOLUS," "RUDENS." Translated by Peter L. Smith. Copyright ©1991 by Cornell University. Used by permission of the publisher, Cornell University Press.

ADAM: THE MYSTERY OF ADAM by Anonymous, translated by Edward Noble Stone. From ADAM, A RELIGIOUS PLAY OF THE TWELFTH CENTURY, translated by Edward Noble Stone, copyright © 1926, University of Washington Press. Reprinted with permission of the University of Washington Press.

THE FARCE OF THE WORTHY MASTER PIERRE PATELIN by Anonymous. Reprinted by permission of Dover Publications, 180 Varrick Street, New York, New York.

THE SUMMONING OF EVERYMAN by Anonymous. Reprinted by permission of Meriwether Publishing Ltd., Colorado Springs, Colorado.

THE TRAGICAL HISTORY OF DR. FAUSTUS by Christopher Marlowe. Reprinted by permission of Dover Publications, 180 Varrick Street, New York, New York.

THE SHOEMAKER'S HOLIDAY by Thomas Dekker. Bald, R.C. (Editor), SIX ELIZABETHAN PLAYS (1585-1635), Riverside Edition. Copyright © 1971 by Houghton Mifflin Company. Used by permission.

A WOMAN KILLED WITH KINDNESS by Thomas Heywood. Reprinted by permission of Dover Publications, 180 Varrick Street, New York, New York.

THE TRAGEDY OF OTHELLO, THE MOOR OF VENICE by William Shakespeare. Reprinted by permission of Meriwether Publishing Ltd., Colorado Springs, Colorado.

THE MAID'S TRAGEDY by Francis Beaumont. Reprinted by permission of Dover Publications, 180 Varrick Street, New York, New York.

THE DUCHESS OF MALFI by John Webster. Bald, R.C. (Editor), SIX ELIZABETHAN PLAYS (1585-1635), Riverside Edition. copyright © 1971 by Houghton Mifflin Company. Used by permission.

THE CONSTANT PRINCE by Pedro Calderon de la Barca. Reprinted by permission of Dover Publications, 180 Varrick Street, New York, New York.

THE CID by Pierre Corneille. Reprinted by permission of Dover Publications, 180 Varrick Street, New York, New York.

THE KING, THE GREATEST ALCALDE by Lope Felix de Vega Carpio. Reprinted by permission of Dover Publications, 180 Varrick Street, New York, New York.

THE LEARNED LADIES by Moliere. Reprinted by permission of Dover Publications, 180 Varrick Street, New York, New York.

BERENICE by Jean Racine. Reprinted by permission of Dover Publications, 180 Varrick Street, New York, New York.

LE BOURGEOIS GENTILHOMME by Moliere, translated by Nick Dear. Copyright © 1992 by Nick Dear. Reprinted by permission of Absolute Press, 14 Widcombe Crescent, Bath BA2 6AH, England.

PHAEDRA by Jean Racine, English version by Robert Lowell. Copyright © 1960, 1961 by Robert Lowell, copyright renewed. Forward all inquiries to Bridget Aschenberg, International Creative Management, Inc., 40 West 57th Street, New York, New York 10019.

THE BEAUM STRATEGEM by George Farquhar. Reprinted by permission of Dover Publications, 180 Varrick Street, New York, New York.

SARA by Gotthold Lessing, translated by Ernest Bell. Copyright © 1991, Absolute Press, 14 Widcome Crescent, Bath BA2 6AH, England.

MINNA VON BARNHELM by Gotthold Lessing, translated by Anthony Meech. Copyright © 1991 by Anthony Meech. Reprinted by permission of Absolute Press, 14 Widcome Crescent, Bath BA2 6AH, England.

SHE STOOPS TO CONQUER by Oliver Goldsmith. Reprinted by permission of Dover Publications, 180 Varrick Street, New York, New York.

THE BARBER OF SEVILLE by Pierre Augustin Caron de Beaumarchair, translated by W.R. Taylor. Copyright © 1922 by Walter H. Baker Company. Permission, Baker's Plays, 100 Chauncy Street, Boston, Massachusetts.

THE SCHOOL FOR SCANDAL by Richard Brinsley Sheridan. Reprinted by permission of Dover Publications, 180 Varrick Street, New York, New York.

SAUL by Vittorio Alfieri. Reprinted by permission of Dover Publications, 180 Varrick Street, New York, New York.

EGMONT by Johann Wolfgang Goethe. Reprinted by permission of Dover Publications, 180 Varrick Street, New York, New York.

A FAMILY AFFAIR by Alexander Ostrovsky. Reprinted by permission of Dover Publications, 180 Varrick Street, New York, New York.

THE DEMI-MONDE BY Alexandre Dumas Fils. Reprinted by permission of Dover Publications, 180 Varrick Street, New York, New York.

PEER GYNT by Henrik Ibsen, translated by Michael Meyer. Reprinted by permission of David Higham Associates Limited, London, England.

GHOSTS by Henrik Ibsen, translated by Eva Le Gallienne. From SIX PLAYS BY HENRIK IBSEN, copyright © 1951 by Eva Le Gallienne. Permission granted by International Creative Management, 40 West 57th Street, New York, New York 10019.

THE POWER OF DARKNESS by Leo Tolstoy, translated by Anthony Clark. Copyright © 1989 by Anthony Clark. Reprinted by permission of Absolute Press, Bath BA2 6AH.

UNCLE VANYA by Anton Chekhov, © Copyright, 1980 by Jean-Claude Van Itallie. All inquiries concerning rights (including amateur rights) should be addressed to the author's agent: William Morris Agency, Inc., 1350 Avenue of the Americas, New York, NY 10019

MRS WARREN'S PROFESSION by Bernard Shaw. Reprinted by permission of The Society of Authors, on behalf of the Bernard Shaw Estate.

THUNDER IN THE AIR by August Strindberg, translated by Eivor Martinus. Copyright © 1989 by Eivor Martinus. Reprinted by permission of Absolute Press, Bath BA2 6AH.

WILD HONEY by Anton Chekhov, translated by Michael Frayn. Reprinted by permission of Methuen London.

THE PLAYER QUEEN by William Butler Yeats. Reprinted with permission of Macmillan Publishing Company from COLLECTED PLAYS W.B. YEATS. Copyright 1924 by MacMillian Publishing

Company, renewed 1952 by Bertha Georgie Yeats.

THE ADDING MACHINE by Elmer Rice. Reprinted by permission of Samuel French, Inc., 45 West 25th Street, New York , NY 10010-2751. CAUTION: Professionals and amateurs are hereby warned that OEDIPUS REX is subject to a royalty. It is fully protected under the copyright laws of the United States of America, the British Commonwealth, including Canada, and all other countries of the Copyright Union. All rights, including professional, amateur, motion picture, recitation, lecturing, public reading, radio broadcasting, television, and the rights of translation into foreign languages are strictly reserved. In its present form the play is dedicated to the reading public only. The amateur live stage performance rights to OEDIPUS REX are controlled exclusively by Samuel French, Inc., and royalty arrangements and licenses must be secured well in advance of presentation. PLEASE NOTE that amateur royalty fees are set upon application in accordance with your producing circumstances. When applying for a royalty quotation and license please give us the number of performances intended, dates of production, your seating capacity and admission fee. Royalties are payable one week before the opening performance of the play to Samuel French, Inc., 45 West 25th Street, New York , NY 10010-2751; or at 7623 Sunset Blvd., Hollywood, CA 90046-2795; or to Samuel French (Canada), Ltd., 80 Richmond Street East, Toronto, Ontario, Canada MAC 1P1.

DESIRE UNDER THE ELMS by Eugene O'Neil. Copyright © 1922 and renewed 1950 by Eugene O'Neil. Reprinted by permission of Random House, Inc.

WAITING FOR LEFTY by Clifford Odets . From the book WAITING FOR LEFTY by Clifford Odets, copyright © 1935 by Clifford Odets, renewed copyright © 1962 by Clifford Odets.

MOTHER COURAGE AND HER CHILDREN by Bertolt Brecht, translated by Eric Bentley. From the book MOTHER COURAGE & HER CHILDREN by Bertolt Brecht, translated by Eric Bentley, Copyright © 1955, 1961, 1962,1963,1966 by Eric Bentley, renewed copyright 1991 by Eric Bentley. Used with permission of Grove/Atlantic Press.

BLITHE SPIRIT by Neil Coward. Copyright © 1942 by the Estate of Noel Coward. By permission of Michael Imison Playwrights Ltd., 28 Almeida Street, London N1 1TD, England.

THE SKIN OF OUR TEETH by Thornton Wilder. Copyright 1942 by
Thornton Wilder. Copyright © renewed 1970 by Thornton Wilder.
Reprinted by permission of HarperCollins Publishers, Inc.

HOME OF THE BRAVE by Arthur Laurents. Copyright 1946 by Arthur
Laurents. Reprinted by permission of Random House, Inc.

WAITING FOR GODOT by Samuel Beckett. From the book WAITING
FOR GODOT by Samuel Beckett, Copright © 1954 by Grove Press,
renewed copyright © 1982 by Samuel Beckett. Used with the
permission of Grove/Atlantic Monthly Press.

THE VISIT by Friedrich Duerrenmatt, adapted by Maurice Valency.
Copyright © 1956,1984 by Maurice Valency as an unpublished work
entitled "The Old Lady's Visit," adapted from "Der Besuch Der Alten
Dame," by Friedrich Duerrenmatt. Copyright © 1958,1986 by Maurice
Valency.
CAUTION: Professionals and amateurs are hereby warned that
THE VISIT is subject to a royalty. It is fully protected under the
copyright laws of the United States of America, the British
Commonwealth, including Canada, and all other countries of the
Copyright Union. All rights, including professional, amateur, motion
picture, recitation, lecturing, public reading, radio broadcasting,
television, and the rights of translation into foreign languages are strictly
reserved. In its present form the play is dedicated to the reading public
only. The amateur live stage performance rights to THE VISIT are
controlled exclusively by Samuel French, Inc., and royalty
arrangements and licenses must be secured well in advance of
presentation. PLEASE NOTE that amateur royalty fees are set upon
application in accordance with your producing circumstances. When
applying for a royalty quotation and license please give us the number
of performances intended, dates of production, your seating capacity
and admission fee. Royalties are payable one week before the opening
performance of the play to Samuel French Inc., at 45 E.25th St., New
York, NY 10010: or at 7623 Sunset Blvd., Hollywood, CA 90046, or to
Samuel French (Canada), Ltd. 80 Richmond Street East, Toronto,
Ontario, Canada M5C 1P1.
Royalty of the required amount must be paid whether the play is
presented for charity or gain and whether or not admission is charged.
Stock Royalty quoted on application to Samuel French, Inc.
For all other rights than those stipulated above, apply to Bridget
Aschenberg, International Creative Management, Inc., 40 W. 57th
Street, New York, NY 10019. Particular emphasis is laid on the
question of amateur or professional readings, permission and terms for

which must be secured in writing from Samuel French, Inc.

Copying from this book in whole or in part is strictly forbidden by law, and the right of performance is not transferable.

Whenever the play is produced the following notice must appear on all programs, printing and advertising for the play: "Produced by special arrangement with Samuel French, Inc."

Due authorship must be given on all programs, printing, and advertising for the play.

WHO'S AFRAID OF VIRGINIA WOOLF by Edward Albee. Copyright ©,1962, by Edward Albee. Reprinted by permission of William Morris, 1350 Avenue of the Americas, New York, NY 10019.

SMALL CRAFT WARNINGS by Tennessee Williams. Lady Maria St Just, Trustee under the will of Tennessee Wiliams. Copyright © Tennessee Williams, 1970, 1972, 1973.

Tennessee Williams: SMALL CRAFT WARNINGS. Copyright © 1970, 1972 by Tennessee Williams. Reprinted by permission of New Directions Publishng Corp. U.S. and Canadian rights.